PUTTING IT ALL TOGETHER
A GUIDE TO STRATEGIC THINKING

William E. Rothschild

A Division of American Management Associations

TO MY CHILDREN:

ROB
STEVE
KAREN
BILLY

Library of Congress Cataloging in Publication Data

Rothschild, William E
  Putting it all together.

  Includes index.
  1. Management. 2. Planning. I. Title.
  HD31.R75   658.4   76-10535
  ISBN 0-8144-5405-4
  ISBN 0-8144-7555-8

© 1976 AMACOM

A division of American Management Associations, New York.
All rights reserved. Printed in the United States of America.

SECOND PRINTING

PREFACE

In the past decade several books have appeared dealing with the concept of strategy and with techniques for quantifying strategic results. These books provide excellent background but are of little help to the business or nonbusiness leader who wants to systematically and comprehensively think through his situation, anticipate change, and determine what strategic options are available to him. This book has been written to present a disciplined, sequential, and integrated approach to strategy development and review. There are several factors to keep in mind as you read.

First, the text is rounded out with "application" sections that invite you, the reader and practitioner, to pause periodically and apply the discussion to your business and institutional environment. I strongly recommend that you take advantage of these opportunities. As you work your way through, keep a record of the key points, insights, and facts that pertain to your industry and your business—its resources, competition, and objectives. This should make the process relevant to you immediately and not just another interesting conceptual framework that may be useful "someday."

A second point to keep in mind is that strategic thinking is a logical exploration and retrieval process, not a mechanistic set of forms or ideas. It is based on disciplined questioning and recording, not on any magic formula that will supply revelations and somehow guarantee success for the user who goes through the ritual. The wave-the-wand approach is analogous to the false expectations many intelligent businessmen had that the computer would of itself make the right decisions for them. Formula planning, like data processing, can be an aid. Strategic thinking, though it links analysis to intuition, relies on sound judgments of hard facts to yield results.

A third point is that the process as I will present it is appropriate to small and medium-size businesses, not merely to corporate giants that can afford sophisticated planning staffs and computerized decision-making models. Lack of such resources does usually limit the extent and complexity of planning and the capacity for strategic change, but the appropriateness of in-depth, integrated, anticipatory thinking is just as great for the small and medium-size company as for the very large. In fact it may make the difference between survival and bankruptcy.

Further, strategic thinking is also needed by the nonprofit institution. All organizations are subject to both external and internal forces, some of which are new and demand new responses. Whether the leaders of universities, hospitals, social service agencies, and even churches admit it or not, they need to be strategists and to exercise a disciplined and comprehensive approach to planning. In my work with decision makers in these types of institutions, I find at least initially a resistance to equating their operation with a business. Some of them seem to think that the suggestion of such a similarity demeans their service and calling. There are differences, of course, but it is my belief that the concepts can be adapted and the appropriate modifications made. I have no desire to undervalue nonprofit institutions; on the contrary I wish to help them continue to prosper and grow. For that reason I have attempted to translate the principles of strategic thinking into terms relevant to the nonprofit organization.

A fourth and final point concerns the practitioners of strategy. Strategy comprises decisions made today that have long-term consequences and that involve the whole management team during the planned period. Therefore this book is aimed not only at chief executives but at their reporting officers from top-level people down through middle managers. Because each management rank contributes to and carries out specific aspects of strategy, the book should be read and understood by all, so that it can serve as a common language and approach to developing, implementing, and reviewing strategic decisions. This provides both the procedures and the language for communicating them effectively. If team members misunderstand what is required of them or use different terminology to correlate their efforts, the output will be garbled and at least temporarily useless for directing the business.

When strategic thinking is understood well and applied intelligently by everyone in an organization who can really influence final results, leaders will be *managing by strategy* rather than *managing by objectives*. The difference is quite significant: The first pinpoints what actions are *feasible* and how they are to be executed, while the second concentrates on the *desired* results and then considers how to reach them. You don't need to be a seer to know that actions may provide detrimental results in the long run if they are not skillfully tailored to the organization's capabilities. Strategic thinking puts the horse before the cart.

I wish to thank my wife, Alma, for her patience and encouragement during the time this book was written. I wish also to acknowledge the contribution made by my friend and associate Kenneth Michel. He provided many insights into the process and much assistance in proving its application.

William E. Rothschild

CONTENTS

1

EVERY LEADER HAS A STRATEGY, SO WHY ALL THE FUSS?

Strategy isn't new. Successful businessmen and nonbusiness leaders have always had strategies. These strategies have varied from unwritten plans in the minds of the organization's leader to detailed blueprints of what is to be achieved and how.

If strategic planning has been around for a long time, why, you may ask, is there such a renewed interest and feeling of discovery in the process of disciplined strategy development? The reason is that leaders in all walks of life have discovered that the dynamics and complexity of the world require more than conventional wisdom and experience; that merely setting objectives without examining what actions are feasible and what alternatives are available isn't sufficient.

For the first time in more than three decades, the American businessman and the nonprofit organization leader find themselves faced simultaneously with new government and social demands, a scarcity (and accelerating cost) of financial and material resources, and worldwide competition—all in degrees that would have been unthinkable a few years ago. In late 1973 all organizations were startled to learn that even energy, which had always been abundant and inexpensive, was not inexhaustible and was becoming critically expensive. Thus the reality of operating a business or school or public enterprise has emerged as even more threatening than the gloom-and-doom predictions of the past. The attitude that "I can do whatever I please" has given way to "Nothing can be taken for granted."

Experience, intuition, and judgment alone aren't enough to cope with these mushrooming complexities. A business must deeply probe all aspects of its environment and its own resources. This is not the work of a day. Every organization functions in a dual setting: There is a microenvironment, made up of customers, markets, related industries, and competitors; and a macroenvironment, a four-dimension overlay of societal, government, economic, and technological forces that affect the organization's operations. Its own resources include all its human and material assets in such areas as planning and design, production, marketing, financing, and management.

If a business is to prosper—and in some cases even survive—its leaders must explore each of these elements through comprehensive and systematic analysis, synthesis, and evaluation. The method I have developed for carrying out this multiphase task is called *strategic thinking.*

The strategic thinking process I will describe differs in sequence and emphases from the decision-making approaches that have been expounded over the last several decades. Those "management by objective" approaches prescribe that the first task to be performed is to develop a comprehensive list of objectives and goals. The next task is to generate a number of alternative lines of action, which are the means of meeting the objectives. In other words, strategies are based on the objectives you choose, not on environment or abilities.

When this sequence is used, it is common to find that objectives have been set unrealistically high, and the alternative strategies lose their credibility. Thus, like Russia and other communist countries, companies set goals and objectives that are so unrealistic that they become, in effect, mere mottoes. In addition, people somehow get the feeling that the objectives are sacred and that challenging them is a sacrilege or a sign of disaffection.

Although the objectives-first approach inclines planners to shoot for the moon when it isn't feasible to get 10 feet off the ground, I do admit that it will work—if you have unlimited resources. The late President John Kennedy said that the United States would land a man on the moon, and it did, but he also committed the resources needed to do the job.

Another problem with the objectives-first sequence is that it fosters a tendency to adopt too many objectives, which restricts the effort and creativity that can be devoted to each.

Another popular sequence starts with the organization's resources and then moves to the question of what it can achieve with them. This I call the inside-out approach, and it too has positive and negative attributes. On the positive side it tends to focus the planner's attention on his company's strengths, or at least what he thinks are its strengths. The problem with this is that we all have trouble being objective about our own firm and tend to view it in a favorable light. We tend to make the environment reflect the positive aspects of our resources, and before we know it, we are convinced the world is ready for us to conquer.

Yet I like this approach in situations where the business is brand-new and has a product that is truly unique. The planner uses this uniqueness to determine what markets may fit the product. Thus the resource helps clarify his perceptions of his environment, and he becomes more selective in evaluating his opportunities. It is also valid to start with resources when you are the leader in your market and wish to monitor factors that can affect your leadership.

If you have an existing strategy with which you are satisfied, then you can start from this and focus on changes that may require a change in it. But as with the resources-first sequence, this will limit your horizons and most likely force you into a defensive, rather than an offensive, mode of thinking.

The strategic thinking process begins with the most important component of your organization's life: you. What is the nature of your business, and what does it want to become? The next analysis concentrates on the source of your business existence, namely, your customers. Evaluations of your industry and markets emerge from your exploration of "the game" you're in, and you turn next to a detailed assessment of your most important fellow players—your key competitors. Equipped with such insights about the external world, you can then evaluate your own organization's capabilities. These analyses make it possible for you to choose the kind of strategy you wish to pursue. Ultimately, they provide an estimation of the risks, costs, and rewards you can expect and a determination of the objectives you can realistically achieve.

Thus I recommend an approach that requires you first to generate feasible alternative actions and then to determine what the alternatives can produce, which in turn yields your objectives.

"So what?" you may ask. It is common for businessmen to feel that sequence is unimportant and merely the concern of academically oriented planners. I strongly believe that the question isn't so academic as it seems. The sequence I propose in the strategic thinking process insures that the planner probes his organization's condition and setting both deeply and comprehensively. It also infuses balance and objectivity into his judgments on the facts he uncovers and the assumptions he makes in his analyses. Finally, it provides him with review procedures to track performance and contingency plans for meeting the unexpected.

Although I encourage you therefore to use the sequence just prescribed, which will be laid out step by step in the following chapters, there really isn't one right way to do the job. I will caution you repeatedly not to get mechanistic in applying the strategic thinking process. Each sequence has its advantages and disadvantages, and the one you select should be determined by how extensively you need and desire to change. Further, the process is reiterative; strategy review, which should be undertaken periodically, will bring your thinking back repeatedly to various phases of your strategy construction. If you don't have the time and change isn't that critical, then start with current strategy and concentrate on factors that may force you to change it. If you want to start with your own resources, this is fine as long as you remain objective and look at all aspects of your environment. The major point to keep in mind is that sequence will affect the scope and depth of your strategic thinking.

SAM MITCHELL'S EXPERIENCE

To begin our description of the strategic thinking process, I would like to construct a conversation with a typical small businessman, Sam Mitchell, president of Midwestern Metalworks, Inc. Let's say it took place in the recent past. Although fictitious, it is quite typical of many I've had over a number of years, and I will treat it as current. Here's how Sam starts our discussion:

"Business has really been terrific! Sales are up 25 percent, and income has set a record. It was really a pleasant surprise, and I hope it will continue. After all, this is my business, and I grew it by myself."

Sam launched his company 10 years ago. Last year sales reached $10 million, and he made a 15 percent return on his investment. Sam began his career as a machinist and worked his way up in the craft, and though he is the owner and manager, he wants to stay involved in line operations—"keep a hand in," as he says.

Like many businessmen in small and medium-size companies, Sam has a problem. He isn't trained in management, nor is he an experienced planner. He has financial consultants and lawyers to guide him in accounting and legal matters, but his company isn't big enough to hire planning experts.

Recognizing the need to work out a plan for the future, Sam has been considering how to do this—where to start, what types of information to collect and analyze, and what to include in his plan. He is looking for some guidance on the planning process and how to undertake it in the most efficient way. He continues:

"Two years ago things began to click. My business has many small customers and two major ones—Aerospace, Inc., and Leisure Vehicles International. Both are located within 50 miles of us and have been using our services since I started. About three years ago both had excellent years but for entirely different reasons.

"Aerospace is a supplier of electromechanical controls for military jet aircraft and space vehicles. When I set up my operations, it was getting most of its orders from McDonnell Douglas and Boeing. As you know, this type of business has some fantastic swings. When the government is spending, there is plenty of work; when appropriations are cut, things are really bad. You'll recall that the aerospace industry was seriously hurt in the late 1960s by the cut in Department of Defense spending, which resulted in canceled and stretched-out contracts. This chain reaction caught my new company in the middle and almost wiped me out. I had just invested in a new wing and new equipment and trained ten new operators.

Within six months my plant was running at 40 percent of capacity, and I was on the verge of bankruptcy."

Sam Mitchell is touching on one of the most critical analyses required for sound strategic planning—*customer analysis.* Of course the description is brief and not comprehensive, but it does point out that we need to understand our customer's problems and how they affect his buying decisions and habits. Sam goes on:

"Leisure Vehicles is a different case entirely. It markets camping trailers through franchised dealers. Since this is a recreation and seasonal business, Leisure Vehicles is affected by consumer spending habits. The company manufactures its vehicles in winter and early spring so as to build large inventories for the peak sales period of late spring and early summer. This practice in turn requires that Leisure's suppliers extend long credit terms—I have to provide 120-day credit in order to get the contract. That takes considerable cash and puts me in a bind.

"Four years ago the recreation vehicle market hit an all-time high, and Leisure participated in the growth. This year is expected to be even better since the peak season has been extended to include the fall, when many people go south with their campers. Of course developments could be turned completely around if we have a further gasoline shortage; growth could be slowed."

Sam is now describing another type of customer—one in the consumer sector. In this case too the customer's business has highs and lows that in turn affect Midwestern's sales, but the reasons for the cyclicality and its duration are quite different. Many businesses need to examine only large customers in depth, as these account for the great majority of sales; many others must classify and group all their purchasers in order to see relationships and to draw implications for strategy. Chapter 3 will describe various ways of classifying customer groups to help identify the opportunities as well as the threats they can present. Further, it will include a checklist of key questions which will assure that your probing is comprehensive and that significant factors are scrutinized and monitored. Customer analysis provides the basis for sound market segmentation and projections, and it is fundamental to any business plan.

Continuing the conversation, Sam discusses other factors that have influenced his organization's progress:

"As I mentioned before, the late 1960s were tough. Because of the effect of a poor overall economy on my major customers and a surplus of machine-shop capacity, my prices reached an all-time low. To make things worse, several of my larger customers began to decrease external subcontracting and rely on their own internal shops. This is normal. When their sales are high, companies such as these can't do everything internally, and so they subcontract. When sales decline, they revert to their own capability. Thus one day a customer is a customer and the next day he is a competitor.

"So all in all, I had a rocky time for a while, but then the picture began to change. The aerospace industry moved frantically upward again and rapidly ran out of capacity, and I was in clover. Many of the independents had gone out of business, and those of us who had survived were left with more orders than we could handle. This didn't mean we could sit back and relax, of course. For one thing most of the competitors remaining are part of larger and stronger national companies. With fewer but more powerful rivals, I've had to rethink my business approach."

Although Sam's comments show merely the tip of the iceberg, he has made several significant points in *analyzing the competition,* an aspect of strategic thinking that will be covered extensively in later chapters. First, he has illustrated how a customer can become a competitor. Second, he has observed that competition changes and that market participants may decrease in number but increase in strength. As the chapters on competitor analysis will emphasize, every businessman must study his direct and indirect competitors, including firms that are vying for the use of limited resources. This process will make it possible to anticipate changes in competition as well as to evaluate a competitor's strategy and gain some insights into how and why he will change. The process will include considerable explanation about the use of data sources and other means of finding out more about competitors.

Sam's next remarks focus on Midwestern's macroenvironment—pressures from the society the organization operates in:

"You probably noted from our last annual report that sales growth exceeded profits growth. The primary reason was the costs we incurred because of new employment and work-site legislation. First, I was required to hire a higher percentage of minority workers.

Then I had to install new equipment and acoustical ceilings in order to reduce the noise level. Finally, six months ago I was forced to get new safety devices.

"Each of these expenditures cut into my profits as well as added complexity to my planning and decision making. Now a businessman must analyze social, political, and governmental demands on his firm along with customers and competition. This comprehensive tracking is very complex and takes a lot of time."

Sam is right. Today's manager must extend his planning work to include a *macroenvironment analysis*. He must evaluate not only government actions at the federal, state, and local levels but also social trends and values. He must carefully scrutinize the effect of the total environment on his own firm and also on his customers, his competitors, and his whole industry. Profitability is now only part of the game. In Chapter 7 I will discuss how a four-dimension overlay of society, government, the economy, and technology can be used to identify changes in these areas and effects on customers, the market, competitors, and your own resources. Further, I will provide conceptual approaches to reviewing the impact of these factors on strategy, and ways of testing viability and establishing contingency alert systems.

In his next remarks about his firm, Sam switches the focus of his thinking from external to internal conditions. These statements are the meat of what I call *resource analysis*.

"New laws were not the only reason for changes in my workforce. Another change, which has a positive impact on profits and sales, was the creation of a small manufacturing engineering department in my organization. During the defense-spending reductions, I was able to hire two bright young manufacturing engineers who had been laid off by Aerospace, Inc. I had second thoughts about employing additional people at the time, but it was a good strategic move. The two men have introduced new methods, a materials flow system, and inventory controls. These are now paying off and have significantly reduced my manufacturing costs.

"Another area I've improved is my financing. A few years ago I was able to negotiate a higher line of credit from four local banks. This has made it possible for me to obtain cash more readily when I need it without fancy paperwork. The extra cash enables me to obtain additional discounts from several suppliers, but its most valuable effect is that it gives me more liquidity during the periods when I have to extend credit to my customers."

Like Sam, managers typically think in terms of tangibles such as men, money, machines, and materials when they are describing resources. But Sam is also aware that his "assets" include intangibles—the know-how of his manufacturing engineers. My approach to resource analysis leads you to assess the ability and experience you and your employees have in all your organization's major functional areas. It takes into account the conceiving and designing of your products or services, their cost and quality, your marketing capability, your command and use of financing, your location, and the management skills at your firm's disposal.

This evaluation probes in depth where you've been, are now, and are likely to be in the future. It enables you to relate the opportunities and threats uncovered in your environment assessment to the resource assets and liabilities you possess currently and hope to have later.

SHAPING A STRATEGY

The conversation with Sam Mitchell has covered enough ground now for me to ask, "Could you briefly summarize your strategy and the results you would like to obtain?" He answers:

"I don't have a written or even a thought-out strategy, but I do have some concrete ideas about where I'm taking the business and how I intend to get there. I plan to improve my profit picture while continuing to expand sales. I want to acquire a small company in the southwestern part of the state and go after some of that new industrial business. There are two shops on the market in this region.

"I recently hired a new marketing manager, and I expect him to help us broaden our customer base so that we won't be so tied to Aerospace and Leisure Vehicles. Instead of purchasing new equipment, I've already begun to initiate a leasing program. This permits me to be more flexible and provides some tax advantages as well. And I've taken steps to obtain some government funds to train minority workers. This will also enable me to land some additional government contracts."

Although Sam denies having a formal strategy, he has clearly and simply described his objectives, outlined where he will invest his resources, and laid some plans for his manufacturing operations, marketing, and financing. In short he has worked out a strategy, if not in detail, and is on his way to implementing it.

A strategy is a statement of an organization's investment priorities, the management thrust, and the ways that it will use its strengths and correct its limitations to pursue the opportunities and avoid the threats facing it. Thus its overall strategy comprises three types of strategic decisions, and they fall on three levels. The first and more general level contains investment decisions, which result in what will naturally be called investment strategy. The second level describes the major categories and extent of resources required and the emphasis to be placed on each business area. The third level is a more specific set of programs describing how resources will be employed to build on strengths and correct limitations.

This fact is important to recognize, since some think that strategy development is reserved to the highest echelons of management and is not the concern of lower levels. This is not the case. Although top executives make the overall decisions on how an organization's financial and human resources will be invested, middle and lower managers know just what resources will be required, as well as the options for obtaining and using those resources, and can uncover alternative ways of building on strengths and correcting limitations. Each decision requires different forms, different people, and different levels of detail. If any of these levels is given short shrift or omitted, the overall strategy will suffer, and possibly the enterprise will fail.

Let's examine the key questions suggested by this breakdown and relate them to the conversation with Sam Mitchell.

1. How will the financial resources of the organization be allocated? This is investment strategy, and Sam has said he intends to increase both sales and earnings by expanding into the southwestern part of the state and enlarging his market scope.

2. What will it take to execute the investment decisions? This is overall management strategy, and Sam hopes to *acquire* new property and broaden his *marketing* thrust for this purpose.

3. How will Midwestern's strengths be used and limitations corrected? This is operating strategy, and Sam hasn't elaborated on the specifics, but he has decided to lease instead of buy and increase his training of minority employees to get government funds and additional contracts.

Thus Sam has answered the three key questions in general. If he explores the following subdivisions of each, he will have a total plan: What will be achieved, how, when, where, and by whom?

In the context of the three levels of decision, strategic thinking must cover all dimensions of a business. It must deal with how the product or service will be designed and developed (engineering), how it will be produced (manufacturing), sold (marketing), and financed (finance), and how these operations will be directed and coordinated (management). Just as a strategy will be incomplete if planners stop at investment decisions and do not include the operating level, it will be ineffective if they fail to include the engineering, financial, or other function of an organization.

Every leader has a strategy, whether it is expressed or not. Some plans are built purely on intuition and judgment, while others are the result of systematic and disciplined thinking—analysis, synthesis, and evaluation. The test of soundness is whether a strategy is consistent with reality and feasible to implement. The process of strategic thinking blends your experience and managerial "sixth sense" with disciplined questioning and recording. It covers strategy formulation, implementation, and review. By leading you to ask continually, "So what?" it will filter the amount of information required to uncover relevant opportunities and threats. By asking how you compare with competitors, it will force you to objectively screen out opportunities that aren't viable. Combinations of ways to use strengths and correct limitations will generate alternatives.

That entire process will culminate in a series of strategic elements which you can review in the light of your objectives. And you can validate those strategic elements in terms of your realistic assessment of past changes and of the critical resources you will need. The future is uncertain and to a large extent beyond our control. Yet we must anticipate and assume if we are to strategize. The key is to identify critical assumptions and be prepared to respond if they are mistaken. In Sam Mitchell's words:

"Of course the assumptions I'm banking on can prove wrong.

For instance, one of my key assumptions is that I can negotiate the purchase of one of those two southwestern machine shops. I could be wrong, since I haven't made a formal offer. It could be rejected because of price, or someone else may beat me to the punch or out-bid me. I have to be prepared to shift my plans radically if one of my major competitors purchases one shop or even both of them."

Throughout the following pages, I will emphasize the need to *think future* and not get trapped by the tendency to base plans on merely an extrapolation from the past. Strategic thinking entails a conscious effort to anticipate future change as well as similarities. Both are important, for planning builds on the past and present to deal with the future. The approach I will detail requires an understanding of who we are and why we have been successful or unsuccessful.

Although strategic thinking is future-oriented, it does not require psychic powers or a gift for predicting. No one can see into the future—except God. But since we must make decisions today that affect our performance tomorrow, we have to know what we assume will happen. Thus it is critical to identify our predictions or assumptions and then track those that have a significant bearing on our potential success or failure. The point is that if we see something occurring that deviates from our suppositions, we must be ready to think through its implications and be willing to modify our strategy. To be specific: Since an underlying premise of every strategy a few years back was that oil would remain plentiful and cheap, it would have been ridiculous not to restrategize when events shook that premise. This is what Sam must do if a key assumption proves to be incorrect.

In closing this chapter let me emphasize again that strategic thinking is continuous and not a time-phased process. Although the pages to come will describe where to start and imply that there is a beginning and an end, strategizing must be an ongoing activity, for the same reasons that interest in strategic planning has revived—the changing dynamics and increasing complexity of the world. As conditions alter and resources are modified, organization leaders must be constantly alert to observe how the changes can affect their planned results and their strategic approaches. This means that a tracking, monitoring, and contingency system must be an integral part of strategic planning.

The following chapters will dissect and expand on each phase of strategic thinking in sufficient depth for you to apply the concepts and steps to your business situation. As we progress I will ask that you stop and apply these in a systematic manner. By the end of the book, I hope that you, like Sam, will have a better feeling for the objectives you wish your organization to pursue and how to get there.

2

LOOKING BACKWARD WITH ONE EYE ON THE FUTURE

Strategic thinking requires data collection, processing, analysis, evaluation, and decision making. Each of these activities is complex and time consuming and requires money and manpower. How much time, money, and manpower will depend on the type and degree of change from the past and present you wish to make in the future. Actually the entire process of strategic thinking is aimed at helping you answer the question of what your organization can and should become.

Each leader, whether business, political, or humanitarian, has a vision and strives to make reality conform with it. Some visions call for a complete transformation; others entail marginal change. The type of vision you have helps define the planning process you should undertake. No one sequence is appropriate for all plans, and yours must be responsive to your situation and expectations.

THE FIVE GENERIC OPTIONS

To illustrate what I mean, I will describe the five generic choices a leader has for his organization:

Holding action:
    Continuing to be what he currently is.

Selective growth:
Growing selectively in the same market.
Diversified growth:
Growing in other markets.
Harvest:
Allowing the business to decline.
Exit:
Getting out now.

Examining each of these options will require an understanding of the organization's present and projected new markets, customers, resources, competition, and societal environment. But one option may require a more penetrating assessment of a particular factor or factors than does another—a closer scrutiny of the competition, for example, or a fuller evaluation of resources and potential threats. Let's look at the five options in some detail.

Hold Your Own

The first and normally most practical option is to hold the position you have in the markets you are now serving. It is the most appealing choice to businessmen who already have a solid share of a market that is still growing. In this situation holding doesn't mean stagnating, but in others it will bring about a decline in sales and market growth rate, though profits may continue to rise.

Many businesses have elected this course of action. Schwinn has continued for years to concentrate on the bicycle market rather than diversify. Fortunately the market has expanded dramatically, and the firm is sitting in the enviable position of being a profitable quality leader in a growth market. Some bigger companies, such as Kodak, have chosen this course with equal success. Although Kodak has diversified to a degree, it is still primarily a film products manufacturer and supplier.

Most often the hold option is appealing when a given market is still moving up the growth curve and a company is in a good position to take advantage of the expansion. Figure 2–1 shows a typical market life-cycle curve. By the use of a time scale, a businessman can predict how long it will be before growth levels off and demand begins to decline. The life span will vary from one market to another, as will the time it takes a market to get from one point to another. Chapter 4 will discuss this subject in some detail.

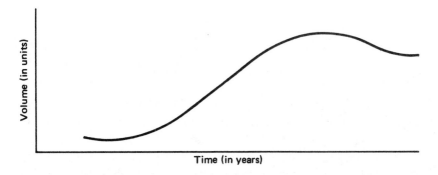

Figure 2-1 A typical market growth curve.

If the holding action seems the best option for your organization, your strategic thinking should emphasize understanding your current market and customers and anticipating any changes in buyers' expectations and needs that can affect your present position. Further, the entry or exit of competitors and your relative strengths and limitations should also be carefully scrutinized. The analysis will be more defensive than offensive.

Grow Selectively

A second option is to grow by entering or refocusing on markets related to, or extensions of, your current market. You might select the new markets because they are growing more rapidly than that in which you are currently participating or because you can exercise some unique ability or strength in them. This activity is commonly accompanied by vertical or horizontal integration.

Vertical integration is what the oil-refining companies did when they extended backward into petroleum exploration and then moved into direct distribution of heating oil and fuel to end-use consumers (individual homeowners and vehicle owners) by operating their own heating oil companies and service stations. In addition, finding that petroleum extracts and byproducts provided other profitable ventures, the companies moved horizontally into chemicals, agricultural, and plastics businesses. In these cases their growth came as a function of knowing their products and developing new applications. In others this type of growth derives from knowing and anticipating customers' needs. For example IBM recognized that its current customers needed typewriters and word-processing equipment such as dictation and transcribing machines. Later it moved into the reproduction equipment market with the same customer base.

In considering the possibility of integrating, you must therefore assess your markets and customers carefully. Another area of considerable importance is competitors. You must recognize that as you move forward, backward, or sideways, you may confront competitors who were customers, suppliers, or dealers of yours. Each type of competitor will have different talents and abilities, and your move will cause changes in these firms that may require new resources in your firm to meet.

Diversify

Growth by diversification is the most ambitious option and the most difficult to achieve. It normally begins with an organization's recognizing that current and related markets won't provide the growth it desires. This means it must either change its expectations or move into foreign waters. The conglomerate of the 1960s was a typical example. H. S. Geneen recognized that he couldn't make ITT an exciting growth company by staying in the regulated telecommunications industry and related fields, so he hired a consultant to seek out new market opportunities and companies that could provide the earnings growth he wanted. The result was ITT's movement into car rentals, hotels, baked goods, and insurance.

On a less ambitious scale, General Motors, Ford, and American Motors moved into appliances, Xerox into education, and Gulf into nuclear energy. When I say "less ambitious," I am referring to the span of the diversification, not the investment and risk.

An organization will typically start searching for diversification opportunities because there is a gap between its current business trajectories and its stated earnings or sales objective. Next, careful assessments of market growth projections, competitive concentration, and new trends in demand help identify the fastest-growing and potentially most desirable markets. In recent years many companies have chosen the acquisition route, but if time permits, a firm should also consider diversifying from within, building its expansion on its current organizational resources.

The batting average of successful diversification efforts is relatively low, since this move requires the ability to perceive things differently and evaluate critically what it will take to be successful in a new kind of undertaking. Often institutions see the pot of gold but fail to recognize what it will take to get there. Ford seems to have failed to make it in appliances, and Xerox (like many others) hasn't done what it said it would do in education. Even the conglomerates have been surprised at the difficulty of moving into new markets and industries. Diversification takes considerably more time, effort, and study than any other option.

Harvest Gradually

Many businessmen find themselves implementing a decision to let an operation decline without really knowing it. If exercised properly, a plan to harvest selectively and to prune dying or dead wood can be very profitable. In a large company that has a variety of business activities, those harvested can fund the growth segments. The secret of success in this option is objective periodic evaluation of all products or segments and decisive action to cut back those contributing least to the organization's well-being. If you are the leader of such a segment and it is healthy though declining in rate of growth, you should begin to return large amounts of cash to the firm. The reason is that the cash and capital requirements should become increasingly lower than needed to satisfy the previous customer population. Unless there is an erratic competitor, market participation should be stabilized, and each supplier should be reaping the benefits. In fact the competition may be declining, since the less successful may be exiting, which may put you in the enviable position of actually enlarging your market share and sales volume while increasing profits and cash flow. There are two major pitfalls in this situation. The leader may overestimate his slice of the competitive pie and invest more than the market or industry demand justifies. Or he may panic and help accelerate the decline or, even worse, erode the profit margins.

Exit

The fifth option is to get out now, even at a loss. This is the most unpleasant of any of the choices available, but it may have to be faced and executed for the long-term good of the whole organization. The unpleasantness stems from the negative impact the option appears to have on all the stakeholders—all those individuals or groups who have a stake in the business and its results, that is, whose future will be affected by the organization's performance.

Stakeholders range from immediate to remote, and in macroeconomic terms, they ultimately include the world. From the more realistic viewpoint of who has a conscious interest in the organization, stakeholders can be classified as stockholders, investors, directors, managers at all levels, other employees and their unions, customers, suppliers, the communities the organization functions in, and the larger public and its governments.

Stakeholder reactions must be taken into account when any of the five options is being explored, as Chapter 10 will discuss in some detail. But the strategy constructed to carry out the exit decision is often the most difficult to implement because of the widespread and potentially intense repercussions. There may be considerable emotional backlash. Managers may be unwilling to think about divestiture because the product, division, or subsidiary holds fond memories and is like one of their own children. Employees will be very upset at the prospect of losing their jobs. Members of the community may fear that this action will start a downhill trend and turn prosperity into doom. Stockholders and investors may see it as a threat rather than an opportunity to get rid of losers and concentrate on winners. There may also be material consequences for some stakeholders that will rebound on the whole firm. It is crucial, for example, to determine the impact of the move on customers, especially dealers, on whom the organization will continue to rely to buy other products and services. Timing too can be vital.

In many instances companies have exited from a market too soon and lost money. An excellent illustration is the vacuum-tube business. Vacuum tubes for radios and television sets were being manufactured by many companies when, as so often happens, a new product using new technology came along, in this case the semiconductor. As it moved up in the market, numerous major producers of vacuum tubes concluded that semiconductors would replace their product in toto and decided to close down their operations. The few concerns left decided for various reasons to hang in there and ride the curve down. Fortunately for these few diehards and unfortunately for those who exited, the market didn't collapse—in fact, it began to grow, as Figure 2–2 illustrates. The reason was the emergence of color television, which needed vacuum tubes. The result was an expanding market with fewer competitors, and those who remained were forced to add rather than reduce capacity.

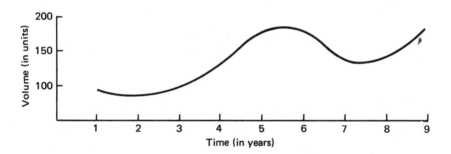

Figure 2-2 The vacuum-tube market growth curve.

A START

The option that management chooses obviously affects an organization's plans from the moment the decision is taken. The process of strategic thinking is aimed at helping you not only make that decision but remain alert to factors that might change your mind as you progress. I would like to suggest some basic guidelines that will help you determine the degree of change in direction you should consider. The guidelines are built on the premise that change is a function of (1) the type of company you manage and how it has operated in the past; (2) the time and human resources you have to carry out the thinking and planning activity; (3) your desires and those of other key stakeholders.

Guideline 1: Know Yourself

First ask yourself this question: "What kind of company am I now managing, and what has it been in the past?" On the surface this sounds like a simple question, but as you think about it and pose it to others, you will quickly find that it isn't so easy to answer. A consultant once said to me that in a client company of his, the past seemed as uncertain as the future. This superficially humorous statement is in reality very significant. He meant that its managers had a difficult time describing the type of company it had been—let alone agreeing on what it should be in the future.

The uncertainty wasn't surprising in this case, because the client was an old and large diversified company whose executives had had a variety of experiences and developed different perceptions of the firm. But I don't think this phenomenon is reserved to big companies. Even in smaller enterprises the view of managers in manufacturing will differ from that of managers in marketing or engineering. The correct picture of what a company has been will usually lie in a composite of these varying perceptions. It may take an outsider to help management come to grips with this tough but key question from the start.

Another factor to consider is past results. How successful or unsuccessful a business has been will often determine the desire to change. If a company has made a lot of money being a components supplier in an industry, it may not wish or have the ability to change to a systems supplier or move into another industry. Changing the name doesn't change reality. I have found that success really does breed inertia and often plants the seeds of ultimate collapse.

If you choose to make the company something considerably different from what it is and has been, the planning process will clearly be complex and time consuming. Also it must be an inside job— no phase of strategic thinking can simply be delegated to outsiders. These points should be obvious, but it is amazing how many businessmen ignore or overlook the complexity of the process and even think they can hire some smart M.B.A. or prestigious consulting firm to work out all the details.

Guideline 2: Appraise Your Planning Resources

Another major ingredient of sound strategic planning is a disciplined allocation of time and manpower. If the chief executive is unwilling or unable to spend time on the thinking and planning process, his options will be limited or will depend largely on luck. A few years ago I discussed this point with a potential client, who promptly informed me that he wouldn't spend more than two or three weeks out of the entire year on this activity. "I'm too busy running the business," he said, "and besides, I don't have the inclination to plan." This was his attitude despite the fact that he had very ambitious objectives that required overcoming strongly entrenched competition in a relatively slow-growing market. His stated mission was to grow through diversification. My reaction was that either he would change his mind and become more involved or he would fail to move the operation as he wanted. Within two years it was apparent that he wasn't going to become committed to strategic thinking, and though he had hired a staff to do the work, he had failed to reach his objectives.

This leads to a second question that will help you determine the option to select: "How much time am I personally willing to commit to strategic thinking?" If the answer is "Little" or "Only what is necessary," then I believe that the best you can expect is to hold or to grow selectively as opportunities arise.

Another time question deals with the dedication and involvement of key operating managers and planning staff. If the business is expected to move dynamically, this will require the continuing participation of other operating managers and a large staff of planners. If the operating managers are firefighting and can't see beyond today, they won't be able to plan, which will limit the degree and type of change the firm can make. The number and mix of planners should also be evaluated. Top-notch planners are difficult to find, and since strategic thinking is part science and part art, you must not assume that you can easily recruit a large, skilled staff. Thus you must assess your current capability and include this in your decision about the reality of the vision you have. The combination of a small staff, firefighting managers, and a limited commitment from you may restrict your business to a holding position or even force you to retrench.

Guideline 3: Assess Your Own and Your Stakeholders' Desires

After you have realistically inventoried your organization's past and present situation and planning resources, you should candidly take stock of your own desires. A chief executive's vision changes with age and the amount of time he has left on the job. If you are 50 or less and can see another 10 or 15 years ahead of you, or if you wish to leave a thriving business to your children, you will most likely want to make the firm grow and continue to prosper. If you are older than 65, you are most likely interested in stability and earnings.

Of course there are some exceptions, and there isn't always a direct relationship between vision and age. I've seen people in their 30s who for all practical purposes were retired, and on the other side of the coin, there are those in their 70s who think and act half their age. But unless you are the owner and wish to provide for your heir, the glamour of growth will quite probably take a back seat to the satisfactions of holding your own and enjoying the fruits of your labor.

Most organizations today are not dominated by one man. The chief executive is immediately responsible to others—his board of directors, his major stockholders, his investors. These stakeholders, along with employees, community members, and other groups described earlier in this chapter, can have a profound effect on his final choice. They can force even the unambitious to strive for the nearly impossible. It is useful at this early stage of the strategic thinking process for you to consider the potential influence of the goals and expectations of those stakeholders on your selection of an option.

If you head a component part of a larger organization, you may be told what to do with your business. You may be asked to diversify; you may be directed to hold position and generate earnings; you may be required to exit in order to provide cash for other, more promising parts of the corporation. I've seen a number of situations in which the top manager was so displeased with what he was told to do that he resigned rather than sacrifice the future of the business for today's profits. But even if you find yourself contemplating such a move, it is important that you honestly assess your component's past and present, its planning resources, and your own desires, since you may have the opportunity to persuade those above you that your mission should be different from what they think.

SEPARATING THE DO-ABLE FROM THE IMPOSSIBLE DREAM

The entire purpose of determining where you have been, are now, and desire to be is to increase the probability that you can achieve what you set out to do. It is useless to pursue an impossible dream. It must be recognized that people are rarely able to change quickly and do things they have never done before. The same thing is true of organizations. They can't be what they have never been without major surgery, and we all know that a serious operation can kill the patient. A knowledge of past performance, present condition, and expectations for the future is as necessary to a business planner as to a physician. Yet I have witnessed or read about many situations where this first step in the planning process was never taken and the organization set out with the probability of failure greatly outweighing the chance of success.

To repeat, strategic thinking begins with your decision on the direction you wish to lead your business in. You reach that decision through what I call *mission development*. This will enable you to foresee the type of information you will require and where to put the emphasis in your analyses and projections. The three key questions for mission development can be expanded to five:

1. What type of business has yours been and is it now? Has it been a supplier of components for a system or a systems integrator? Has it been domestic or worldwide in scope? And so on.

2. Does it have any unique features to build on? These are normally strengths that are well recognized and not subject to argument, such as unique technical, marketing, or financial resources. They provide a running start and should be used.

3. What are your planning resources? These, as I said, should include the abilities of your key managers and planning staff members as well as your own.

4. What are your personal ambitions and expectations? Do you wish to expand the business, or do you want to cash in your chips and get the reward you deserve? Are you mainly interested in "the good life," or would you like to move to other pastures, like public service or office?

5. What are the interests and desires of the major stakeholders? Making a quick pass at this assessment, which will be carried out more systematically at a later phase in the process, will help you avoid surprises.

APPLICATION TIME

Throughout this book I will periodically request that you stop reading and apply the process of strategic thinking to your own situation. This application will enable you to test your understanding of the approach and to gain an appreciation for the type of thinking and discipline that is required. The way to do this is to use the theory in practical applications and not merely to be a passive viewer. Since considerable thought is required, it is better for you to spend the time as you go rather than shortcut the process in order to get through more quickly.

Stop now and answer the questions just summarized. It will be helpful if you get into the habit of recording your thoughts so that they will be available for later reference.

SOME THOUGHTS ABOUT THE
NONPROFIT ORGANIZATION

The same logical process just outlined for business firms pertains to nonprofit organizations. Whether we are talking about hospitals, social welfare services, research centers, universities, government agencies, or religious bodies, mission is important. Let me take a few examples.

Religious orders. I have witnessed the problem of mission change in many religious orders of the Roman Catholic Church. Orders dedicated to supporting the Catholic education system began some years ago to lose confidence in their product—Catholic schooling. They questioned the continuing viability of their work, and many began to rethink their purpose. Some orders pulled out of education and moved into new areas, such as social services for the poor. Of course there were already orders providing these services. Often the mission changes represented big deviations from the past, and some don't appear to have been well thought through. Numbers of the new undertakings have failed, and others are close to foundering.

Universities. Following World War II colleges and universities moved aggressively toward expansion. Many small liberal arts institutions added graduate departments. Other schools branched into business and education specialities, choosing diversified growth. But many of these moves were made without strategic thinking. The institutions did not adequately explore what they were, why they had succeeded in the past, what resources they had, and where they wanted to go. Today they are paying for this. In some cases even survival is in question.

Mission Development	
Type of Company	What kind of organization has yours been? (Include the markets served, extent and type of participation, and strategy executed.)
Planning Resources	What type of planning support is available? How much time and effort do you wish to commit?
Uniqueness	What uniqueness does your organization have? (This is a preliminary listing of assets which will be confirmed later.)
Your Vision	Describe the type of organization you wish to manage in the future. (This may utilize the five generic options available. It begins to address the strategic questions you will select later, after your evaluation of environment, competition, and resources.)
Stakeholders	How do your desires compare with those of other decision-making stakeholders?
Output	This is a statement of direction and an indicator of the type of information you will analyze and anticipate.

Research centers. There are many single-purpose institutes that focus on one disease or one medical specialty. They grow and prosper as they work toward the results for which they were established. These are excellent examples of organizations with specific vision and purpose. But they too have a problem. What happens when they achieve their objective? Do they exit, harvest, or strike out toward new growth? Most often the institution's main purpose is survival, and it moves into new areas of research. Unfortunately this will duplicate efforts if the area is already being investigated by others. This puts yet another group in competition for scarce resources.

The point is that mission development is equally important for all organizations, whether their activities result in a profit or not. The key steps in mission development are outlined in the accompanying checklist. (To consolidate the elements of each phase of strategic thinking, similar checklist summaries will be given at the end of most subsequent chapters.)

3

CUSTOMERS DETERMINE THE
SUCCESSFUL STRATEGY

More than 20 years ago, Peter Drucker wrote, ". . . business is not determined by the producer, but by the customer."* This quotation had been universally approved; 99.9 percent of the businessmen you speak with will agree it is correct. Yet most businessmen act as though they are in full command of the situation and the customer will merely buy what they offer.

If businessmen practiced what they say they believe, they would recognize that strategic thinking must begin with a comprehensive study of their customers. On the contrary many begin their planning with an invention or market data. Thus they lose sight of the fact that customers—as individuals and in groups—make a product successful and expand markets. In this chapter I will describe an approach to customer analysis that will emphasize who customers are, why and how they buy, and what changes can influence their purchasing habits, among other considerations. The analysis will yield a better understanding of how markets are segmented and ultimately how the entire market is shaped. Here are some of the questions that will provide the pictures:

Who?
Who are your customers?
How can they be classified?

*Peter Drucker, *The Practice of Management*, New York: Harper & Row, 1954.

Which classification is most important to you and your competitors?

Will this classification still be most important in the future? *Why?*

Why do customers buy when and as much as they do?

What are their objectives?

Which objectives are most important?

Are the reasons for purchasing and their ranking in importance likely to change?

What if . . . ?

What could cause a change in customers' objectives?

What information will help anticipate these changes?

So what?

What are the implications of change in customer behavior and objectives?

Will the impact be positive or negative on you relative to the impact on your competition?

What then?

How will this customer classification add to your understanding of the total market, size, mix, growth rate, and timing?

CLASSIFYING CUSTOMERS

Since it is ordinarily impractical to analyze each customer, I will suggest that you classify your major customers in groups. An easy method and one that will yield strategic insights is to classify customers according to the reasons they buy the goods or services your industry provides.

Fundamentally customers make their purchases for one of three major reasons: (1) to use themselves, (2) to include in another product or service that they sell, or (3) to sell to someone else in the same form but in varying quantities.

Customers Who Buy for Their Own Use

Consumers. This term is applied to purchasers who consume the product themselves. We are all consumers of some products or services. We buy a car to drive, regardless of whether for pleasure or business, or a washing machine to use in our own homes.

Industrial users. These companies or institutions use the product or service in their operations. It may be the same one bought by consumers—a washing machine, rubber gloves, a window-cleaning service—but industrial users make their buying decisions differently and should be grouped accordingly. Commercial purchasers of air conditioners for example would be willing to pay more for higher-performance units than homeowners because they would calculate the payoff period and determine when they would recoup the larger investment with smaller operating costs. This can be very significant from the standpoint of building a strategy.

Regulated users. These are similar to industrial users but should be classified separately because special constraints and motivations influence their buying decisions. The constraints, in the form of special laws or regulations, may dictate how they buy, how they pay for their purchases, or how they will be paid for their services. This is now well known by most consumers of electricity, who have learned how the utility companies are able to recoup their investments through higher rates. Among other regulated users are telephone companies, water and gas utilities, railroads, airlines, and trucking and transfer lines.

Government users. This classification includes all levels of government—federal, state, county, and municipal. These users purchase a product or service in order to promote the public good. It might be police equipment, fire apparatus, or public relations consultants for various agencies. Like regulated users, government customers operate under special constraints and must make their purchases in accordance with specific procedures. The supplier must understand these characteristics thoroughly in order to anticipate change.

Customers Who Buy to Incorporate Another Product or Service

Original equipment manufacturers. The OEM company purchases parts, components, or subsystems from another manufacturer and incorporates them into its own product. Examples are the lawnmower producers who buy the motors they install in their machines and the air-conditioner makers who use other manufacturers' compressors. The component or subsystem loses its identity and becomes part of the larger. The cardinal point in assessing this group of customers is to anticipate whether they will find it more economical to produce the component or part for themselves, thus withdrawing their business from you or perhaps even becoming a competitor.

Contractors. Contractors are another type of customer who purchases components, parts, and supplies and includes them in his services. A building contractor may buy complete kitchen units and incorporate them into the houses or apartments he puts up. The whole concept of modular construction revolves on a builder's purchasing pieces and assembling them rather than fabricating each unit from scratch. The military business was built on the practice of using prime and supporting contractors, each adding his own value and each making a profit on his contribution to the total product or service.

Customers Who Buy to Resell

Consumer distributors. These concerns purchase large quantities and often many kinds of products and repackage and sell them in smaller lots to dealers or directly to consumers. There are many types of distributors, and they provide a very valuable service to small businesses. Larger producers have generally found that it is more economical and efficient to have their own distributors, which they frequently own.

Industrial distributors. These are similar to consumer distributors but concentrate on industrial rather than consumer products and sell to industrial users or OEMs. They too are becoming less important to large companies but are still key to small businesses.

The importance of distributors varies from industry to industry and will be discussed in the following chapter, which presents industry analysis. Some companies have created or purchased their own distributors, as I just mentioned, and these must be carefully scrutinized when you undertake resource analysis in Chapter 6.

Subdividing the Classifications Further

Once customers are grouped by use of your product or service, they can be described and classified with more precision. Consumers, for example, can be analyzed by demographic and personal characteristics such as age, sex, occupation, location, income level, marital status, and knowledge of products. Industrial users can be grouped according to the specific types of products they turn out. For instance some of your metal-producing customers may specialize in steel, others in aluminum, and still others in tin or copper, and some may be generalists that participate in several of these areas. Another group may be involved in synthetics, while still others may provide communications services. The Federal Government Standard Industrial Classifications (SIC) are an excellent source for guidance on grouping customers, and they are used by government publications to provide historical trends and projections.

Regulated customers can be classified according to the kind of service they provide, but even more important to know are their ownership characteristics and funding basis. Some electric utilities are wholly or partially government-owned. Some are quasi-public and though government-supported operate like private enterprises. Still others are stock companies and must consider their stockholders' interests as well as provide service. Then there are cooperatives, and new forms of utilities are appearing on the horizon. The key strategic issue facing companies serving these groups of customers is whether they will change and what mix of private, quasi-public, and public ventures will exist in the future.

Government users can be broken down into levels and types. Federal customers may be classified according to the branch they belong to (executive, legislative, or judicial) and then according to department or agency (Department of Defense, Federal Trade Commission, and so forth). These affiliations may be critical to later evaluation since each government body has its own regulations and ways of doing business. In some cases these purchasers are competitive and may not desire to use common suppliers, thus pre-empting a piece of market. Customers belonging to state governments may be subdivided in similar ways. Local-government users are also an important customer group that may or may not be homogeneous. For instance some cities centralize purchasing whereas others decentralize it. Each type of government customer has different powers, requires specific services, and operates under particular constraints as to how and when it makes purchases.

I wish to caution you not to get carried away in grouping customers to the point where you are classifying for the sake of classifying. You should subdivide only as far as you need to uncover factors that may require a unique resource to provide a strategic advantage. This is a point that must be kept in mind if you have a planning staff or hire an outside research firm to do a study of your customers. Such specialists can be so enamored of collecting and codifying data that they lose sight of the purposes of the job, which are to examine the reasons for past success or failure and to anticipate the future.

Classification—A Means, Not an End

Many businesses use a customer classification scheme such as the one I have just described but fail to relate it to either their current operations or their strategy. After you have identified your major customer groups, use these subdivisions to determine their relative importance to you, to your competitors, and to your industry in general. This comparison can be of considerable help in answering vital strategic questions and unveiling potential changes and their impact. Do you rely on the same types of customers as your competitors, or are yours different? If your buyers change, will you alone feel it, or will it affect some or even all other suppliers? Let's illustrate these issues with a realistic if simple example.

Suppose you make small motors for the kind of equipment used in machine and hobby shops. About 25 percent of your sales go to consumers directly, and the vast majority of these buyers are in the northeastern United States and are men between the ages of 25 and 35. Another 25 percent of your product is bought by industrial users, and these are primarily steel fabricators. The remaining 50 percent goes mainly to OEMs producing machine tools.

As you review these statistics, you begin to wonder how your percentages compare with those of the past and how they stack up against the figures of others in the industry. A survey of your preceding five years shows that your sales to OEMs have declined from 65 percent while sales to consumers directly have increased from 10 percent. Thus you realize that a change has occurred of a strategic nature, a change that has affected how you do business. It leads you to ask: What will these percentages be in the future? This projection is relevant because your manufacturing and marketing practices vary for different types of customers. This information also helps you think about customers' uses and objectives, which in turn can provide a means of anticipating changes.

You now compare your sales mix with the industry average and with that of your major competitors in order to determine how similar or dissimilar your customer base is and how vulnerable you are to change. You find the percentages that appear in Table 3-1. They show that your sales breakdown is rather similar to the industry's and not far from being a replica of competitor Y's, while competitor X has concentrated more heavily on OEM sales. Each company has segmented the market, and the results have changed the mix and the vulnerability to change. OEM sales are essential to all of you, but X has more to lose or gain if they shift in the future. If this market segment grows at the expense of the consumer or industrial user group, you and competitor Y are more vulnerable than X. Knowing more about OEMs seems important. You should probe the reasons for and the effects of the objectives and purchasing habits of OEM customers.

Table 3-1. Customer mix comparison.

Types of Customers	Your Sales	Competitor X's Sales	Competitor Y's Sales	Industry Average
Consumers	25%	15%	25%	24%
Industrial users	25	20	20	30
OEMs	50	65	55	46

There are many illustrations of the need for customer classification to be found in recent business history. In the past five years, we have witnessed American Motors concentrating on the small-car consumer, while the rest of the industry fought it out in the large-car consumer segment. AMC took a gamble and was able to hold share in 1975, while Chrysler took the opposite approach and has lost share to the small-car imports. There are several companies in the appliance industry who choose to concentrate on supplying components to producers of consumer goods. They have been increasingly troubled by backward integration as more producers have undertaken to make their own compressors, motors, and controls.

CUSTOMER OBJECTIVES

Now that you have a classification of customers and an understanding of which are most important to your company directly and indirectly, you can *selectively* probe as to why they buy when, as well as what is critical to them.

Obviously customers purchase goods and services to satisfy specific objectives, which vary from one type of customer to another and may change for one type in degree of importance over time. For purposes of analysis, customer objectives may be divided into three kinds: economic, functional, and psychological.

Economic motives may dominate purchasing decisions in periods of economic uncertainty or inflation. In mid-1973, for example, American housewives became concerned and angered about the price of meat and intensified their comparison shopping. Families began eating more meat substitutes. Economists call this "price elasticity," which means that demand correlates inversely with price. If a market were perfectly elastic, every percentage increase in price would be matched by an equivalent decrease in demand. All markets have some elasticity.

There are times when the functional attributes of a product become more important than cost. A motorist with a flat tire on a highway will probably pay whatever he must to get it repaired or replaced. He doesn't run around comparing prices. Industrialists confronted with safety legislation and the potential legal and monetary repercussions are motivated to satisfy the legal requirements regardless of costs.

The third category is psychological motives, which are primary in the purchase of prestige-oriented products and services. In these cases the utility and cost of a product may be of reverse importance. The fad purchaser is motived in this way. People buy to demonstrate to their friends, neighbors, or colleagues that they are financially successful enough to own such a product as a Cadillac, Lincoln, or Rolls-Royce. The fact that they are large, uneconomic, and expensive to purchase, service, and operate isn't significant. This motivation can also stand behind the purchase of inexpensive items. In the early 1960s the Volkswagen was a prestige-oriented product even though it was cheaper than other cars. This came about because many members of the young sophisticate group decided to make the Volkswagen a status symbol, one that signaled not wealth but intelligence and "being in."

Let's examine each of these sets of objectives in more detail.

Economic Objectives

Many businessmen think that economic factors are the most important if not the only ones that need to be explored. It is true that price must be considered in determining a marketing and business strategy, but it is not the only motivator. Moreover cost to the customer comes in many shapes and forms, and most buyers take these into account to some degree.

First, there is the initial purchase price. The government requires many of its suppliers to submit bids and then chooses the lowest bid that also meets functional and quality specifications. Some consumers are very price-conscious and allow their buying decision to be influenced too much by this factor. There are industrial users, distributors, OEMs, and contractors who also fall in this category.

Second is the cost of operating the product or service. The customer may be looking at how much use he may have of his purchase—for example whether he will need it for two or ten months a year or whether it will last five or 25 years. This is true of industrial users, which evaluate operating time and life span very carefully. In the nuclear energy field, this is a major factor in the selection of generating systems. Consumers became very aware of operating costs as the price of gasoline doubled in a few months in late 1973 and early 1974. The cost of power has affected home-owners' evaluations of heating and cooling systems. Suddenly air conditioners and heating units with high efficiency ratings began to be gobbled up while the less efficient units stayed on the store shelves.

A related cost depends on the complexity of the product's operation. If the equipment is so difficult to use that it takes highly trained and skilled personnel, then the customer may factor that into his decision. This may also become a strategic consideration in determining the marketing and service pricing elements of your strategy.

A third economic factor is the cost of service and maintenance. Again some customer groups carefully scrutinize this expense in making their buying decisions. This became a recognized problem for many foreign producers who entered or reentered U.S. markets after World War II. They may have had lower prices and been able to demonstrate lower operating expenses, but they were at a serious disadvantage because of a lack of service facilities, relatively high prices of replacement parts, and a shortage of trained service personnel.

Industrial users and other business groups are also aware that the time it takes to repair a product can critically increase service costs since it reduces operating use. The additional expense is compounded if other equipment must be leased or rented in order to fill the gap so that business will not have to be turned away because of lack of capacity. This has happened to many electric utilities when their generators have broken down or plant operations have had to be suspended for maintenance work. It has cost money to purchase power from other utilities, and in some cases suppliers have had to reduce power, thus losing revenues.

Functional Objectives

The functional attributes of a product or service relate to customer needs and expectations. Each group of customers look at function from their own point of view. A pleasure skier may select skis for their durability and adaptability to various snow conditions, while a novice may be most enthusiastic about ease of use and safety. A professional skier may view capacity for speed as most important.

A small businessman may want a car that is practical for making deliveries but attractive enough to use as a family car too. A salesman may look for driving comfort and the high quality needed to sustain excessive highway use. A car dealer may be interested only in models that sell quickly and provide high profit margins.

As I said earlier, customer objectives may change over time. A change in functional expectations may be due to a buyer's experience or age, or it may be due to factors outside his control. An excellent example is the effect the gasoline shortage had on the type and number of automobiles sold in the United States. Even salesmen who use cars for their work modified their preferences. They became more interested in the small car, which requires less gas to operate than the larger cars they were used to.

Further, a product's functional appeal may change as it moves along the maturity, or growth, curve. In early periods its newness or innovative characteristics may differentiate it from competitive lines. The first metal ski had unique properties and appealed to professional and recreational skiers alike. As its market matured and fiberglass came into use, the metal ski began to move into the commodity category. Products in the commodity category are so similar they cannot be easily differentiated and are therefore viewed by customers as being virtually the same product.

Psychological Objectives

Psychological motives relate to intangible aspects of a customer's perceptions such as the satisfaction he gets simply from owning or using a product or service. As I said before, an obvious factor is status enhancement, which may well provide a greater impulse to buy than do economic or functional considerations. In the late 1950s and early 1960s, the big, fin-adorned, high-horsepower automobile was regarded as a reflection of the owner's affluence. More recently the large-screen color television set and the stereophonic sound system with massive, even ugly speakers were "in" things. Companies have purchased the biggest, most complicated computers because they wanted to be considered progressive and dynamic. These factors shouldn't be overlooked as you evaluate each customer group since they may suggest unique opportunities. But you shouldn't forget that psychological objectives also change with time. The big car lost its status appeal and the small sports car took its place. Color television developed a mass market and no longer had significance as a sign of its owner's exclusiveness. Stereo may be replaced by the quadraphonic sound system as the prestige product in its industry.

CAUSES OF CHANGE

Strategy deals with anticipating change. It is vital to try to foresee what may change your customer base and why. The question to ask yourself next is therefore, "What may happen to cause groups of customers to develop new objectives and different priorities?"

There are three major sources of change in customers' purchasing patterns and ranking of priorities: environment, resources, and strategy. In essence these are the same factors that may prompt you to alter your plans. Because of this similarity a supplier's managers can confuse the buyer's problems with their own and fail to assess his actual situation.

The Customer's Environment

The first place to look for factors of change from the environment is the economy. If it is advancing and inflation is under control, the customer, whether an industrial user, an OEM, or a government agency, may be bullish and accelerate the timing and size of purchases. Given a downturn, he may demand new terms and conditions, delay buying, or even stop ordering altogether.

A change in the competitive scene can also influence purchasing behavior. If your customer is an industrial user or OEM, competition can affect his willingness to take risks. If he is forced into a price war and his profit margins are declining, he may choose to concentrate on cost savings and decrease his concern over function and quality. The individual consumer is also subject to competitive forces that may siphon off his money and move him into the economic arena.

Government, as we all know, is an increasingly important constituent of the business environment. Customers are affected by taxation, legislation bearing on work conditions and operations, and fiscal and monetary policies. On the tax side customers may find that they have additional cash because of special investment credits or deductions. This may increase their desire to obtain delivery quickly so that their outlay on the purchase will be eligible for the tax break. Conservation and safety laws may have inflicted heavy expenses on many of your customers. Industrial users have been forced to add pollution-control equipment—a fine boost for those in this business but a serious drain on other vendors. Government and regulated customers must also comply, so they too have diverted funds to this activity. Fiscal and monetary policies have had major impacts on the cost of money, and many of your customers may have been driven to curtail or delay acquisitions because they couldn't obtain financing or afford the attendant expenses.

I could go on, but I think the point is made: in order to anticipate changes in your customer base, you will need to spend some time identifying the crucial environmental factors that can alter your buyers' desire and need to purchase.

Abilities and Resources

Another group of factors that can change a customer's purchasing habits relate to the abilities and resources at his organization's command.

High on the list is the buyer's ongoing ability to finance purchases. In recent years some very powerful industrial concerns have gone bankrupt. Some companies—Rolls-Royce and Penn-Central Transportation, for example—have been put into receivership, and the profits of many suppliers went with them. For a variety of reasons, cash-paying class A customers may become oriented toward terms and conditions, or outright purchasers may become lessees. The timing and size of orders may change radically. There are techniques for analyzing the financial abilities of some of your industrial and government customers. These are the same as the methods for evaluating the financial potential of competitors, and they will be described in a later chapter.

You may also lose a customer because he develops your product or service himself. A buyer's ability to conceive, design, and produce what he has been purchasing from you obviously has strategic implications for you. Any of several considerations may decide him to make rather than buy—economy, supply conditions, a desire to increase performance or contribution margin. Whatever the reason, not only may a major customer disappear, but a new and strong competitor may appear. Ford's decision to buy Philco had an impact on independent radio producers like Motorola. Sam Mitchell's remarks in Chapter 1 told how customers did their own machining during a period of recession, which reduced the volume of his business.

Another factor that may alter a customer's objectives is his growing familiarity with a product or service—his ability to decide what he needs, when he needs it, and who should use it. When a product is new, the customer's need for presale counsel and guidance is high. There are numerous examples of this. In the early years of computers, IBM capitalized on users' inexperience and provided them with extensive help in selecting equipment, converting manual data processing into computerized systems, training operators, and creating programming. The results are well known. When Howard Head introduced metal skis, he made sure that his salespeople were well acquainted with the sport, and he trained the owners and managers of specialty ski shops to help the consumer make his choice. And as electronic controls replaced electromechanical, electronics manufacturers helped their OEM customers create the necessary new designs.

Thus suppliers of a new item adopt a package approach and include a variety of services in the sale or leasing agreement. But as customers become more experienced, they learn how to provide such extras for themselves or procure them from other outside sources. This affects the way you sell as well as the resources you require. It also opens the market to new, aggressive, unintegrated competitors who can offer the product alone, without the expensive backup services.

The person who makes the customer's purchasing decisions and how he makes them can have strategic implications for you. In some organizations, due to the size and magnitude of the purchases, the decisions on what, when, and how to buy are reserved to the top executive levels. In others the decisions are carefully scrutinized by teams of multifunctional experts. The background, interests, and perceptions of decision makers influence their organization's purchasing objectives and must be anticipated.

More than a decade ago a large electrical-products manufacturer concluded that it would be able to obtain a significant share of the electric utility data processing market because it had excellent relations with electric utility customers. However, the manufacturer overlooked the fact that although the utilities were the same, the decision makers were not. The manufacturer's traditional products were sold to the technical management of the utilities, whereas data processing equipment was sold to the financial management. This overlooked factor contributed to the manufacturer's inability to significantly penetrate that market.

Another important aspect of the customer's decision-making process is the criteria used to evaluate the purchase. At certain stages of a product's life cycle, economy is paramount; at others quality or performance tops the list. An illustration can be taken from the nuclear power business. In the early 1960s nuclear energy plants were judged primarily on economic grounds. Then as ecology pressures gradually evolved and the price of fossil fuels rose, more emphasis was placed on questions of the reliability and availability of nuclear power. This change had a marked impact on the strategies of all the major suppliers of nuclear fuel and systems.

Strategies

A third set of factors which can change a customer's purchasing habits derives from his investment management and operating strategies. When major purchasers or customer groups decide to change their strategies, these new directions must be carefully noted. Let's look at a few strategic changes by customers that can force you to change your strategy.

You might find that steel companies you sell to are gradually moving their production facilities abroad. This means that they are perhaps geographically closer to other sources of supply. Or an electronics manufacturer to whom you sell may have decided to move into mass production and cut back on the variety of products it has been turning out. Customer groups that have been relying on internally generated funds might be switching to long-term debt. Rather than requiring cash on delivery, they may be offering their buyers extended terms and demand the same from you and other suppliers. The customer likewise may change his attitude toward debt and demand longer periods to pay. Finally, new practices in the customer's organization may affect you. A customer may decide to hire people from the outside for some key jobs rather than promote current employees. The new executives may come from different industries and have different perceptions and expectations. Your long-term relationships may disappear and in fact become obstacles to overcome rather than assets.

IMPLICATIONS OF CHANGE

Each element of a customer's strategy can have a pronounced impact on you, opening new opportunities and threats for your business. Even a small change in a buyer's strategy, environment, or resources may trigger a chain reaction that will ultimately affect how he and perhaps his whole customer group make their purchasing decisions. Your analysis of your buyers up to this point has thrown light on who your major customer groups are and what segment of the market you stress; what their objectives are and how these are ranked by each group or key individual purchaser; and why they have these objectives and what factors in their environment, resources, and strategies may cause them to change. Equipped with this knowledge, you can now explore how changes in their buying patterns may affect you.

The question that you ask at this point, as you will periodically throughout the strategic thinking process, is: "So what?" What are the implications of a switch in sales from one customer classification to another? What will it do to you if a customer begins to emphasize the quality of his purchases and show less concern over price? Will new legislation regarding equal employment opportunities cause a change in your customers' purchasing power? What difference will it make to you that your buyers' markets are moving to third-world countries and away from industrialized nations?

As you begin to delve into the possible effects on you of such changes—and you should also explore what lack of change might mean—you will see that some will be positive and others negative and that some will be felt by you alone and others by your competitors as well or even your entire industry. Of course the force of the impact on you and your rivals may vary, so it is important to distinguish opportunities and threats that pertain only to you from those of a broader nature. The strategic thinking process entails the need to be as thorough as you can in each phase of analysis. Probing the implications of customer change in depth reveals that some opportunities and threats are likely to repeat themselves because they are reinforced by another aspect of customers' situations; for example a reduction of the prime lending rate may coincide with new and more liberal tax provisions to give certain buyers a better cash position at the end of their tax periods. On the other hand, if a unique opportunity or threat arises that you are not prepared to handle, your company may lose a chance in a lifetime or stumble into disaster.

ADDING UP THE PIECES

Customer analysis is a basic building block in the whole structure of strategic thinking. It provides you with an overview of not only your own clientele but the entire market you are operating in, as these little equations illustrate:

Customers + customers = groups
Groups + groups = market segment
Segments + segments = total market

Approaching your market analysis, therefore, you will have grouped customers according to type (based on location; objectives; use of product; decision maker; or strategy), explored their needs and wants, and probed potential changes in their buying habits. This aggregate information will allow you to visualize market segmentation accurately and will also demonstrate emphatically that customers, not products, cause demand to grow, hold, or decline. It will have given you considerable insight into each market you serve or plan to serve. You will now be in a position to develop a marketing plan that is aimed at the right targets.

By quantifying the pieces of qualitative data you have collected, you will have the material you need to quantify the total market picture as well as its parts:

- Total market sales in both units and dollars.
- Segment sales in both units and dollars. Include both the segments you serve now and the ones that may prove attractive enough for you to enter later.
- Growth rates for the segments and the total market. This will enable you to compare the growth rates of various segments. Are yours among the winners or the losers?
- Pricing trends and distinctions from one segment to another.
- Cyclicality and potential causes and effects of change in it.
- Sensitivity of demand. In an earlier part of this book I mentioned how price can influence the growth of a market. If a market was perfectly elastic, it would mean that demand for the product was directly related to its price. In recent years I have found that the demand for a product is also sensitive to service, features, and external forces.
- Captive customers. In some markets the key customers are so integrated that they pre-empt a significant part of the market, thereby preventing the independent supplier from penetrating it. This will be discussed more fully in a later chapter.

Using customer data as a base will help you avoid the damaging strategic pitfall of fixating on the size and projected growth rate of a market or segment. I have often seen managers who were so swayed by the dollar earnings in a market that they completely lost sight of the customers' needs and wants. This approach also puts you in a position to do comparative analyses of competitors and to know where they are concentrated and positioned. It also furnishes useful perspectives on industry characteristics. Finally, it generates information on how your industry and the total market might be affected by social, governmental, or other forces of the macroenvironment.

A WORD FOR THE NONPROFIT ORGANIZATION

If you are trying to strategize for a nonprofit organization, the translation of some customer classifications in Table 3-2 may help. Classifying users is no more difficult for a nonprofit organization

Table 3-2. "Customer" classifications for nonprofit organizations.

Types of Customers	School	Hospital	Government	Places of Worship
Consumers	Students	Patients	Citizens	Congregation
Industrial and regulated users	Companies that pay tuition or sponsor training	Companies that pay patients' bills directly or through insurance	Corporate taxpayers	Corporate donors
OEMs and contractors	Unions, professional associations, vocational counseling services	Insurance companies	Other government bodies	National religious councils

than for a business firm. Consumers for example can be easily described by demographics and vital statistics, whether the product or service is educational, medical, or spiritual. Yet though the data are available, they are often not arrayed or analyzed properly.

An institution that fails to keep its customer information up to date can get a shock. In my community, it was found that the number of families with children was declining more rapidly than the national and state averages and that this wasn't merely the result of a declining birth rate. The data showed an exodus of families far exceeding past and anticipated trends. This had repercussions on the schools, the fire and police departments, and the other services the community needed. Of course it opened up the whole issue of why the families were leaving. Were their objectives changing? Were they moving out because of dissatisfaction with community services? Was the cause economic—were they migrating to more affluent communities or poorer ones? These are truly strategic questions for a community. But they are often overlooked because the data aren't systematically analyzed from a planning point of view or because the issues are too sensitive politically.

Let's think about the effect of customer objectives on colleges and universities. Why do students seek higher education? Again, is it because of economics, since it is a known fact that college graduates earn more in their lifetimes than those who have less education? Or is it because of their egos—does going to college make them feel superior? Or is it functional, that is, are they really interested in learning? If colleges do not know what attracts their students, they cannot be prepared for changes in their customers' objectives.

Most members of the clergy or religious orders don't want to admit that they are selling a service and have customers, but in fact they are and have. This in no way detracts from their value and dedication. They need to understand why people attend their places of worship or service centers if they are to know, as many wish to, whether to accept or try to change "consumer" motivations. As a starter this will require information on the identity of the members of their congregations and periodic checks for attendance and contributions. If they fail to go after these data and to stay abreast of any change in the mix of their "buyers," their religious function will disappear.

APPLICATION TIME

Now take some time and apply the discussion in this chapter to your business. The first step is to group your customers by type. You might begin with a simple classification scheme and flesh it out in more detail as required. Remember that the subdivisions should be only as refined as is necessary to explain where you have been and are now.

Next, compare your mix of customers with that of your major competitors and with industry data. Competitors' customer information may be difficult to obtain, and you may have to approximate these figures and confirm them as you progress. In some instances industry publications can help you make these approximations. A later chapter will provide some guidance on where and how to obtain information on competitors.

CUSTOMER ANALYSIS		MARKET EVALUATION

Consumers	*Industrial, Regulated, and Government Users; OEMs and Contractors; Distributors and Dealers*	Total dollars or units
		What is the best way to segment:
		  By customer type
		  By location of customers
		  By price levels
		  By product type and features
		  By decision criteria or decision maker
		  By customer strategy

Demographics	Types of users	
Personal characteristics	Size/geographic location	
Buying habits	Buying habits	
Objectives and expectations	Objectives and expectations	
How products are used	Product use	

Economic factors	Economic factors	Size of segments
		  Dollars
		  Units

How important is product?	Importance?	

Pre- and post-sales service required?	Service required?	Growth rates
		  Total/segments
		  Dollars
		  Units

Financial abilities	Financial abilities	
Can do without?	Can do without?	Pricing trends
Personal strategy	Business strategy	Cyclicality/seasonality
Loyalty of key decision maker	Decision maker loyalty	

Quantity	Quantity	Sensitivity of demand
		  Price
		  Service
		  Features
		  External forces

Frequency	Frequency	
Terms/conditions	Terms/conditions	
		Captive market, not available to independents

With these particulars in hand, focus next on examining the customer groups or key purchasers that make the greatest impact on your business. As I have just cautioned, be thorough but don't get lost in details. Your purpose is to concentrate on only the customers who can swing your sales figures or profit margin.

You may find it helpful at this juncture to get some assistance from others either inside or outside your organization, especially from someone who is objective and will not be biased by his preconceived notions. Their objectivity and different view should help you spot the reasons behind customers' buying habits. A description of purchasers' past and present practices without an explanation of these wouldn't be complete. Let me urge you again to record this information for further reference and monitoring. I have seen many instances where thinking has not been documented and confusion has arisen later over the grounds for a decision based on it.

The checklists summarize the key points made in this chapter. Use them as an aid in analyzing your company.

4

THE NAME OF THE GAME

Now that you have assessed where your organization is presently
and should go and have evaluated your customers' characteristics,
expectations, and purchasing habits, you are ready to look carefully at others who have objectives similar to yours and who compete for the customer's sales dollar.

To begin the analysis of competitors, I have found it helpful to
get the lay of the land in the whole industry. This survey includes
how the industry behaves, what changes seem to be on the horizon,
and what positive or negative effects—opportunities or threats—to
expect from these changes.

Just as in professional baseball, where teams are classified as major league, AAA, AA, A, and so on, it is useful to classify the various industry participants—in this case, as to type, mix, and size.
You will recall that this kind of differentiation was recommended
earlier, in customer analysis, and it applies equally here. These
groupings provide a means for describing what has happened, where
you stand now, and what you might anticipate for the future. Further, you can begin to get an appreciation for the results, costs, and
risks inherent in the industry.

In business as in sports, it's important to recognize who the
strongest contenders are and whether there is a chance to unseat
the champion. The concentration of command over the market
has a great deal to do with an industry's attractiveness. Do three
companies control 85 percent of the market, as in the U.S. automobile industry, or does one competitor have 75 percent of the

pie, as IBM is reputed to have in computers? Depending on your current position and objectives, these statistics can mean the difference between profits now, five years from now, or never.

TYPES OF PARTICIPANTS

Industry participants can be divided into two fundamental types: those who are focused on one or two kinds of enterprise and those who are highly diversified. Of course this is simplistic, and it must be recognized that firms have varying degrees of focus. But companies do tend to fall into these categories. Clearly IBM concentrates on data processing, even though it offers other types of equipment (electric typewriters, transcription and copying machines). It is a single-industry competitor. The second type I call multi-industry competitors. These range from Beatrice Foods, which has businesses in food, sporting goods, garden and lawn supplies, and trailer homes, to well-publicized major conglomerates such as ITT and Litton Industries.

The main reason this split has strategic value is that it enables you to determine the commitment of the participant to the industry in question. It also enables you to spot whether there is a trend in a business field from many small, concentrated, single-industry companies to large, diversified competitors who might be able to take a loss in one line for a sustained period because of high profits in others. The aim of this analysis is to anticipate when the single-industry leader is beginning to weaken, a change that is often signaled by an increased invasion of a market by multi-industry competitors.

Geographic location and target market provide subdivisions for both categories:

U.S.-based, focused on the domestic market.
Foreign-based, focused on the home market.
U.S.-or foreign-based, focused on international markets.
U.S.-and foreign-based, focused multinationally.
These firms, though headquartered in one country,
acquire and integrate products from many countries.

Table 4–1 gives a view of where some leaders in the television industry belonged according to this subdivision scheme in 1973. The arrows show how several changed classification in 1974—Admiral by being acquired by Rockwell International and Motorola by merging with Panasonic (Motorola is now called Quasar Corporation).

Table 4-1. Classification of some televison receiver industry leaders in 1973 and 1974.

	U.S.	Foreign	International	Multinational
Single-industry	Zenith Admiral			Sony Panasonic
Multi-industry	Rockwell RCA General Electric Motorola Sylvania	AEG-Telefuncken	Siemens Philips Hitachi	

Single-Industry Competitors

In the early stages of a market's life cycle, the single-industry participant tends to be small and to be headed by a strong, knowledgeable entrepreneur. Quite often such a company is willing to grow with the market, having found a niche and stuck with it successfully. While the entrepreneurial leader is in command, he strongly resists moving outside his area of expertise. Later, if demand begins to shade off or he steps aside, the firm will look for more fertile though related opportunities.

The fact that the single-industry company is knowledgeable about the market—and sees its entire future as resting with its success in that market—makes it a tough competitor to beat. If the industry is dominated by a few of these specialists, it will become stable and the rules will be well known by the participants. Normally only the entry of a new competitor, some discontinuity like a new technology, or a serious change in the customers will rock the boat. A few examples may help demonstrate these patterns.

Kodak has been a strong specialist in the camera and film industry. It has concentrated primarily on photographic equipment and supplies and developed a large market. Most of its competitors have also been specialists, and even after Polaroid's entry—through product innovation—the industry continued to grow in a stable, consistent manner.

General David Sarnoff, equipped with strong patents and technical advances acquired from the original owners—General Electric, Westinghouse, and Marconi—concentrated on the radio and later the television market. His company, Radio Corporation of America, advanced the state of the art and dominated the industry for many decades. It wasn't until the General moved aside and his son took over that RCA moved aggressively into other fields and became a multi-industry company.

The computer business is dominated by a single-industry specialist—IBM. The multi-industry entries into the market have had a hard time competing both in the United States and abroad. These companies include several that in the early days of electronic computers were many times the size of IBM, for instance Siemens in Germany, General Electric and RCA in the United States, and English Electric in the United Kingdom.

The foreign version of the specialist firm is quite similar to its U.S. cousin except that it may be more closely tied to the national government, which in fact may have created it. When such a company ranks high on its government's priority list, it may be impossible to beat. Japan provides many cases of this. Since it is an export-oriented country, it has done a great deal to protect its companies' home markets, and it also subsidizes their export activities in a variety of ways. An excellent example comes from the history of consumer electronic products. U.S. and European companies were excluded from Japan, which enabled firms like Sony and Matsushita (Panasonic) to build cost and volume strength. As a result they were able to later penetrate overseas markets, primarily in the United States, at the expense and even the demise of many U.S. producers. The list of casualties included RCA and Motorola, both of which were pioneers in the radio industry but couldn't compete against the high-quality/lower-priced products of the Japanese.

The multinational company is relatively new. Unlike U.S. or foreign concerns focused on either the home or export markets, they transcend national borders. They buy, produce, and sell where it makes financial sense. Thus their strategic decisions can be based on economics and on business opportunities. They are not distracted by national loyalties or priorities. The number of single-industry multinationals is increasing. For instance a new computer company, Unidata, was formed in Europe by a merger of the resources of Siemens, CII of France, and Philips. One reason for the creation of these new coalitions, as they are called in much of Europe, is to reduce the cost of participating in attractive but capital- and cash-intensive markets as well as to reduce the risk. Another is to gain access to new and sophisticated technologies.

The multinational single-industry company will tend to be more flexible than any other type. It is able to finance through a variety of currencies and take advantage of monetary fluctuations, differential tax regulations, and favorable exchange rates. Petroleum companies such as Shell, Texaco, and Mobil have been classified as multinationals. They have learned how to deal with many governments and to negotiate highly favorable tax and depletion allowances. Some have located refineries close to their markets and have built foreign-flag tanker fleets to transport their oil and byproducts around the world. They minimize risks and share costs through elaborate joint-venture agreements, including the foreign governments as partners. In most instances these companies have concentrated on oil and other energy-producing materials, but in the early 1970s, many began to diversify more broadly.

Multi-Industry Competitors

By definition multi-industry concerns participate in several industries. Like single-industry firms, they can be differentiated by geographic location and target market as U.S., foreign, international, and multinational. This type of organization is largely a post–World War II phenomenon, and most have developed since the early 1960s.

If a multi-industry company has a strong portfolio of products and businesses, it is in a unique position to manage its sales and profits growth and to fund some losers by using the income generated by winners. The term "manage profits" used here may seem to be harsh, but there is no question that many of the glamour Wall Street favorites of the early 1960s had managed their profitability growth. What it takes to accomplish this feat is a strong, centralized, financially oriented management and a series of businesses with short- and long-term profit cycles. These factors appear to have been behind H. S. Geneen's success in his management of ITT. By adding a conglomeration of businesses in a variety of industries—bakeries, car-rental agencies, hotels, insurance firms, parking lots—to ITT's communications enterprises, he was able to make the tradeoffs necessary to show consistent and sustained growth.

This kind of company is difficult to analyze since it can group its businesses in ways that make it nearly impossible to determine how and where it is earning and losing money. (The foreign multi-industry corporation is even more difficult to appraise since it may have accounting methods that can overstate or understate its profits.) In fact multi-industry companies are fighting the SEC and other federal agencies on the issue of disclosure of data, for they don't want to be measured or reveal how their pieces are doing; they want to publicize only total results. Unfortunately a number of concerns that have practiced this type of deception have been darlings of Wall Street and have for many years had undeservedly high price/earnings ratios (stock prices in relation to earnings per share).

The ability of this kind of company to sustain large losses in one sector over a long time while constantly appearing to be solvent in toto is a great asset. About four years ago Gulf Oil decided to make a strong bid in the nuclear reactor market. It obtained a foothold by acquiring General Atomics from General Dynamics. General Atomics was the primary promoter in the United States of the gas-cooled reactor, while other major suppliers stressed the water-cooled reactor. General Dynamics had suffered heavy losses in the nuclear market and finally recognized that the cost of even staying in the game was too great, especially since its share was minuscule. Gulf realized that it needed considerable capital and cash resources in order to achieve its ultimate stated goal of a 20 to 30 percent slice of the market, and so its managers went out to obtain additional financing. They got some of it from joint-venture partners, some from the federal government, and some from within Gulf by using accounting practices that could increase cash flow. During the windfall profit era, the oil crisis of 1973–1974, Gulf used part of its newly found cash and profits to fund this new venture by writing off heavy losses. The fact that it was participating in several industries gave it the financial elbow room to do this.

Some multi-industry companies are interested in diversifying primarily as a means of managing financial results, and they make their acquisition and merger decisions on this ground. They seek financial synergy. Others wish to capitalize on a strength, perhaps in marketing or engineering, and are seeking to purchase complementary talents, or are simply pursuing opportunity markets. A few years ago the leisure industry was growing fast, and companies like Beatrice Foods went out and made a series of acquisitions to participate in this arena. Its new businesses, some of which I referred to earlier, included a trailer-home manufacturer, a garden and lawn supply company, Hart Skis, and a luggage firm as well as additional food companies.

I normally differentiate these two approaches and call the first kind of multi-industry company a conglomerate and the second a diversified firm. Knowing which type you are competing against can indicate the strategic response you should make. The conglomerate may have short-term objectives and may give you opportunities to enhance your position while it is "milking" a business. The diversified company usually has longer-term plans that may require you to be positioned for a long, bloody fight.

Changes in Type and Mix

By using the classification scheme just described and plotting the past and present along with your assumptions about the future, you are able to visualize the competitive climate you will face and the consequences of changes that may occur in it. Figure 4–1 illustrates a 20-year period in a hypothetical industry. Since a decade ago, competitors A and B have become parts of larger multi-industry participants. Company A has been bought by a conglomerate; B

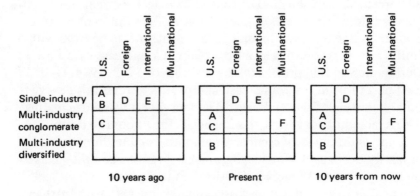

Figure 4-1 Changes in classification of participants in an industry in a 20-year period.

has joined with a firm that in your opinion gives it potentially greater financial, marketing, and engineering strengths than it had before. These are threats, of course, and yet both changes may open opportunities for you because the new parent management in each case is new to this industry and could cause the acquired business to falter. Even more interesting is the expectation that only competitor D will remain a specialist over the longer haul.

These observations will enable you to draw implications about your competitive position, develop a listing of opportunities and threats, and think out your strategy. Will the industry continue to be financially rewarding? Will the new competitive forces reduce or increase the need for innovation and capital investment? These and many other questions should be investigated carefully, since the aggregate answer might be that the cost of merely staying in the industry is beyond your means.

To convert this phase of strategic thinking into practical terms, let's take an illustration that vividly portrays the kinds of changes that do occur and need to be anticipated: the Head Ski case, which deals with Howard Head and his company. From its inception until 1967, the company concentrated on the high-quality/high-price segment of the ski market, which it led with approximately a 50 percent share. There were four major competitors: Hart (20 percent), Kneissl (9 percent), Yamaha (6 percent), and Fischer (6 percent). Thus 91 percent of this segment was controlled by five participants, with 70 percent of it concentrated in the hands of two. All these competitors were single-industry specialists except Yamaha, which was and is also in motorcycles. Head and Hart were U.S.-based and at that time had small exports; Kneissl and Fischer were European, and Yamaha was Japanese. Head, the innovator of metal skis, priced on value* and strongly influenced sales and distribution patterns, utilizing price maintenance (also called fair trade) and specialty ski shops. The industry followed Head Ski in its value pricing practice.

Within four years the competitive situation had become radically different. Head itself had diversified into other sporting goods markets, having added tennis, gymnastics, and archery equipment to its portfolio as well as ski clothing and accessories. It was moving more aggressively into Europe. The segment leader had become a multi-product, less specialized company. By early 1968 Hart had also changed, becoming part of Beatrice Foods, as mentioned earlier. So the No. 2 company was now a division of a billion-dollar multi-industry corporation. Other large firms were beginning to penetrate this segment. AMF moved into it with a new line of fiberglass skis. Then in 1972 Head disappeared altogether by being merged into AMF.

Thus in a short five years, the quality equipment segment of the ski market changed from one that was dominated by specialists to one that consisted primarily of U.S. and foreign multi-industry competitors.

Changes in type and mix of competitors can be precipitated by changes in an industry's capacity—its ability to meet its customers' demands. As you will recall from your elementary economics course in school, when supply is less than demand in a free pricing situation, profits are normally high. This factor encourages existing competitors to add capacity and new competitors to enter. The combination of new capacity and any normal cyclical downturn

*There are two fundamental ways to price your product or service: on cost or on value. In cost pricing you evaluate the cost and mark up from it. This is ordinarily what is done when a product is older and becomes a commodity. In value pricing, you base your price on the value you think the product has to the customer, regardless of cost. Normally, value pricing is used for prestige-oriented or new items.

results in an oversupply, which in turn can lead to price erosion and lower profits. Thus you can readily see that current and future capacity levels have significant strategic and financial implications to you directly as well as indirectly from their effect on the composition of your competition.

ANTICIPATING THE NEW ENTRANT

I have just described how you can group participants in your market and indicated that the makeup and mix of the competitors can have a profound effect on the way business is done and its related costs and risks. But your analysis can't stop here. The next step is to try to anticipate new competitors who may enter the scene and who may make a heavy impact on your results.

Newspapers and business journals are full of stories about the entry of companies into new markets and industries. These reports often allude to the fact that the existing participants seem to have been surprised and unprepared for the new entrant. Strangely enough, to you and me, the outsiders, such moves may often seem obvious and easy to predict. Why are companies caught unprepared, and how can they be more alert to these possible developments? The following discussion presents an orderly and disciplined approach to watching out for "a new kid on the street."

The Most Obvious Place

The first and most obvious potential new competitors will be firms that serve other geographic regions of the country or indeed other parts of the world. Quite often these are companies that have concentrated on their home markets, where you have not participated, and that now decide to invade your territory. Since you haven't met them in your region, you may have forgotten them and failed to consider them as possible future rivals. Textbooks are full of cases like these, and none are more revealing than those concerning Japanese enterprises.

The Japanese were underestimated by many U.S. producers. Sure, they were strong in Japan, but American concerns were convinced they couldn't penetrate U.S. markets. The reasons for this viewpoint were several. It was "obvious" first of all that Japanese companies couldn't ship bulky objects across the ocean and be price-competitive; shipping costs were just too high and would remain that way. In addition, everyone "knew" that Japanese goods were of poor quality and inferior to those made in the United States. Finally, American tastes were "of course" different from those of the Japanese, who "therefore" couldn't style products for our people.

Because of these assumptions (which were considered facts) most American companies sat back and didn't worry about any threat from the Japanese. The results are now a matter of history in the consumer electronics market: By 1972 the Japanese were the leaders, using the semiconductor and integrated circuit technology of the United States, and most of the radios, tape recorders, and stereos sold here were Japanese-made and distributed under Japanese labels.

Developments in the American automobile market have been quite similar, though the final results are still not in. The Japanese did fail in their first attempt to penetrate, but the second time around they captured a significant share of the market. By mid-1975 that share had grown to 8 to 10 percent of the total market. Although there is a vast difference between World War II and the battle for the marketplace, it appears to me that as at Pearl Harbor, the impossible became reality, and the American businessman, like his military counterpart, was caught unprepared and vulnerable. The lesson we can learn from this is that we must look at the total market—the *world* market—and at each segment of it in order to identify possible future competitors, even if we don't serve those regions.

The reverse of this point suggests another place new competitors can come from—other segments of our own market region. It is quite usual to find a company that has specialized in one product level moving onto another. It may have sold only low-price items and then decided to move into the medium- or high-price range. Thus the specialist may expand and become something of a generalist.

Concerning the quality of market served, another potential problem arises. I have seen many businessmen lulled into a sense of false security because they have arbitrarily defined their market as the one they have chosen to serve and have ignored all others. They have a large share of their served market and don't record the total market and its overall leader. "We aren't worried about companies X, Y, and Z because they will sell to anyone, while we have a higher-quality product and concentrate on only the upper-income groups." These words seem ridiculous, but I have heard them many times. They can represent a fatal flaw.

The Second Most Obvious Place

The second place to look for possible future competitors is related or bordering industries. These include companies that lie in front of you—your industry's immediate customers; those behind you—your suppliers; and those alongside you—firms that serve associated parts of your industry.

Your customers. Customers may turn into competitors for many reasons. They may become unsure of their supply lines or begin to worry about having only one supplier, and so they decide to provide their own materials or parts. Or they may want to increase their contributed value, which will increase profits; "Why pay those exorbitant prices to a vendor?" they may argue. No matter what the reason, the customer may disappear and a new, unexpected competitor appear. This has a twofold effect, as the conversation with Sam Mitchell in Chapter 1 indicated. It decreases the size of your market, and it increases the competition for what is left.

Sears did this several years ago in the appliance industry. The company had made private branding an integral part of its marketing practices, and it must have decided that having equity in the suppliers of its private brands would be more profitable. Further, many of the leaders in appliances didn't provide private-brand products. Sears thus began to acquire its suppliers in whole or in part, with the result that it became a major participant not only in distribution and retailing but also in manufacturing. Thus changed the willingness of many manufacturers to allow Sears to stock materials carrying their own labels.

Another example of backward integration comes from General Motors. GM bought up many of the suppliers of its vehicle components and parts—manufacturers of spark plugs, transmissions, batteries, headlights. But these suppliers continued to sell to other automotive firms. Later Ford did the same thing, purchasing Autolite, Philco, and several other companies supplying components for automobiles.

You must therefore look carefully at your customers and ask whether they are likely to integrate into your markets. This evaluation will guide you on the prices you will be able to charge if they do and the profits you can expect to make. It will also make you question how much you should count on a particular customer's continued sales. If you find that you depend too much on one customer or group, then it may be time for a change, or at the very least you must formulate a contingency plan. The same goes if you discover that you possess a virtual monopoly, since the customers may not wish to be so dependent on you.

Those who feed you. Another group of potential competitors lie at the other end of the spectrum—your suppliers. Some of them may feel that they possess the critical resources and skills required to participate in your business. They may then decide to move forward in order to increase the size of their sales or to assure that they have access to the ultimate consumer.

There are numerous illustrations of manufacturers that have expanded into distribution and of subsystem and component producers that have decided to become total-system companies. Chapter 2 mentioned the oil companies that moved from refining to exploration and then into the direct sale of gasoline and home heating oil. General Electric moved into the business of mass-transit cars because it became apparent that the electric systems had become the most expensive part of the car and represented the largest contributed value. The integrated circuit manufacturers, such as Texas Instruments, moved into calculators and watches.

It is worth keeping an alert eye on your suppliers and thinking about their potential or actual desire to reach into your area. Important indicators are the percentage the suppliers contribute to your end product and the complexity of their operations relative to yours. Once their contributed value or degree of complexity exceeds yours, you can anticipate the entrance of a new competitor. I don't mean that this will happen automatically, since your industry may not be as profitable as the supplier's, and the supplier may be unwilling to risk losing the financial position he has in his own field. Further, the skills required to suceed may be very different. Thus the probability of new competition from behind you may be small. But the wise manager will be prepared for the eventuality.

Looking to the side. Another possibility, and one that commonly occurs, is the entry of companies from related industries. IBM provides a case in point. Commenting on the firm's announcement that it would move into cash registers, *Business Week* said, "IBM's move . . . makes sense. The company has the lion's share of the computers in the accounting departments of large retailers, and its salesmen have been eager for the add-on business that point-of-sale equipment might bring."* Thus IBM decided to take advantage of its sales presence and build from its position of strength.

An earlier section of this chapter noted how Head Ski moved from ski equipment into clothing and accessories. Like IBM, it based its move on marketing strength, judging that its dealer network and distribution system were capable of handling these goods too and that the Head name would pull the new lines through to the same affluent and discriminating customer. Thus the ski clothing manufacturers found a new competitor rising not from the sportswear ranks but from the ski equipment ranks.

A manufacturer will integrate horizontally because it feels that it has some skill or resource that is transferable to the new field. This may be reputation; it may be a sales force that can add to sales; or it may be the necessary technological expertise to participate. Or a company may simply feel that its prospects are limited in its current market and that this avenue of expansion is the least costly and the most likely to be successful.

Beyond Your Horizons

At times your analysis must go beyond your immediate industry. The potential competitor may lie in markets that seem far removed but that are still related. Ski products illustrate this as well. Many of the major competitors in 1973 weren't in ski equipment in the 1960s but were in other sporting goods markets. AMF was in the

---

*"IBM: Time to Cash In on Cash Registers," *Business Week*, August 18, 1973.

bowling industry and decided to move into other sporting goods. General Foods, a packaged-food leader, turned to fast foods in the late 1960s.

The search for potential competitors must therefore take in your broad surroundings and your total industry. This principle parallels Theodore Levitt's suggestion, expounded in *Marketing Myopia,* that a company think of itself in the broadest possible sense. I am not proposing this as an approach to developing your own strategy, because it tends to force you to think too generally. But I do think it is a way of identifying others who may enter your market. Thus in looking at the ski segment, your surveillance would move to suppliers of sporting goods, recreation equipment, and finally other leisure-time products or services. Your list of possible competitors might then include companies furnishing tennis and baseball equipment, camping and hiking products, and bicycles as well as hotel, restaurant, and resort interests. Any of these may decide to diversify and move across industries and markets. Such moves are forms of horizontal or vertical integration but are more extended than ordinary.

The truly unexpected. So far I have described how to anticipate the appearance of competitors who have some obvious or related connection with your field of business. But what about forecasting the entry of a conglomerate from an unrelated industry? Is there a way to anticipate the emergence of this kind of competitor? There isn't any simple answer, although conglomerates have shown a pattern in their acquisitions and mergers. Most companies of this type have selected partners purely for financial reasons. H. S. Geneen seemed to choose firms that would help him continue his upward trend in earnings per share. He was interested in growth companies to give him sales expansion and in some relatively stable companies to provide the earnings. He was willing to sell off if the need arose.

I don't know of any sure way to anticipate moves like these, but I can suggest some general guidelines. If you are in an industry that is growing rapidly in either sales or income by comparison with the gross national product, and some of its participants don't have the financial or managerial resources for the long haul, then be on your toes for someone to come in and take them over. Or if your industry isn't growing rapidly but is very profitable, an outsider may look for a participant to take over in order to tap the earnings potential.

In connection with the threat from conglomerates, keep your eyes open for the reentry of a corporate division as an independent business. In the 1960s many small firms were acquired by larger concerns. The founding fathers of these small companies were attracted to selling out because they were promised large fortunes via stock swaps, and also were usually given the opportunity to continue to run their firms as divisions of the larger corporations. Within a few short years, the dreams came to an end when the exchange stock stopped growing and began to decline. Further, the small-company president found that he was now constrained in his operations and began to want to return to his former status of running his business independently. An article, "The Unhappy Entrepreneurs," in the September 1973 issue of *Dun's* summarizes this situation very well. The article includes a half-dozen case histories of entrepreneurs who decided to buy back their old companies from conglomerates. The trend has continued, adding to the state of flux in the competitive scene, and changes of this nature must be tracked and anticipated.

OTHER FORMS OF COMPETITION

New entrants into your own business domain are not the final elements of this phase of competitor analysis. You will need to survey two other types of potential rivals: the functional rival and the indirect competitor.

The Functional Competitor

Have you ever heard businessmen argue about other products or services that compete against theirs? For example, in today's society there are four main ways of heating your house: by oil, natural gas, electricity, and steam. Each provides the same function—it warms. Each has its own advantages and disadvantages. The oil company has to compete against suppliers of these different heating agents as well as against other oil companies. In order to be successful, it must know the customer's needs and then be able to compare the substitute products with its own. The same is true of service industries. For example, instead of considering itself a railroad, a company should recognize that it is in transportation, thus not limiting its vision to the means of serving the customer's need but focusing rather on the service itself.

The major problem in analyzing functional competition is that we tend to deceive ourselves into thinking that our method of providing the function is the best and that other methods are inferior. Unfortunately the customer doesn't always agree and may switch from ours to another. Therefore it is important to recall the customer's objectives and priorities and to put ourselves in his place.

This analytic perspective can have the strategic effect of requiring cooperation among companies that sell the same service or product. This is the reason for industry advertising, such as that sponsored by the Home Heating Companies of America promoting the use of oil.

An excellent example of functional competition comes from the early days of incandescent lighting. Thomas Edison recognized that the integral natural gas industry was his key competition. He set out to get institutional customers and ultimate consumers of gas—cities and homeowners—to switch to his way of lighting. To achieve this substitution Edison carefully analyzed the gas industry. Since he realized that most people are reluctant to change their habits, he made sure that electric lamps and systems were as close to gas equipment and processes as possible. The results are well known, and today gas is rarely used to illuminate cities and homes.

Several further points need to be stressed. One is that substitute products may not exist at the time you are planning but may arise on the scene in your forecast period. Another is that the innovator of a substitute may be a company outside your industry. The reason for this phenomenon is that current participants may not wish to change the economics of doing business. The outsider, commonly an entrepreneur with only a small share if any, has little or nothing to lose and everything to gain. Edison had nothing to lose since he had no stake in the gas market. Haloid (later known as Xerox) had only a small position in the duplicating industry and was committed to promoting dry-copy technology. The leading current participants weren't interested, and many of them turned down the opportunity to pick up Xerox patents even at bargain prices. When the "unknown" began to put xerography across, most of the leaders—Addressograph Multigraph, Kodak, A. B. Dick—were caught by surprise. Ultimately they were forced into follower positions and even had to license from the newcomer. It will be interesting to watch the market progress of the Wankel engine.

The major precaution to observe in this connection is not to get complacent. Nobody has all the answers. You must keep alert to the possibility of a better way and be on the lookout for the substitute that may change the very name of the game for you.

The Indirect Competitor

There are three other important forms of competition that may have strategic implications. Two focus on money and one on human resources.

1. Competition for the customer's discretionary dollar. Every customer has a choice of where and how he spends his discretionary dollars. Assume that a consumer has saved $1,000 over the past year. He has many ways he can use this money. He may decide to spend it on a vacation to the South Seas, use it as the down payment on a new car, buy a membership in a country club with it, or just keep it in the bank. Businessmen often forget that they are competing against other forms of products and services in addition to other companies supplying the same products. The consumer's freedom of choice can have a significant impact on the size of the market, its growth rate, and its profits. This fact will play a role in your decision on what to promote and how strongly to try to influence the consumer. Just as with other types of competition, it is necessary to be anticipatory and to track consumer preferences and trends.

2. Competition for investors' money. Another arena of competition that can affect your strategy encompasses the investment dollar. We all recognize that the investor has many choices in where he places his funds. Like any other critical and scarce resource, investment dollars are subject to a great deal of competition. There have been many cases in which entire industries have been classified as unfavorable risks and investors have refused to put their money in them or have demanded high interest rates and collateral. Railroads have earned a poor-risk reputation over the years and now find themselves with limited means of obtaining financing. It might be argued that industrial stocks have fallen into disrepute and currently have limited value to companies in their financing strategies.

Managers must therefore understand the reputation their industry has in the financial community and then anticipate the trend and cost of financing in the future. This type of competition isn't normally considered and can cause some unpleasant surprises.

Another point to be considered in light of the real and potential shortage of capital is the financial characteristics of your industry. Some industries require capital for long periods of time. Their return on capital is low, and only those who have access to large capital sources can participate. Other industries are cash intensive, that is, they require large amounts of cash to support required levels of inventory or receivables. Thus, the type of financial resources varies from one situation to another.

3. Competition for manpower. Industries and companies also compete for manpower. Their image and reputation can affect their ability to attract and retain the quality and type of personnel they need.

In the 1960s the aerospace business was riding high, and almost everyone was interested in this dynamic and challenging industry. The attraction permeated all age, education, and income groups, and many of the country's top minds and creative talents were drawn to the industry. Aerospace companies had little difficulty obtaining large numbers of applicants; their main competition came from other aerospace firms. Toward the late 1960s, however, the industry began to lose favor, both because of reductions in government funding and because of the unpopularity of the Vietnam conflict. This resulted in significant cutbacks in employment and ultimately in a disenchantment with the industry and its participating companies.

OTHER STRATEGIC FACTORS

In addition to competitive factors there are many other characteristics of strategic importance about the industry in which you participate. These factors determine the cost of participation and the extent and type of changes which you and your competitors can make. These factors include the nature of the industry leaders and standard setters, distribution and dealer networks, service requirements, warrantees, capacity size and ultilization, and the type of management in the industry. Each of these topics is discussed so that they may spark your analysis and anticipation.

Trend Setters

The analysis we have just completed enables you to identify the share leaders in your market. They are quite often the industry trend setters that specify the terms and conditions of industry participation. For example Head established marketing, pricing, and quality norms for ski equipment, and others followed. IBM set the pattern in computers by leasing rather than selling and by including significant service and software provisions as part of the initial sale. RCA began to grant an option to purchase a service contract, and others were forced to offer the same in the color television market. Sears adopted the strategy of marketing its own brands and guaranteeing performance and service. This ultimately led most large chains to offer private-label merchandise.

In some cases the trend setters are not the share leaders. For example Chrysler, in the No. 3 position, was the first to offer a five-year warranty on automobiles. Others, including General Motors, followed, and the entire industry was burdened with extensive new costs and the need to strengthen dealer service facilities. In 1972 American Motors gave car selling a new twist by including the guarantee that a consumer would have access to another car if repairs took a long time. Although AMC appeared to be using this tactic to increase its market share, others did not follow.

At times trend setters can apply such pressure and increase the cost of participation so much that competitors can't sustain the effort and are forced to exit. A most dramatic case in point involved General Electric and RCA. Despite extensive technical and financial resources, they found that the cost of staying in computers was too high for them. In independent projections based on public data, both estimated that the IBM trends would require them to raise more than $500 million in additional investment money just to provide the next model change. You could also argue that the trend set by General Motors and Ford—the planned obsolescence of automobiles, via style change every two or three years—increased the cost of participating in this industry to a level that drove many car manufacturers out of business. On the other hand, if you are a trend setter, keep in mind that you must be responsive to customers and able to get them to follow your lead or else you too may fail.

Distributors and Dealerships—An Industry's Life Cycle

Each industry has its own distinctive distribution system. It is important that you understand the types of distributors and dealers doing business with you. In some industries they are mainly independent dealers who carry a variety of products and brands at a number of locations. In others they are owned by the suppliers or manufacturers. Still other industries distribute largely through general department stores and other unspecialized merchandise centers. As with customers and competitors, distributor changes may have significant strategic implications and should be anticipated.

There appears to be a significant correlation between the type of distributor and dealer networks servicing an industry and the place the industry appears to be in its life cycle. Products and services, like people, go through stages of development. These can be illustrated graphically by a curve, as was shown in Figure 2–1. The shape of this curve and the time periods along it vary from industry to industry. Some consumer products may complete the whole cycle in a few months; fad products can move from birth to death in less than half a year. High-technology businesses, such as the nuclear energy industry, may take decades. Even today, after 20 years, the nuclear energy field as a whole is merely a "teenager," and some aspects of it are still in their embryonic stage.

When you analyze the type of distribution network servicing you in the light of your industry's stage of maturity, you may see a pattern that will provide a means of anticipating what type will emerge next.

When an industry is just getting started, its distributors tend to be trained specialists. Often they become dealers because they have an interest in the item; it may previously have been a hobby. There are many examples of this. In the early days of television, sets were sold in television stores. These dealers guided consumers on what to buy, installed the set and antenna, and offered or contracted to provide repairs. This is a natural service package in the introductory stage of a market life cycle since the user of a "young" product doesn't know what to look for in it or how to repair it. Further, prices are ordinarily high, and customers expect distributors to be experts.

As an industry moves into its "teen" period—its rapid-growth phase—the dealer and distribution network will change. Less specialized dealers normally begin to enter the scene. In the case of television, appliance stores began to add sets to their lines, for it became apparent that TV customers were quite similar to buyers of their other kinds of merchandise.and could be served with only a small increase in business expenses. Further, as the product became better known and its reliability increased, the consumer needed less presale counseling and after-sale service.

The next stage of the life cycle is middle age. The black-and-white television market is already in this phase. Although it is still growing, its rate of growth has declined, and within the next decade it will move into old age. During the middle period of a product's market life, dealers become price-oriented and very generalized. Today for instance discount and full-line department stores sell TV sets, emphasizing price rather than service. The consumer knows what he is doing, and the product is so reliable that repairs become a secondary concern. In fact the purchase price may drop so low that buying a new set becomes cheaper than repairing an old one.

The strategic importance of determining what types of dealers are serving your industry is that different types require different forms of cooperation from you, which affects your costs. Some dealers maintain small stocks and have to get shipments rapidly. Some insure that they will obtain a minimum profit by means of a guaranteed margin on the product. This means that a customer will pay the same price for the item regardless of where he shops. For example, he will pay $15 for a particular Chanel cologne whether he buys it from a premium store or from a discounter. Other dealers require advertising and promotion support. Many require all these aids but in varying degrees. The specialist may call for a guarantee that he won't have to compete on price. A generalist may ask for margins to support extensive advertising. A discounter may need national "pull" through brand advertising and pricing flexibility.

As the mix of distributors changes, a manufacturer is confronted with several strategic questions. Should he concentrate on the type of dealer or distributor networks accepted by and leading the industry, or should he try to enforce a change? Should he work only through franchised dealers, or should he start his own distribution centers? Should he promote margin protection ("fair trade") or should he merely suggest retail prices and let the dealer decide what to charge? Should he design specific brands to serve selected market segments or different types of dealers? Should he go into private branding?

Thus the composition of dealers and distributors affects how you price, promote, and label your product. These considerations in turn make an impact on your financial resources.

Service

Another industry variable is service. In some cases service is included in the original price or leasing charge. For instance, when you lease a copier, you obtain service as part of the lease. In others service is "unbundled" and must be paid for separately.

The type of service that is built into an industry depends on several factors. One is the sophistication of the user and the complexity of the product. As I said earlier, television dealers ordinarily offered service with purchase when the market was in its youth. Another factor is competitors' practices. If all participants provide service as part of the initial price and this price is relatively low, you must go along or get out of the business.

A final factor revolves around whether purchasers can find alternatives. If parts aren't available or trained service people are in short supply, an industry will suffer and the market may fail to grow. Our television illustration demonstrates this last point vividly. As more sets began to be sold by department stores and discounters than by specialty shops, a service crisis arose, for the general merchandisers sold on price and volume without service provisions and the specialists often refused to repair sets bought from these sources. This presented a dilemma to consumers and manufacturers alike. Gradually it forced producers to provide factory or company service centers. Today most television manufacturers have their own repair services, and many even offer insurance policies for service. When Japanese firms invaded the U.S. television market, they had to provide service in order to participate.

An area related to service concerns warranties and guarantees. The type and duration of such backups can drastically affect an industry participant's attractiveness. I previously mentioned that Chrysler led the trend in the automobile industry toward the five-year warranty and that other manufacturers were forced to follow. Most consumer goods carry some guarantee on parts, ranging from five years down to 90 days, and many underwrite service for a given period as well. If these terms are extended or reduced, they can seriously affect the ability of a firm to continue to participate.

The Industry's Value Structure

Industries, like societal groups, can be described by their values and ethical conduct. The garment industry is widely considered to have a cutthroat, dog-eat-dog approach to doing business. The banking industry is regarded as practicing a gentlemanly and relatively unaggressive code of conduct. This does not mean that banking is less competitive; it merely means that the expected behavior involves a high degree of courtesy. There are some industries where the rules of the game lead members to be more cooperative and less combative. The cooperation need not be collusive or illegal. It is primarily the result of the participants' accepting established patterns of interaction. Of course values and industry standards change; they can't be considered eternal. At times the change results from external forces such as government intervention. At other times it results from a change in management or the entry of a new type of competitor.

Foreign industries also have different standards from comparable American industries. For example, stockholders and investors in Europe measure management differently from their counterparts in the United States. Europeans may judge managerial performance on the basis of the ability, not to increase profits, but to create jobs or to handle stockholders' equity instead of external debt.

Cartels offer another example of divergent cultural standards, being acceptable in Europe but not in the United States. The same is true of payoffs, a common, legitimate practice in many parts of the world. Many Americans were shocked by revelations in 1975 that American businessmen had used payoffs to close business deals in Middle Eastern countries. Those who condemn the use of payoffs and similar tactics in those circumstances fail to recognize the reality that the values of a nation affect the conduct of business in that nation. As the old saying goes, "When in Rome, do as the Romans do," and I might add, "or don't go to Rome at all." I am not suggesting here that American businessmen should not practice ethics, but that they should recognize that ethics are relative and that if they can't adapt to the requirements of a given country's businessmen, then that business may be unavailable to them.

Suppliers

In addition to its primary manufacturers or service companies, an industry comprises firms that supply major components and materials to them. Key strategic questions arise from the nature, type, number, and long-term viability of the supplier companies. In numerous cases an entire industry has been forced to change because of a change in supply lines. At times multiple supply sources may be reduced to a single source. This may be the result of acquisitions or mergers, bankruptcies, or exits, or it may develop from monopolistic, collusive action on the suppliers' part.

The whole world was given a traumatic demonstration of how crippling a change in supplier relations can be when the Middle Eastern oil-producing nations forced the manufacturing nations to their knees through a unified boycott. This boycott has resulted in a global escalation of the prices of crude oil, refined petroleum, gasoline, and petroproducts such as plastics. The experience should have brought home the old lesson of the danger of relying on a small number of sources—and all the more on a sole source—for a vital material. I say "should" because I'm not sure it really has. After the boycott everyone relaxed and forgot about it. Moreover few people seem to understand how dependent this country really is on remote sources for other critical materials, such as bauxite, platinum, gold, and copper. Every businessman should ask, "How dependent am I on my suppliers, and what if anything can I do to reduce this dependence?"

In some cases the federal government has been willing to intervene to protect suppliers from being forced out of business. At other times it has put companies into business by requiring suppliers to share their expertise and patents. It is to assure itself of multiple sources that the federal government doesn't award a disproportionate number of contracts to any one contractor.

Supplier analysis need not be elaborate. In many industries it can be limited to these data:

- The number of suppliers there are currently, and whether it has increased or decreased in the last year and five years.
- The types and sizes of suppliers.
- Ownership interconnections between manufacturers and suppliers.
- Are users buying them up? This has the compound affect of not only strengthening your supplier-owning competitor but also reducing your sources.
- Locations of suppliers. Are you becoming more dependent on foreign sources?
- The financial condition of each major supplier.
- The degree of integration of suppliers. Do they go back all the way to the mine, or are they merely middlemen and dependent on others for their supply?

At times supplier analysis may require an in-depth probe of individual sources. This process is similar to the procedure for analyzing competitors that I will describe in the next chapter.

TRANSLATING THE PROCESS INTO NONPROFIT TERMS

Since the discussion in the last chapter dealt with communities, schools, and religious centers, let's see how this phase of strategic thinking relates to hospitals first. With regard to classification, hospitals are traditionally regional in nature, and today most are generalized. Once they could be split according to ownership into private, religiously affiliated, and public institutions, but over time they have consolidated, and some have chosen to specialize. Moreover, helped by the advent of Medicare, a new market segment has evolved—quasi-public hospital care of the aged. These changes can be charted as in Table 4–2, which shows the classifications and patient capacities of seven hospitals in a region.

Table 4–2. Changes in classification and patient capacity of a region's hospitals in a 20-year period.

	10 years ago	Present	10 years from now
Private			
A	150	250	300
B	200		
Public			
B			450
C	500	600	650
D	1,000	1,250	1,300
E	750	850	1,000
Religiously affiliated			
F	350	300	
G	500		
Quasi-public			
B		350	
F			300
G		500	500
Total patient capacities	3,450	4,100	4,500

The size of the hospital industry in our hypothetical area has grown since a decade ago and is anticipated to grow in the future. Moreover the complexion of the competition will change dramatically. Suppose you are A. You are expanding, and you will be competing against only public and quasi-public institutions 10 years hence—in fact you expect to be the only private hospital left in the area. This means that you will become unique, a condition that has both minuses and pluses. You will be competing against potentially stronger rivals, which will affect your ability to attract personnel and have the best, most up-to-date equipment. On the positive side you may be able to cater to the more affluent patient, which may allow you to charge the rates necessary to be medically sophisticated. All these implications emerge as you gain understanding of the industry and its changing characteristics, and all have a bearing on strategy.

The nonprofit organization needs to watch not only for changes in the composition of its present competition but also for new entrants into its field of endeavor. Let's consider colleges and universities in this connection. It is possible that more of their institutional users, such as corporations, governments, and trade associations, will decide to enter the education business and move from customer to competitive ranks. For example numerous companies, among them IBM, Motorola, and Western Electric, have opened their own training centers. Students at the General Motors Institute can earn both a bachelor's and a master's degree in engineering. Of course the purpose of such programs is to train the company's own employees, but it would be quite simple to extend them into the external market and offer them to other firms, institutions, or even the public at large. If these corporations didn't enter the market alone, they could join with an existing education organization and offer degrees through the partner. This would give them access to degree offerings and would combine the power of the commercial concern with the nonprofit status of the education institution.

There is also the possibility of suppliers becoming competitors, because education comes in many shapes and forms. This is in fact already happening; as textbook publishers are entering the programmed instruction market and packaging home-study programs and extension services. These suppliers have integrated into the end-use market and cut out the middleman, the college or university. Most educators would retort that this isn't the same, that no packaged course or programmed material can take the place of the formal classroom and the guidance and motivation provided by the professor. This is probably true, but it misses the point—that students have various objectives and some may be very happy to buy a prod-duct that won't require them to attend classes and permits them to make their own schedule and learn what suits their individual needs.

Geographic penetration is also possible. Certainly we have seen state-owned schools move into new regions of the state and open branches. What is to prevent nationally known private colleges from moving into other states? And why shouldn't they go international? In fact some have, through cooperative agreements with overseas governments and universities. Further, if U.S. education institutions move into overseas markets, what is to prevent overseas schools from moving into our home market? Again some have, through exchange programs that offer our students specialized work, particularly in foreign languages and culture, not obtainable in U.S. schools. As more corporations become multinational and language barriers decline, all these changes will make increasing sense.

The point, let me repeat, is that strategic thinking is as relevant to nonprofit institutions as to businesses. The types of competitors are changing, and new institutional configurations are evolving. It is vitally important to look around and spot new competitors, since they will cause changes in how an institution provides its services and measures the results. Further, competition for the limited discretionary and investment dollar must not be forgotten. This is growing more and more acute on all levels of society. Money used for education is siphoned from medical care. There is only so much money available for charities. Government spending isn't unlimited. The same is true of manpower. If the brightest of our young people become disenchanted with public service and refuse to enter it, then the quality of government will decline.

To paraphrase the well-known IBM sign, if you wish to help your organization prosper or perhaps even survive, you must learn to *think strategically* about your competitors.

APPLICATION TIME

Take some time now to apply the process of industry assessment to your business situation. To help you in this, the key points are summarized in question form, as follows:

Classification of Competitors
1. List all of your current major competitors ar 1 then classify them in terms of the following categories: United States, foreign, international, multinational; single industry or multi-industry.
2. Anticipate changes which you think may take place over the next five to ten years.
3. What are the positive (opportunities) and negative (threats) implications of these changes?

New Entries
Draw a diagram depicting:
1. Competitors in other geographic regions or other segments who do not currently, but may decide to, compete in your markets or segments.
2. Customers served by your industry. Note those who may want to move backwards, and consider the reasons why such a move may make sense.
3. Suppliers to your industry; note movement and reasons.
4. Companies on the periphery—those who serve the same customers with different but related products. This might include other pieces of equipment related to yours or equipment that would be included in a broader definition of the market. It is impossible to list all related items, but those of closest proximity should be included.
5. Any other companies that might be enticed to serve your customers or markets. This should include conglomerates or diversified companies that might be attracted by the growth, size, or profitability of your markets. Choose the most likely new entries and quiz yourself about what you know about them and their strategies.

Substitutions and Innovations
1. List other products or services that provide the same or a similar function. Record the percentage of total market sales for each substitute product.
2. Anticipate product innovations which can replace or reduce the sales of your products. When do you think these products will be commercially feasible? (Note: Information

about potentially competitive products can be found by searching the U.S. Patent Office or foreign patent offices.)

Other Forms of Competition

1. Think about your industry's and product's ability to compete effectively for the consumers' dollar and how this may be modified in the future.
2. Identify the type of financial resources required, and evaluate the ability of the industry to obtain capital and at what cost.
3. Record the image your industry has and how this can impact on its ability to attract the quantity and quality of people it requires now and in the planning period. There is also a cost dimension to this aspect of competition, since people can be bought.

Other Industry Characteristics

1. Who are the trend setters?
2. Will a new practice be introduced which will force you to follow? What is it and what is the likely cost of this change?
3. Describe the current type of distribution prevalent in the industry. What changes do you anticipate? What about the mix of dealers? Will this mix change?
4. How about the pre- and postsales service requirements: Is service bundled (that is, included in the purchase price) or unbundled?
5. Are there any changes in the types of warranties or guarantees?
6. Describe the level of capacity utilization now and in the next five years. Does the industry anticipate demand and add capacity in advance of demand, or does it react and cause an oversupply situation?
7. What type of people lead the industry? Do the behavior and values vary from segment to segment?
8. List key suppliers, including type, size, and location. Are suppliers increasing or decreasing in number, or are they holding? What is the financial condition of key suppliers?

Remember, description is only part of strategic thinking. You must anticipate what may happen and then draw inferences, both positive and negative, for your own future. The phases of the strategic thinking process pertaining to your analysis of your industry are outlined in the checklist.

THE NAME OF THE GAME

Competitive Scene

Participants
    Types
    Number (Level of concentration)
    Size
    Location
    Exits

New Competitors
    Other regions
    Related industries
    Customers
    Suppliers
    Horizontal integration
    Conglomerates
    Diversifiers

Other forms of competition
    Functional substitution
    Innovators
    Discretionary dollars
    Investors' dollars
    Manpower

Industry characteristics

Trend setters
Distribution
Dealers
Service
Warranties
Capacity
Values
Suppliers
Financial characteristics

5

COMPETITORS: "GETTING TO KNOW ALL(?) ABOUT THEM"

Have you ever heard of a successful coach who was merely content to know the names of the teams in his league, their standings, and their won/lost records?

Of course not. A successful coach wants to understand how and why the opposing teams operate as they do. He wants to know their strengths and limitations and the array of game plans they utilize. He tries to anticipate changes in their strategies and tests his team against the game plan he thinks it will meet when it plays each opponent. He uses scouting reports in developing his own plans.

Yet businessmen often fail to give more than a passing thought to competitive factors that may affect their own behavior and management planning. If they recognize the need at all, they may go to the expense of obtaining competitor studies and then never use them to formulate and test their own strategy. Competitors are vital elements of the environment and can change the opportunities and threats a company meets as well as enhance or inhibit its strategy and performance results.

In this chapter I will outline the major ingredients of a sound competitor evaluation, suggest key questions to be answered, and specify some sources of information on competitors. The discussion will emphasize the need to make and track key assumptions concerning your principal competitors' objectives and strategies.

All these elements will necessarily be based on limited information, since you can never know everything you might desire to know about a rival company, and the data you can get will be difficult and expensive to obtain. You must therefore focus on information that will help you anticipate changes of objectives or strategy.

To do an effective, strategically oriented evaluation, you should determine the following about each major competitor:

- His results in terms of how *he* measures *himself.*
- His past strategy (how he went about achieving those results) as well as any environmental or internal resources that may have strongly influenced his success or failure.
- His major past assets and liabilities and anticipated changes in these.
- His most likely strategy in the future.

The way you evaluate and summarize the competitor's evaluation will vary depending on whether the competitor is single-industry or multi-industry, and on the type of international focus he has. Begin by assuming—as is true—that the environment is largely the same for all of you, since you participate in the same markets and industry. Although the environment is the same, however, the implications affecting, and the perceptions of, each competitor will not be seen uniformly by all, because each competitor has different abilities and experiences and will perceive different opportunities and threats. These differences will result in a variety of responses, expectations, and strategies. Were this not the case, all participants with rational approaches and similar data would implement almost identical strategies.

As you progress through the evaluation process, try always to put yourself in the competitor's place and attempt to see the world from his viewpoint. Although difficult, this effort is vital in competitor analysis. I have found it useful to set up several teams and have the members of each develop the subject company's strategy as they think the competitor would perceive it.

THE FIRST PHASE: EXPLORE PAST RESULTS

The first question to ask is, "What has my competitor achieved, and how satisfied do I think he is with those results?"

Any company's track record can be evaluated from many points of view. You can measure performance in absolute terms. You can count total dollars in sales, profits, or cash flow. Or you can focus on growth of sales, profits, or market share. Ratios such as return on investment, return on assets, and net income to sales are also commonly used as yardsticks. Measurements can also be relative. For instance you can compare a participant's achievement with that of the competition or the total industry. Each index provides a different perspective. Annually *Fortune* magazine publishes statistics on the top 500 U.S. and 100 foreign companies. *Forbes* classifies firms by the industry in which they participate. This kind of information can give you some insights into how companies have performed. But to make it really useful, you must probe how each participant keeps its books and records its profits. Some companies stress earnings; others report their condition in such a way as to delay the payment of taxes; still others bookkeep to increase cash availability.

These measurements are important because they may affect the company's ability to procure financing and attract people as well as influence stockholders' and investors' satisfaction with current management.

Of course it is always important to remember that rarely does an organization show success by all measures. An aggressive strategy will normally mean a decline in profits and perhaps an increase in debt. The key to assessing performance is how a competitor's managers, investors, and stockholders measure the firm. In this regard you should see whether these measures are in concert or at odds with each other. For example a manager may be striving for short-term profits, but the stockholders may be interested in the long term. At times managers may be satisfied simply with earning large salaries and showing a break-even performance. Thus you should try to find out how a competitor concern sets its objectives and what motivates it.

You may retort, "That's easy to say but difficult to do." But it may not be. It is instructive—and fascinating—to see how chief executives broadcast their objectives and measurements. The reason they do this is that businessmen, like most people, need recognition and obtain a great deal of satisfaction from telling others how well they have done and plan to do. By studying their speeches, other public statements, and annual reports, you can uncover their priorities and self-evaluation systems. If there is deviation in their words and promises, this may help identify a flaw in their armor. This flaw may mean that the company is in trouble and there will ultimately be a change, whether in objectives, strategies, or management.

THE SECOND PHASE: RECONSTRUCT PAST STRATEGY

What strategy has the competitor followed in the past to achieve present results? This question focuses on the company's game plan. There are several points that should be emphasized.

Most importantly, reconstruct his strategy—don't take his word on it. In the previous section I pointed out that what a competitor says should be scrutinized in order to understand his objectives and discern changes in his *statements.* Here I am urging you to reconstruct his strategy to see whether he is *implementing* the plans he has publicized. By reconstructing the company's actions, you will be able to discover whether a deviation exists and then probe to determine its cause. Sometimes this will enable you to spot a limitation in the competitor and will open up an array of opportunities for you and others.

The reconstructed strategy should include a description of all functional elements—how the firm has carried out conception and design, production, marketing, financing, and management. Further, you should try to identify the opportunities and threats it has targeted. Explore functional coherence closely; the observation that the competitor has followed "a technologically oriented strategy" tells you nothing about whether the elements have been supportive of each other. It isn't uncommon to find a company that stresses one strength, such as technological leadership, following strategies in other areas, such as manufacturing and marketing, that detract from its ability to optimize that strength. By being comprehensive and specific, you can begin to evaluate the company's resources and possibly explain why the competitor has decided to pursue the course it has chosen. This will then permit you to determine how a change in resources may affect a change in strategy and whether the opportunities of the future match the competitor's capacities.

An example may clarify these points. Let's suppose you are a manufacturer of lawn products. One of your major competitors, Company X, has been following the strategy outlined below. It is a single-industry firm, focused on the domestic market, and is entrepreneurial (family owned).

Investment Strategy: Heavy investment to grow share.

Management Strategy: Marketing centered.

Operating Strategy:

Conceive/design: The company has improved existing products to make lawn care easier and more efficient. Its main development thrust has been to redesign and package commodities to demand a premium price.

Produce: The firm has small regional plants and maintains tight quality control but slight inventory control. It has added capacity in advance of demand.

Market: The company appeals directly to consumers and has fostered an image of high quality and willingness to stand behind its products. It engages in considerable national advertising to build brand consciousness. It sells only through franchised lawn-care and gardening dealers, refusing to distribute through price-competition department stores or discount stores. It enforces "fair trade" prices, thus not permitting discounting or retailer initiated sales, though it has "factory authorized" sales to increase turnover before and after peak seasons.

Finance: Since production requires large cash outlays that are not available from receipts during preseason periods, the firm finances its operations through short-term loans. It does long-range financing through stock issues, which are made attractive by the high price/earnings ratio resulting from rapid sales and income.

Manage: The company has a small managerial and supervisory staff and promotes internally.

Obviously, Company X has a management strategy driven by marketing. Everything is aimed at keeping up its image as a high-quality, innovative producer. All other strategy elements are geared to this aim. A good overall strategy integrates the strategic choices that have been made. If the elements of your competitor's practices don't match, there may be a flaw, and it should be flagged. For instance suppose the lawn-care concern just described were using a large, mass-production plant with low quality control. This would be detrimental to its marketing strategy and might provide an advantage to its competitors.

THE THIRD PHASE: EVALUATE COMPETITORS' RESOURCES

Analyzing a competitor's resources is tough to do, for several reasons. First of all, information will always be skimpy and quite often second- or third-hand. This means you must make hypotheses and then establish a monitoring system that will confirm, reject, or modify these as you progress. Second, the data will have varying degrees of importance, and it isn't enough to settle for merely what is readily available, what appears on the surface; you must learn to seek out and focus on what has strategic implications. The next few pages will outline some of the key questions that should be answered and suggest some sources that may prove useful. The questions I will provide are aimed at pinpointing abilities that have influenced past strategy and that will cause a modification of future strategy if they change.

It will be important to keep in mind that evaluating resources demands more than simply listing the physical, financial, and human assets the competitor possesses; it includes assessing how well these assets have been and will be used. Resources are dynamic. They can and will change in time. A failure to consider the past and future application, not merely the existence, of abilities will lead you to over- or underestimate your competitor. There are many illustrations of companies with large financial reserves that didn't put them to use. Possession of a large patent portfolio didn't keep some major companies ahead of the industry.

The discussion of resources that follows will focus on the same five key areas of functioning as the investigation of past strategy:

(1) conceive and design, or the technological abilities of the competitor; (2) produce, or the ability to meet customers' needs by getting quality products and services to them on schedule; (3) market, or assets such as the sales force, distribution networks, and advertising staff as well as intangibles like image and customer acceptance; (4) finance, or the ability to raise and manage capital and cash; and (5) manage, or the ability to direct and plan for the use of all the human and material resources in the business operation.

Conceive and Design

The competitor's ability to design, develop, and engineer his product or service is often crucial for business success, but it is difficult to track, since creativity rarely conforms to a schedule. One of the key questions to ask is how and where this function is performed. Some companies buy or license ideas or patents. Others expend considerable internal effort on research and development. Sometimes a departmental engineering group accounts for a significant portion if not the majority of innovations. Sometimes a single person takes a central role. In one company I studied, one man directed the organization into most of its growth areas; though not an inventor, he was the driving force behind numerous patentable ideas and an invaluable ingredient in the firm's success. Another key question involves the extent and age of laboratories and equipment.

In addition to the type, depth, and location of technical skills, it is important to obtain details on the competitor's patent portfolio, assess its age, and determine how dependent on it the firm is. If you find that a few critical patents are largely responsible for the competitor's success to date, hypothesize what it is likely to do when the patents run out and whether it is prepared for this event.

Other issues concern the company's licensing practices. Does it license from others, and if so, how much does it rely on these inputs? Conversely does it license to others to generate revenue? Licensing may provide a market opening to you if you know that a competitor has an interesting patent portfolio and needs ready cash.

There are several ratios you can calculate to determine the conception and design strength of another company. One is the investment in research and development as a percentage of sales. Comparing this figure with your own and with the industry average gives you an indicator of relative positions. The word *investment* is important. An investment reflects commitment to the future and in addition reveals something about how a competitor keeps his books. Some companies capitalize R&D whereas others expense it, and the choice of procedure has an impact on profits and cash flow. Along with the investment/sales ratio, you may wish to calculate what proportion of the competitor's research and development funds comes from government sources and whether these funds are used to develop commercial products. This is a conscious strategy used by several companies I have studied and should be noted, since it is difficult to carry out and may show a potential limitation.

Where to look. Finding out about a competitor's ability to conceive and design may be easier than you think. Technical people are quite open and gain recognition by sharing their ideas with their professional colleagues. You can determine what competitors are developing and how far they have progressed from papers presented at technical meetings, surveys, industry publications, and the patent files of the U.S. and foreign governments. All this information is public and is available to anyone who is willing to take the time to retrieve it. Analyzing it of course requires effort and skill. You must translate the raw data and disjointed facts into the terms of your competitor evaluation in order to obtain useful intelligence.

Produce

The production evaluation enables you to assess how flexible and efficient the competitor is and will be in manufacturing his products or providing his services. Here are some key questions:

Does he manufacture the product himself?
To what degree is he vertically integrated?
Does he subcontract, undertake joint ventures, or work with manufacturing associates?
How much power does he exert on those who manufacture for him?
Does he make long- or short-term production commitments?

An increasing number of companies have gone the sourcing or contracting route to be able to provide their products—that is, they have changed from producers to marketers. Observing the success of many Japanese companies in the United States, many long-established radio and sound-system manufacturers decided that they couldn't compete and began to buy products from the Far East and Japan to brand as their own. Some firms have entered the market without any production capability. They merely specified the design and engineering of their product, set up buying offices overseas, and established a strong marketing organization. This practice might spread farther than it has beyond the consumer area. It is important to identify who the competitor's suppliers are and how able they are to provide quality products in sufficient quantities and on time.

If the competitor does his manufacturing himself, where, what size, and how modern is his plant? Is he well located to bring in raw materials and components? Is he near the market, or does it take time to transport finished or semifinished goods to buyers? In the last few years, the logistics of getting shipments from suppliers or to customers has become a serious problem. Many companies have discovered that any savings they have effected have been eroded by the increase in transportation costs, to say nothing of the added expense due to extra insurance coverage and the expanded inventories necessary to keep incoming pipelines full and outgoing loads worth the freight.

Has the competitor focused on reducing labor costs? Has he adopted automated processes and modern methods? Is he unionized? The answers to these questions give you some idea of how progressive he is as well as how flexible he might become. If he is locked into expensive facilities and automated approaches or if he has a militant union, he may not be able to move with the industry. He may be forced to keep on manufacturing products that have lost their appeal or to stay with high-cost methods and locations. Knowing the type of pension and lack of work obligations of the competitor may also provide insight into his flexibility. Some companies have such a high pension or unemployment liability that it is too expensive to exit a product or business, and thus such companies may have to remain in a marginally profitable, or even unprofitable, situation.

How would you describe the nature and sophistication of his manufacturing personnel—supervisors, engineers, purchasing clerks, line workers, transportation people?

In general what can you learn of his production policies that will give you some strategic insights into what he is doing and will do in the future? It is also helpful but not critical to have some notion of his fixed and variable manufacturing costs; his contributed value is a somewhat more important figure to isolate.

Where to look. Converse with suppliers who serve both you and your competitors. Obviously you cannot ask for any proprietary or confidential information. But suppliers can tell you order quantities and can comment on the quality of the materials they sell to which purchasers. You should also buy and analyze the competitor's products. This will enable you to determine approximately how much it costs him to make them—that is, *his* purchase costs in *his* plant using *his* methods. Your manufacturing people will have informed opinions about his methods and processes as well as knowledge of his degree of integration and any union problems facing him.

The competitor himself will describe his facilities, equipment, and workforce in his staff and plant newspapers, annual reports, and trade media. Industry publications will often describe his wage rates, number of employees, and skill mix. Additional data can be garnered from marketing sources.

Market

Marketing factors include the competitor's sales force and distribution network, image and reputation. Let's look at some key factors in this area.

What type of sales organization does the competitor have? How big is it, and where is it located? A sales force can consist of anything from a large in-house staff to a single outside independent representative, from national to regional, from salaried to compensated by commission. How the sales force is rewarded will influence the sales focus. The composition of the sales force should conform to the company's size and strategy. The mixture of accounts, from small to large, will also affect the salespeople's efforts.

The background of sales employees may also provide strategic insights. Some companies require a technical education; others prefer experience with customers' financial problems. Turnover is a useful indicator of training and dedication. It is important to determine whether the sales force meets customer needs and expectations.

Distribution and dealer networks can greatly influence a competitor's strategic decisions. In fact I have seen companies show more concern for the protection and enhancement of the distributor than for the satisfaction of the ultimate user. The reason is that these companies have spent years cultivating their dealers to get loyalty and easy repeat business from them, and don't want anything to change this. Obviously the customer does decide how and where he buys and sometimes helps create new channels.

As discussed in Chapter 4, an organization may distribute through company-owned dealers, franchised dealers, agents, or independents; general merchandisers or discounters; or any combination of these. A firm may use only company-owned centers in an effort to control its distribution or to reduce the number of distribution competitors. Franchises and agency agreements have proved to be very effective as long as the franchises don't lose ground to other channels. When discounters appeared on the scene, they penetrated markets served by small franchised dealers, and in time the sales of some firms' products went overwhelmingly to them. This presented a dilemma to other companies with tightly controlled, often price-protected franchises. The issue arose of whether to switch, hold to their practices, or compromise. How this issue was resolved offered new opportunities or threats.

How about market research and planning? Some competitors concentrate on these areas, some don't. Some companies give the impression that they are committed to the task but in reality do very little. Of course this type of research isn't equal to strategy, but it can orient marketing practices very effectively. General Foods has earned a reputation over the years of being able to anticipate demand and consumer preferences. It has developed new products, created new brands, and increased sales. It is also interesting that General Foods has had trouble developing and packaging a successful chain in the fast foods market to compete successfully against McDonald's and other fast foods chains.

Consider your competitor's service and sales policies. Does he provide before- and after-sale service? How does he back the quality?

Does he offer warranties beyond industry norms? On the financial side does the competitor offer liberal and flexible payment conditions or quantity discounts? Remember, terms such as these may be underwritten by an intermediary, like the government or a subsidiary. After World War II, American companies had the benefit of highly favorable sales support from government-sponsored programs, like the Marshall Plan and AID, which specified that a country had to buy from American suppliers in order to qualify for the funds and low-interest payments offered by the program. In today's market U.S. firms no longer have as significant an advantage, and new types of financing, like barter agreements, may be easier for other countries to implement than the United States.

Quite often, policies like these spell the difference between marginal and outstanding performance. Your probing must go beyond the competitor's practices, to uncover the reasons he is able to continue them.

How a competitor involves his top management in carrying out various marketing functions indicates his degree of commitment as well as the need for your own team to be directly involved. It is interesting to observe the extent to which Japanese firms use their top managers to make contacts and improve trade and business relations. In 1973 the Japanese sent a delegation to Brazil comprising the top men of more than a dozen of their major corporations to negotiate and consummate favorable trade and merger agreements. A lower-echelon employee such as a salesman has a hard time competing against the big guns of the adversary.

Several ratios give you an indication of a rival firm's marketing and advertising commitment. Relating the dollars it spends on marketing in toto to its sales provides a ratio that can be calculated again over time to show how its investment at one point compares with that at another and with the industry's. A similar ratio using advertising expenditure enables you to see how important the competitor considers this marketing element. If the ratios are consistent, this denotes that the competitor has a sustained interest in the industry; if they are highly erratic, then his effort and strategy might be weak and merely opportunistic. I have seen several computer models that utilize the advertising ratio and other key expenditure ratios. These models permit you to assess the sensitivity of profits to each expenditure and also to evaluate what would happen if the expenditure were increased or decreased. Knowledge of competitors' ratios and expenditures may enable you to project the earnings impact of changes in expenditure or shifts in strategy emphasis. One model with which I am familiar, the PIMS (Profit Impact of Market Strategy), is described in the *Harvard Business Review,* and copies are available to subscribing companies.*

Where to look. Marketing information can be obtained from several sources. Your own marketing and sales divisions have knowledge of the size, type, and skills of the competitor's. They can help you reconstruct his marketing emphasis and approach. Your customers can provide considerable insight into his pricing policies and before- and after-sales services. Obtaining information from this source requires sharp questioning and attentive listening.

Advertising literature communicates what the competitor considers important and how he focuses his marketing thrust. Industry shows and exhibits, combined with annual reports and industry association data, will highlight the products that are being pushed and enable you to compare your marketing expenditures against the competitor's. Also look for quotes from the competitor's managers in industry and general business literature.

Normally none of these sources is conclusive by itself, but taken together, they enable you to draw some conclusions to track and build on.

Finance

Knowing how a competitor finances his company has vast strategic implications. His ability in this area affects his other resources and the extent to which he will be able to grow.

Some companies are very successful, as we pointed out before, in using some products to fund others. Does your competitor have this type of portfolio? Does he have more cash absorbers than generators? Which products are his cash suppliers, and do you have any that can be used to erode his base?

The use of accounting practices to provide cash or inflate earnings figures has long been a very popular tactic. By switching from

*S. Schoeffler, R. D. Buzzell, and D. F. Heaney, "The Impact of Strategic Planning on Profit Performance," *Harvard Business Review,* March-April 1974.

one inventory system to another, a competitor can change his tax requirements and pick up extra short-term cash—short-term because ultimately it will have to be paid. Another gimmick is to change the method of research and development accounting. Some companies capitalize R&D and others expense it. By capitalizing it, a competitor will inflate his reported earnings and possibly be able to convince investors that he is a growth company and should have a high price/earnings ratio. The depreciation method and the actuarial rates used to establish the contributions to the pension fund can also affect earnings and cash flow. When you are analyzing a foreign company, you must be particularly careful to study its accounting methods since these vary from nation to nation. German firms for instance tend to understate earnings through their treatment of reserves and contingency funds.

It is important to know the competitor's credit and capital ratings. These determine the extent to which he can finance and the interest rates he pays. Several ratios reveal a company's financial health.

Debt to equity indicates degree of leverage, or to put it another way, how much of someone else's money a competitor is using to nurture his business. Three forms of this ratio will provide leverage information:

$$\frac{\text{Total debt}}{\text{Total assets}} \quad \text{or} \quad \frac{\text{Long-term debt}}{\text{Capitalization}} \quad \text{or} \quad \frac{\text{Total debt}}{\text{Net worth (equity)}}$$

The current ratio measures a company's ability to meet its short-term obligations:

$$\frac{\text{Current assets}}{\text{Current liabilities}}$$

Most businessmen believe that the higher the ratio, the better. But this may not always be true since it may mean that management is using others' money, via liabilities, to finance company growth. The quick ratio is another measure of liquidity. It is determined by dividing current liabilities into the sum of cash, marketable securities, and receivables.

A ratio relating interest to income is calculated by dividing the interest paid on debt into the net income before taxes and interest.

This indicates how much the cost of servicing debt is covered by net income. If the turnover is rapidly declining, it may signal problems ahead. I think this information is particularly important at times when interest rates are rising fast, especially regarding competitors who are highly leveraged and rely on debt just to survive.

Several other ratios provide insight into the competitor's financial well-being. For instance how much inventory does he have on hand? You can translate this into an inventory turnover number by calculating

$$\frac{\text{Net sales}}{\text{Average inventory}}$$

How many days of receivables does he have? This is determined by the formula

$$\frac{\text{Accounts receivable}}{\text{Sales per day}}$$

Financial measures such as the ones I have described are useful only if they are compared with the industry averages. Is 100 days of receivables standard or atypical? What is the average inventory turnover? Is the entire industry highly leveraged or only the competitor you are analyzing? Any measurement has to be set against a yardstick comprising a whole. An inch of rain is a shower in some parts of the world but a flood in others. A doctor can't intelligently evaluate a blood-pressure reading or pulse rate unless he knows the patient's age and weight. The same is true of financial ratios. In some industries 50 percent debt is unusually low while in others it is highly risky and a sign of potential disaster. In organizations I have studied, less than 60 days of receivables means that the company is in danger of losing business since this credit term is the standard for customers in its market.

Companies that obtain funds from stock issues can be assessed by their price/earnings ratio. A high P/E ratio normally reflects growth shares, but the stock market is fickle and the ratios may change very quickly. An excellent example of an abrupt change can be found in the history of conglomerates. In the late 1960s these companies enjoyed ratios of profits 20 to 40 times earnings; in 1973 they were averaging between 5 and 8. The decline has

affected their ability not only to attract equity funds but also to
retain managers and hire new people. The reason is that many of
these firms induced executives to join them by offering them attractive stock options. As the stock fell, it was highly demoralizing
for these managers to see their paper millions go down in flames.

Where to look. Except for privately owned companies, financial
information on firms is a matter of public record and can be analyzed from annual reports, reports to investors, and documents filed
with the Securities and Exchange Commission. At times the information isn't available in the depth or form that makes the analysis
easy, but by using several sources, you can approximate to the level
necessary for determining strategic implications.

Manage

Some companies with extensive strengths do poorly, and some
with mediocre abilities do well. The difference lies in their management talent. In business as in basketball, it takes a combination of
good players and good coaching to make a winning team.

Assessing the competitor's management begins with evaluating
the executives' interest in the firm, their ability to organize and
motivate the workers and the supervisory force, their performance
review skills, and their planning capabilities.

Determining who makes the competitor's decisions and how is
valuable. The speed of decision making can spell the difference
between success and failure. If authority is centralized in a company that is large or diversified, the process may be complex and
slow.

The type of consulting service used may be a key to anticipating
changes in the competitor's behavior. Every consultant, whether
an individual or a firm, seems to have a favorite theory, and if you
know your competitor has hired an outside adviser, it may be easy
to figure out what he will do next. Of course it's important to find
out whether your competitor's management takes advice or merely
listens and then acts the way it wanted to in the first place.

Knowing the values of the key managers can provide considerable
insight. There are companies led by ruthless and unethical people
who will do anything to win. There are also those whose executives
look beyond profit and desire to make a social contribution. This

may have a lot to do with the personal wealth and ambitions of the company head. Managerial values also vary from culture to culture, which should be kept in mind regarding a competitor with a foreign base of operations or foreign origins.

Succession policies can also affect a rival's future and strategy. Knowing whether the company tends to promote from within or to reach outside will help you predict the extent and type of change. Inbreeding has its advantages and disadvantages. If a company has ignored a need to train and develop its manager, this may mean that it has traded its ultimate future for a short-term gain.

How are managers rewarded and punished? This question can affect a competitor's planning and future options. If the company rewards its executives for high return on investment, this will evoke different behavior from an emphasis on sales growth. If a company is risk-oriented, its managers will be aiming at different opportunities from those pursued by the risk-avoiding firm. Every business leader subscribes to a particular hierarchy of measures, and he will usually tell the world what it is in his speeches and published interviews.

Finally, you should check to see whether the competitor's actions and his management measurement system are consistent and reinforce each other or whether one negates the other. If you spot an inconsistency, this may provide a competitive advantage to you.

SOME SPECIAL CASES

The analysis I have presented pertains to all types of competitors, but for the multi-industry or foreign rival, you may wish to add several other elements.

A basic fact about the multi-industry competitor is that he has to balance his business portfolio. He may be using the organization that competes against you to generate cash for other growth opportunities. His commitment for the long term to the industries he participates in may vary in degree. This will affect his willingness to invest or to sustain losses in yours. If he is counting on it for main growth, he may be highly committed and refuse to be intimidated. In short, try to discover how dedicated he is to your industry and markets.

Quite often a clue to this dedication is the background of the chief executive of the parent company. If he comes from the business against which you compete, it's a good bet that he will support it even if it is a loser. If he doesn't have any attachments, then it may be easy for him to remove from his must list.

The relationship of a foreign competitor to national goals and to his government may be strategically important. The kind and quantity of incentives, financial aid, and other supports he is given should be known. In some cases these may not be obvious and must be probed for.

Another series of questions relating to the foreign competitor concerns his freedom to move across borders, especially into U.S. markets. A switch of strategy should be noted in this connection. Originally Japanese television manufacturers looked at the United States as an export market. As they grew they began to think multinationally. They set up manufacturing in the United States and became quasi-American, which changed the nature of the competition in our domestic television market. Sony for example opened a plant in San Diego, and Panasonic acquired Quasar from Motorola. Thus two key foreign manufacturers moved into our neighborhood.

In some cases, to really understand a particular group of foreign competitors, you may have to examine their entire environment. What is happening to their domestic market? Is it stagnating? Have they been receiving government support, and if so, what is happening to it? Are they being urged to merge and consolidate? Are they in a business given priority by the government? What about labor costs, social costs, pressures from ecologists? Yes, the same questions we pose about ourselves apply to the competitor from overseas, because all such factors have become international; they are not reserved to the United States.

APPLICATION TIME

Now take some time to analyze your key competitors. The following (page 102) may assist in the evaluation.

Summary of Competitor Analysis*

Conceive/Design	Produce	Market	Finance	Manage

Technical resources
Concepts
Patents and copyrights
Technological sophistication
Technical integration
 	
Human resources
Key people and skills
Use of external technical groups
 	
Funding
Total
Percentage of sales
Consistency over time
Internally generated
Government-supplied
	Physical resources
	Capacity
	Plant
	  Size
	  Location
	  Age
	Equipment
	  Automation
	  Maintenance
	  Flexibility
	Processes
	  Uniqueness
	  Flexibility
	  Degree of integration
	
	Human resources
	Key people and skills
	Workforce
	  Skills mix
	  Unions
	  Turnover
		Sales force
		Skills
		Size
		Type
		Location
		
		Distribution network
		
		Research
		Skills
		Type
		
		Service and sales policies
		
		Advertising
		Skills
		Type
		
		Human resources
		Key people and skills
		Turnover
		
		Funding
		Total
		Consistency over time
		Percentage of sales
		Reward systems
			Long-term
			Debt/equity ratio
			Cost of debt
			
			Short-term
			Line of credit
			Type of debt
			Cost of debt
			
			Liquidity
			
			Cash flow
			Days of receivables
			Inventory turnover
			Accounting practices
			
			Human resources
			Key people and skills
			Turnover
			
			Systems
			Budgeting
			Forecasting
			Controlling
				Key people
				Objectives and priorities
				Values
				Reward systems
				
				Decision making
				Location
				Type
				Speed
				
				Planning
				Type
				Emphasis
				Time span
				
				Staffing
				Longevity and turnover
				Experience
				Replacement policies
				
				Organization
				Centralization
				Functions
				Use of staff

*If *multi-industry*, examine portfolio of businesses (sizes, priorities, importance to company) and resources provided by parent company. If *foreign*, examine national priorities of home country; degree of government ownership; supports and incentives; home-market environment.

Identification

Who are your current key competitors? Which of them has the greatest effect on you or the segments in which you participate?

Evaluation (for each key competitor)

1. Record past results—his sales, profits, growth, share. Is he satisfied with his performance?
2. Reconstruct his past strategy, including:
   (a) Investment, management strategies.
   (b) Operating strategies (conceive/design, produce, market, finance, manage).
3. Identify his current and future resources. (The checklist is a good reference.)
4. Note his areas of strength and limitation in each of the key resource areas.

Implications

Ask, "So what?" Does the competitor's performance, strategy, resources, or strengths and limitations provide any opportunities or threats to your company?

It is important to record your thoughts and note key characteristics of customers since these will be used later when you determine your management and operating strategies.

If you wish to refresh your understanding of financial analysis, there are numerous reliable texts and handbooks you might consult. See, for example: Robert N. Anthony and Robert H. Hermanson, *Management Accounting,* Homewood, Ill., Learning Systems Company, 1970; David E. Hawkins, *Financial Reporting Practices of Corporations,* Dow Jones–Irwin, Inc., 1972; and Erich A. Helfert, *Techniques of Financial Analysis,* Homewood, Ill., Richard D. Irwin, Inc., 1974.

6

KNOW YOURSELF: RESOURCE ANALYSIS

The first five chapters have probed your external world and set up procedures for assessing what may happen in it, who may make moves that influence your business, and how you can handle the resulting opportunities and threats. But to be in a sound strategic position and to develop effective strategic alternatives, you must analyze your organization's own abilities. From this stage of the process, you will come to *know yourself.*

The sequence is the same as recommended repeatedly before. First, you will describe what you have been in the past, what you are now, and what you think you will be in the future. Based on your assessment of the future, you will ask, "So what?" and record both present and projected major assets and liabilities. I use these terms rather than "strengths" and "limitations" to emphasize the relativity of these concepts. You must view yourself in three contexts:

- Compare your resources with those of others aiming at the same target.
- Weigh them against the requirements of the specific opportunity or threat you are or will be pursuing.
- Assess them in the light of the elements of strategy already suggested by your customer and competitor analyses.

The relativity of your assets and liabilities must always be kept in mind as you evaluate yourself. Quite often managers start out appraising a positive attribute in relative terms, but before they know it, they begin thinking of it as an absolute superiority that makes their firm invincible. This is like a basketball coach who thinks his players can beat every other team just because two of them are 6 feet 10 inches tall. A team with big men can be superior—if it competes against a less competent or slower team. But shorter opponents who play the fast break and outrun the bigger men may be the winners despite the height difference. Similarly in business a company with only limited financial resources may beat a more affluent firm because of the way it operates or the market segment it has chosen to concentrate on. This does not mean that financial superiority isn't an asset; it means that how and where the money is used determine whether the asset is a real strength.

WHAT TO EVALUATE

Resource evaluation concerns itself with the same abilities outlined in the discussion of competitor analysis. The major difference is that you now probe your own capacities in more detail. Your self-scrutiny will identify areas that need to be improved regardless of the strategy you choose. This list is a fringe benefit and can be very useful. For example you may find that you need to beef up your credit and collection operations since your accounts receivable are getting out of hand. This is an area that needs attention whether you decide to pursue an aggressive strategy or to relax and slowly liquidate your business.

In particular you will look at which of your resources will provide you with competitive leverage or a head start, both in themselves and in combinations that can increase the odds of your winning. As outlined in the previous chapter, there are five major functional areas in your organization that you need to appraise: (1) conceive/design, (2) produce, (3) market, (4) finance, and (5) manage.

Ability to Conceive/Design

In some industries the ability to conceive and design is the key to not just success but survival; without it the participant will fail.

But regardless of its criticalness, you should inventory what you can and cannot do. This inventory should cover your basic, applied, and advanced research strengths and your engineering function.

Basic research attempts to advance the state of the art or develop new insights into existing theory or practice. This is science as distinct from engineering. Most companies are weak in basic research, since it is expensive and is often considered economically unrewarding. Until World War II few major industrial companies were skilled in basic research; the two that most easily come to mind are Bell Telephone Laboratories and General Electric's Research and Development Labs. Since the war, many other organizations have been formed to take advantage of the vast research funds available especially from the federal government. Among these are nonprofit institutes and university centers that provide public access to their findings. Therefore, when you evaluate your basic research capabilities, also think about taking advantage of data that are in the public domain and available to you from independent bodies.

Applied research moves concept and theory to demonstration. It may take up basic research done by others or by you for other purposes. An excellent example is the application of semiconductor or integrated circuit technology to products other than those originally incorporating it.

Advanced engineering is the next step in a product's evolution. It moves a prototype from its laboratory environment to the factory in order to show that it is technologically possible to make. *Design engineering* translates the item into quantity-produced goods. It varies in complexity from one industry to another, and in some cases it consists in merely replicating the designs of others in a legal and ethical manner.

In each area you need to inventory the types and degrees of skills and talents as well as the facilities you have or will acquire. Since it is rare to find the same level of competence across the board, you should evaluate where you are strong, where you are weak, and where you have no ability at all. It isn't unusual to find a company with an impressive list of patents but a dismal track record in execution. It is also important to identify the most productive R&D people. Are there only one or two who have turned out the majority of the patents your company holds? How old are they? Do you have other innovators coming along?

You should also assess the size, type, location, and sophistication of your laboratories. Improper equipment will hold back even the best talent in the race for superiority. As in your assessment of your competitor's dedication to R&D, it is useful to look at how much money you have spent on this function and how consistent the amount has been over the last five years. Further, have you been using your money or relying on others to finance your research and development work? If you have been living on government funds, you should be careful not to think of this as an unending source.

In short, you should objectively determine who have been the technological leaders in your organization, the type and extent of talents you have had, the size and sophistication of laboratories and equipment, and the funding in terms of size, consistency, and source. A matrix such as Figure 6–1 might be useful in this total evaluation.

	Basic	Applied	Advanced	Design
Technology, technical skill				
Key people (age)				
Funding (last five years, year by year)				

Figure 6-1 Matrix for technical evaluation.

Ability to Produce

Most businessmen recognize that production capabilities are crucial. Yet I have found many who sit back and assume a degree of good health and well-being in this area when even a cursory review would show them otherwise. Any smart leader of any type of enterprise needs to take a reading periodically of his organization's ability to produce its product. The questions to ask center on costs, productivity, and capacity/readiness to serve.

Costs. Materials costs are a large part of the price of manufacturing any product and must be held in line especially in a time of inflation. Thus your production evaluation will include how well your purchasing agents negotiate in various supply areas—with both U.S. and foreign producers, both direct sellers and commodity merchants, and so on. Their skills should not be measured on grounds of materials costs alone, since availability and quality are also vital to successful functioning. In addition you should assess how well your organization can substitute other, less expensive or perhaps more plentiful materials if the need arises.

Labor costs are another focus of evaluation. These include the costs of hiring, training, and retaining workers as well as paying them. Production workers earn less per hour in some parts of the world than in others, but the training and retaining expenditures may far outweigh the wage savings.

The costs of inventories of supplies and in-process and finished goods should be reviewed. Is your staff skilled in systematizing inventories and keeping the proper levels? These costs are particularly important when financing is expensive and it may pay to increase stocks as a hedge against inflation. Are your inventory methods responsive to changes?

Productivity. The types and age of your equipment bear heavily on your productivity. Are you highly automated? Can your machinery be adapted to change, or is it locked into using specific materials or processes? What is the cost of capital to expand your capacity? Is your manufacturing engineering organization skilled in process design, work measurements, and tooling?

Another area of productivity, one often overlooked, is the ability of your foremen, supervisors, and managers to motivate the workforce and keep your productivity high. Many managers think that adding labor-saving equipment does the job, but it also takes a continuous effort to assure that the worker feels he is part of the team.

What kind of labor organization do you face? Whether the union you deal with takes a militant stance or tries to be cooperative can make a large difference in productivity.

Capacity/readiness to serve. The degree of capacity utilization helps determine your ability to meet customers' demands. If you are already operating at 90 to 95 percent of capacity, you can't add much more without increasing fixed costs. What is the optimum level of capacity utilization? It may be 95 percent in some businesses but only 85 percent in others. When a plant is working beyond its optimum capacity, it will usually find itself paying a premium for the extra output. Incidentally this situation can result from ignoring maintenance or pushing the workers to the point where they strike or slow down just to get a rest.

Other factors that affect your ability to serve are the type of suppliers and the degree of integration you have. If you rely on distant suppliers (in such places as Taiwan, Singapore, and Korea), the time necessary to obtain supplies can inhibit your ability to respond to increased demand. If you have a large contributed value and a high degree of integration, you may be in a good position to add capacity but be less able to reduce it. On the other hand, the lower your degree of integration, the less you may be able to insulate yourself from sudden cost increases.

Your ability to produce should be studied on the three time dimensions of the past, present, and future, and you should not merely extrapolate the future from the present, much less from the past. Today's low-cost supplier or low-wage country may not remain so in the future. Witness the effect of devaluations and revaluations on the Germans and Japanese. The cost of ocean shipment has risen. So don't become complacent and think that the position you are in now will continue forever.

Ability to Market

Many businesses have highly salable products and are able to manufacture them efficiently but are unable to penetrate markets successfully. When I discussed in Chapter 5 what to look for in a competitor's marketing efforts, I stressed the need to assess his sales force, types of dealers and distributors, market research, and incentives to dealers and consumers. You should survey the same factors in your own operations but in more detail. To begin with, however, let's return to your market segmentation analysis, which you began in Chapter 3.

Segmentation. The use of a segmentation breakdown such as Table 3–1, which looked at the total market for certain kinds of small motors and the competitors' penetration of various customer groups, shows you where you fit in industry sales as a whole and relative to your rivals. Do you have a particular marketing sector targeted, or do you try to serve all types of buyers equally? How have your marketing people chosen the segments they emphasize? This series of questions helps indicate the level of sophistication and planning in your marketing operation. I have been amazed at the lack of planning that many marketing managers demonstrate. Their thinking seems to stop when the orders are received.

Sales force. Describing the innovative capabilities in a firm's research and engineering functions, I pointed out that a few people may account for the majority of new concepts, patents, and copyrights. The same is likely to be true of your sales force. Many businesses find that perhaps 80 percent of their orders are accounted for by 20 percent of their customers and that these are being served by only a few salesmen. Do you have other dynamic people coming into the stream if and when those key men leave?

Distributors. Have you relied on a few independents to carry the load? What is the likelihood of their continuing their relationship with you in the future? Are they capable of withstanding changes in the sales and competition mix? Do they have adequate staff, or are they one- or two-man shows that will die when the principals retire? An outline of the location and size by sales volume of distributors, set up as in Table 6-1, will help you assess the solidity of your present distribution network. A companion table projecting figures for, say, five years hence will indicate regions where weaknesses may develop.

Table 6-1. Your present distribution pattern.

Location of Distributors	Size, by Units Sold			
	0-100	*100-250*	*250-700*	*700-1,000*
East				
West				
North				
South				

The key questions just formulated, combined with those suggested in the previous chapter but equally applicable to your own marketing and distribution resources, probe your assets and liabilities in these critical functions. An alternative approach is to investigate your operations under the following five headings:

- *Knowledge of customers.* Knowing who are and can be your buyers allows you to forecast their needs and expectations in general. Market research pins down what these mean in terms of specific products.
- *Response to customers.* This area includes the quality and scope of your products, the type of distributors who handle them, your warehousing system, and your transportation arrangements.
- *Influencing customers.* Start by assessing your sales force. Then examine your advertising—national, regional, and cooperative programs—and such special promotion devices as quantity-purchase discounts and display arrangements.
- *Servicing customers.* Survey what you offer in before- and after-sale services, including installation, application engineering, and repair. What is your policy on supplying spare or replacement parts?
- *Financing customers.* These include your practices in granting long-term and short-term credit. Your receivables inventory and nonmonetary forms of sales financing should also be appraised.

Ability to Finance

In the domain of financing, you again need to identify the assets and liabilities your organization has and their strategic implications. Here are the major points you should cover:

Your ability to obtain funds, both long- and short-term. This means assessing your credit ratings, your lines of credit, the types of borrowings available to you and the interest on each, and the image and attractiveness of your stock. These are a function of the nature and extent of debt you already have and the market performance and dividend record of your stock. The trends of your financial ratios are indicators of your financial health and are reviewed by leaders and investors.

Your ability to control costs, fixed and variable, direct and indirect. In addition how well have you been estimating future expenses and anticipating cost trends?

Your ability to finance sales at the lowest possible level. This means reining in credit lines and controlling accounts receivable. Review your dating program and days outstanding.

Your ability to minimize taxes. Check that you are paying only what is required and that your tax-related accounting practices are in tune with the law and provide you with the highest possible cash flow and operating income.

Your ability to anticipate changes in monetary rates on a worldwide basis. This will enable you to use deposits in overseas banks to buy and sell foreign currency advantageously.

As I have said before, it is important for every organization to know where it stands and what it is doing in terms of financing its operations. Financing is both absolute and relative. It is absolute in that if you can't pay your bills or borrow to do so, the game is over and bankruptcy will result. It is relative in that when your financial resources are poorer than those of other participants in your industry, you are at a competitive disadvantage.

Ability to Manage

Many executives lose sight of the need to analyze their own and their management team's abilities. They may keep close tabs on the engineering, marketing, and financial capacities of the business but forget that many resource-rich companies have failed because of managerial ineptness. What you are interested in here are the qualitative aspects of your managers (yourself included), not merely their names, ranks, backgrounds, and number.

Values and objectives. Some companies have set high standards of ethical behavior and find it difficult to compete in industries whose value structure is less demanding. Then too there are managers who place their own career objectives significantly above the welfare of the company. Every person puts personal concerns before organization goals to some degree, and I think this is healthy and normal. But the type I'm referring to takes self-interest well beyond acceptable limits and will do anything to make a splash with little or no regard for the consequences. If a management team is more opportunistic than is good for the business, this can constitute a serious liability.

Turnover and experience. If management is inexperienced and turnover is large, your company can be expected to make many mistakes. These factors may make the difference between winning and losing the game. They can be offset, however, by the abilities of those below the management level. If there are veterans in the ranks and management is willing to listen to and accept their advice, then the lack of seasoning may not be that much of a problem.

Planning ability. Is your managerial team interested and skilled in both long- and short-range planning? As I mentioned in Chapter 2 when dealing with mission development, competence in planning affects the nature and degree of change you can make from the past. It isn't easy to enhance this ability, and if managers are deficient in it, the organization should work to build it up. Another task in this evaluation is to determine whether there is a disequilibrium between short- and long-range plans. There is no question that an organization interested in long-term growth must have an integrated set of immediate and remote objectives. Strategic thinking is the link between the first and the second and includes both.

Staff utilization. Having inadequate or no staff can be a serious limitation. Underusing or misusing staff capabilities can be just as serious. I have already discussed how the lack of a planning team can inhibit the strategy options you can investigate. The lack of financial staff can inhibit the range of financing you can obtain or your ability to control receivables and inventories. Legal expertise is vital in this period of history when there are so many laws and regulations hedging business operations. This doesn't mean that you must have a large staff on your payroll, but it does mean that you should have access to these and other types of talent and counsel.

Control and measurement. Does your company have tight or loose controls? Can you reduce costs or change directions easily and quickly? Are your measurement and reward systems responsive to the environment and human needs? What type of motivational philosophy is being utilized? Does it emphasize the carrot or the stick? Are your managers rewarded for performance or for loyalty? What do your personnel policies aim at achieving? Are you interested in attracting bright young people to develop and promote for a life-time career, or are you considered to be a hire-fire company?

Management assessment is difficult if not impossible for managers to do themselves and usually requires outside consultants. The services of an industrial psychologist may be fruitful. In using this type of evaluation professional, you should check out his credentials to make sure he understands the dynamics of business organizations. It is even better if he has experience in your industry. Such a background will equip him to provide realistic comparative assessments rather than merely describing your resources in terms of some general theoretical model.

LET'S TAKE AN EXAMPLE

Let me pause for a few minutes to illustrate how to apply the resource analysis approaches I have been discussing. Suppose we are top executives doing this analysis for our firm, Data Processing Corporation (DPC), which provides services to city and state governments. Our hypothetical company has been in business for 20 years.

Ability to Conceive/Design

DPC has no research ability or need, for both basic and applied research are performed by the hardware producers and not software firms such as ours. The languages used by the computers are developed mainly by the manufacturers of the machinery. More than 80 percent of DPC's work entails the use of IBM equipment.

Basic engineering is limited. DPC has three systems analysts who keep abreast of the state of the art and track what is happening in the hardware companies. Dick Wilson is the senior member of this team and has done most of this surveillance over the past 10 years. We assume he will stay with us for the 10 years remaining before he reaches retirement age.

Design engineering is the heart of our company. The department contains a 50-member staff whose job it is to develop the master programs. Most are customized to suit the needs of the client ordering one. DPC has a good reputation in this area. There is about a 15 percent turnover of our master programmers per year, and many of those who leave us are picked up by our competitors.

As we stand back and look at these facts, we can discern some assets and some liabilities. On the assets side we can list the design engineering staff and Dick Wilson with his expert knowledge. Both of these have been pluses for DPC, and *if* we hold on to these resources, they should constitute strengths in the future. This is a tough issue—will we be able to retain them? How can we increase the chances of doing so? We recognize the need to plan how to retain key people as well as physical resources. We know we can't merely sit back and expect them to stay available by chance alone.

On the liabilities side we see that we have deficiencies in the basic and applied research areas. We are not saying that we should correct the situation, since in our case that would be too costly. But we are dependent on the manufacturers for these functions and could one day wake up to find that they are changing their policies and refusing access to their proprietary processes and languages.

Ability to Produce

This area will require some adaptation for a service-type company. The traditional plant and equipment are not our key production resources. In our kind of business, we are more concerned with our human than our physical resources. The questions we are asking ourselves involve mainly our people's capacity and our quality control. DPC has a four-month backlog of work orders, and people can do only so much programming. So if we want to add capacity, we will probably be required to add employees. If we don't turn out programs that run properly, we won't be in business much longer.

Our workforce is generally young, educated, and mathematically inclined. All employees have at least two years of college; 75 percent have a bachelor of science degree and 15 percent a master's degree. They range from 21 to 35 years of age, with the median age of 28. Half are married, and 65 percent are women. Average service is three years and average overall experience seven. In reviewing the costs of the product, we find that it averages about $5,000 a program delivered and tested.

Among our production pluses, therefore, is the staff, well educated and ranking high in math aptitude. However, as seen by some of our executives, that same staff might be considered a liability, containing as it does such a large percentage of women. In the judgment of those managers the turnover rate for women employees is higher than for men and may contribute to the relatively low service level. On the other hand, this attitude may be rigorously challenged by women's liberation groups as being bias, pure and simple. Of course to arrive at a useful, objective conclusion about turnover rates, we will have to compare the statistics for the men and women in our workforce to see whose turnover is greater and why. Further we must remember that even if the charge against women employees can be substantiated, the data may change in the future as women become more liberated. In any event, we should be constantly aware that in the asset and liability area we are often dealing with judgments, and these will vary from one individual to another. The same factor or piece of data could find itself on either side of the ledger depending on the opinions and biases of the evaluator.

That data we've been working with here are limited and subjective, of course, and we can't determine whether our assumptions about our strengths and limitations are correct until we see how we compare in education level, turnover rate, and other findings with our direct competitors and industry participants as a whole. We may find that in most programming companies the average education level of production people is higher. But we have isolated some critical characteristics and will compare them with the industry and our competition later.

Ability to Market

Again, marketing a service is different from marketing a product. For example, at DPC we have no formal sales force; in fact, selling is done by us the management and by our key programmers. We have neither market research personnel nor promotional expertise, relying instead on the quality of our output as the means of continuing sales. Our marketing approach consists of personal selling to a few key accounts in the public sector and guaranteeing customer satisfaction by redoing work or customizing to his specifications. This approach has brought us premium prices and also advance or progress payments.

DPC's greatest assets in the marketing area are its personal management-led selling and its proven reputation for quality work. A quality image is hard to beat in a service business, but it depends on our ability to keep a solid workforce.

However, our lack of a dedicated marketing and sales force has its limitations. As a small company, we often get so involved in running the business that we fail to maintain a backlog. Another drawback is our overdependence on selling to state and local governments, which are very vulnerable to politics and a change of administration. In addition, our financial terms and conditions are both a plus and minus. On the positive side, they reduce the cash flow requirements, but on the negative side, they permit a more aggressive competitor to buy share by offering more favorable conditions. This is particularly true at the time this book is being written, since municipal governments are in a liquidity bind.

Ability to Finance

We have a good credit rating and a reputation for promptly paying our bills. This had led to a $150,000 line of credit at prime plus one percent. Our company has been successful in selling its stock, over the counter, at 30 to 35 times earnings, and this has even continued during the recession of 1974–1975. We are considered a solid growth company by most investment analysts and are on their recommended *buy* list.

DPC has done well in maintaining cost controls. We have been able to limit receivables to less than 30 days, and in fact we receive 25 percent of our fees at the beginning of the project. Since we deal with government bodies, we have two individuals assigned to their collections alone. We are now in an excellent cash position.

Since there is little need for capital equipment and most of our terminals are leased to us, we have no funded debt. All of our profits are reinvested in the business.

DPC has an impressive list of financial assets. Our credit rating and cost of money are both positive. Our cost and financial policies are also beneficial to DPC's continual growth. However, the size of our line of credit and our inexperience in debt financing could be a limitation. Further our tendency to get prepayments could also be a problem, as was discussed in the marketing analysis.

Ability to Manage

DPC's management resources have to some extent already been discussed, both directly and indirectly. For instance, it was indicated that management is the prime sales force, and that DPC is an efficient, cost-controlled organization. But there is, of course, more to say:

Our organization is operated on a top-down basis, and Dan McGregor, our president, is the focal point. Dan developed the company himself, starting it as a one-man programmer operation. Though 62, he has no intention of retiring. We have two other members of top management, both vice presidents. Both men are young (38 and 42) and have been in the industry for over 15 years. The older of the two, Tom Hockmeyer, is our financial veep. Tom has excellent banking connections; it was he who negotiated the line of credit at those favorable interest rates.

Salaries are 10 percent above the industry average, and our profit sharing plan accounts for 10 to 15 percent of the total compensation. We have hospital benefits and an unfunded pension plan. The organization is dynamic. We purchase all legal and auditing services.

Dan McGregor is both an asset and a liability. He represents our company's past and present, and is still calling the shots for the future. The two vice presidents appear to be assets, but we must consider the possibility of their leaving the company. Our dependence on a few key men, the existence of a clouded line of succession, along with a compensation system based on profit sharing are real or potential problems. There is no question that our growth is limited by the management characteristics of the company.

The DPC illustration was intended to highlight the need to evaluate yourself in order to arrive at key conclusions. However, since objectivity is vital but very difficult to achieve, you may find it necessary to obtain the services of a professional consulting organization.

SELF-ASSESSMENT IN NONPROFIT ORGANIZATIONS

Resource analysis is equally critical for the nonprofit institution and follows the same sequence. All nonprofit organizations have some level of innovative skills. They may possess some unique ability that has contributed significantly to past success. This resource may consist of a few key people who have taught brilliant courses or made major advances in music or medicine. These people may leave or retire, and with them will go their ability and reputation. Their departure should be prepared for.

Production costs must be kept in line by the nonprofit organization. If the costs of delivering a service exceed the current income financing them, ultimately new sources of funds will have to be found or the amount or quality of service must be reduced. This is the main reason private institutions transform themselves into public or quasi-public organizations.

Productivity and capacity must also be assessed. How many students can attend each class; how many patients can a doctor treat per day; how many cases can a social worker handle in a week? If teachers instruct less and get paid more, salaries will rise or hours of instruction will decline. All institutions must consider how to enhance productivity. Can human talent be replaced or its utilization intensified by mechanized equipment? Capacity for a college includes a survey of the physical plant—classrooms, dormitories, laboratories, library facilities. The number of beds in a hospital and its out-patient diagnostic and treatment rooms are the major components of its physical space.

On the financial side, as all nonprofit institutions have become painfully aware, there is an increasing need for professionalism and vigilance. Many of their leaders today function as full-time fund raisers. All such organizations must stay alert to the sources of their income. What percentages of revenue come from government bodies, alumni or other private individuals, business enterprises or industrial associations, and the institution's own endowment fund or investment portfolio?

Each of these sources is erratic and can't be counted on to continue its contribution consistently. We have all seen the impact of changes in government funding practices. Private and business donations are affected by taxes, inflation, unemployment, and other economic trends. Investment income isn't assured. Institutions that switched much of their safe, low-return bonds for swinging, high-reward stocks have been hurt by the long market downturn, which decreased the earnings that were expected from these shares.

The type of leadership an institution has affects its present condition and its ability to respond to change. Some colleges have highly respected academicians at their head. They build a school's reputation but may make business errors. Some institutions are led by first-rate promoters or marketing-oriented people, but they may be a liability in building a sound professional reputation for the organization or increasing its professional excellence. Like any other resource, the management of endeavors such as these can have various combinations of positive and negative characteristics.

Thus you can see that with slight modifications the key questions proposed for profit-making businesses can help identify the nonprofit organization's assets and liabilities.

APPLICATION TIME

Now it is time to do the job of describing your resources and determining your pluses and minuses. The chapter has provided you with a broad sample of questions to ask about all your ability areas. Let me remind you that though all the questions (and others they may suggest) should be asked, they are not all of equal weight in themselves or in relation to every type of business. Some may be glossed over quickly; others may require more study than you can give them now. When you have completed your analysis, you will have:

- A listing of your resources themselves and your main assumptions about how they will look in the future.
- A listing of assets, or positive features that provide competitive leverage if properly utilized.
- A listing of liabilities, or negative factors that need to be corrected or counterbalanced depending on the strategy you select.
- A listing of problem areas that should be improved regardless of the stragegy you choose.

The checklist for this chapter sets out in abbreviated form the points to cover in your appraisal of your resources.

Summary of Resource Analysis

Conceive/Design	Produce	Market	Finance	Manage
Basic Research	*Materials*	*Knowledge of Customers*	Cost of Forecasting (Estimating)	Overall leadership
Concepts and studies	Key people and skills	Forecasting needs and expectations	Total Cost Analysis	Specialist leadership
Emphasis	Sources	Market research	Acct. receivable management	Turnover/experience
Key people and skills	Substitutes	*Response to Customers*	Credit collections	Values/style
Ability to convert to application	Flow planning and transportation	Products' quality and scope	Financial analysis	Strategic emphasis
		Distributors	Obtaining long-term financing	*Organization*
Applied Research	*Physical Resources*	Locations	Auditing	Type
Findings	Capacity utilization	Size by volume	Flexibility of acctg. policies/procedures	Size
Emphasis	Time/Cost of adding capacity	Warehousing	Expense control	Location
Use of external vs. internal research	Plant	Transportation	Monetary management	*Control*
Key people and skills	Size	*Influencing Customers*	Tax accounting	Financial
Ability to convert to prototypes	Location	Sales force		Human
	Age	Key people and skills		*Decision Making/ Planning*
Basic Engineering	Equipment	Size		Type
Prototypes	Automation	Type		Degree
Emphasis	Maintenance	Location		Time horizon
Key people and skills	Flexibility	Advertising		Location
Ability to convert to product designs	Processes	National		Contingency
	Uniqueness	Regional		Criteria used
	Flexibility	Cooperative		
	Degree of integration	Promotion devices		*Staff*
	Manufacturing			Type
				Use

Design Engineering
Designs
Patents and copyrights
Emphasis
Key people and skills
Ability to design for
  production

Funding
Size
Consistency over
  time
Sources
Own organization
Parent corporation
Government
Other external source

Engineering
Key people and skills
in process and tool
design, cost im-
provement, time
standards

Quality Control
Key people and skills
Standards and specifi-
  cations
Supplies inspections
Product inspections
Audits
Vendor evaluations

Shop Operation
Key people and skills
Work requirements
Workforce
  Skills mix
  Utilization
  Availability and
    turnover
  Costs
  Unionization
  Productivity

Service Policies
Before-sale
After-sale

Credit Policies
Long-term
Short-term

7

A FOUR-DIMENSION OVERLAY: SOCIETY, GOVERNMENT, THE ECONOMY, AND TECHNOLOGY

Once upon a time a businessman could formulate his strategy by considering his customers, his competitors, and his market in particular and industry in general. The world was simple, and it wasn't changing that rapidly. But for the past three decades, the world hasn't been that simple. Now we find many strategic issues emanating from areas that were once reserved for the attention of academicians and theorists. In this chapter I will review how society, government, the economy, and technology impinge on your customers, competitors, market, and industry, and I will discuss how these forces result in changes that open up new opportunities and threats for organizations.

SOCIETAL CONCERNS

Society, or if you prefer, the public, has caused significant changes in what customers expect of the products and services they purchase. We now find countless sorts of groups urging people to demand products that are safer, last longer, have fewer defects, and cost less. Groups have appointed themselves judges of products and rank them in terms of performance and quality. This has had a significant im-

123

pact on methods of competition. Companies have gone to considerable lengths to change products in order to enhance their ratings. Entirely new distribution channels have evolved from these changes.

There have been other effects as well. Many groups have been formed to protect the public from pollution and preserve natural resources from waste or misuse. These efforts have resulted in new and more restrictive legislation and more stringent enforcement of existing laws, which in turn has affected the economics of doing business. The list is staggering and has hit all industries. Electric utilities have been delayed in putting nuclear plants on line; in fact some have canceled their plans for these entirely. Steel companies and other metal-producing firms have been forced to add pollution control devices or to convert processes. Paper suppliers have been deterred from using public forests. The whole agricultural industry was forced to stop using DDT because it was found to be unsafe for wildlife.

No longer can companies dump wastes at will into streams and rivers. Polluting gases must be filtered and their toxic content reduced. Noise levels must be kept down to a stipulated level. Legal steps are taken to assure conformity with the new standards, even to the point that managers have been held personally responsible and put in jail for their company's noncompliance.

The major problem in all this lies in determining which spokesman to listen to. Like any complex issue, the ecology controversy has many sides and many spokesmen. Who really represents the public? Who will have the most influence and cause change? These are tough questions to answer, but they must be probed.

I would like to point out that such struggles have always been around. To go back only to the early 1900s, reformers who fought against abuses in the food and drug industries and the monopolistic practices of business giants succeeded in getting the government to impose food and drug regulations and to split up trusts. The principal difference between then and now is that the time lag between verbal attacks and legislation has contracted. Today it may take only two or three years for change to occur rather than 20 or 25 as previously. Sometimes politicians try to anticipate the next public concern and run to lead the effort, which shortens the time span further.

The key to staying abreast of societal trends is to develop the practices of reading and listening to those with their fingers on the public pulse. Then ask, "How might this new issue affect my customers, my competitors, my market, and my industry as a whole?" This demands objectivity. You should resist the temptation to shrug the issue off as "ridiculous." Sound strategic thinking includes anticipating changes and working to harness them for the benefit of your organization.

GOVERNMENT ACTION

Business history documents that the attitude that prevailed until recently in the American economic sector was, "Government has no right to intrude into industry." And yet like death and taxes, it has become a presence in every company's life. It has laid down guidelines, regulations, and laws that pervade every aspect of business operations. The list is far too extensive and complex to record in any detail, but let's look at some of the things that have taken place in the last decade.

Environmental Legislation and Regulation

I just described some of the legislation generated by the pressure of environmentalist groups. Laws and regulations dealing with the use and abuse of water, air, and land cover how these resources can be used, who can use them, how they must be protected, and how they must be replenished. There are laws at all levels of government—federal, state, city, county, and town. How have these affected where you can locate your plants and how you can operate them?

People-Related Actions

There has also been a continuing effort to protect the worker through legislation on occupational health and safety. More wide-reaching has been the renewed emphasis on equal rights. Originally aimed at increasing employment opportunities for ethnic minority groups, government concern has spread to sex (including the homosexual) and age. There have been laws and statutes dealing with wages and salaries and with the rights of workers to join or not join unions and their opportunities to organize and negotiate. Recently an awareness has grown of the problems of workers obtaining pensions, and shortly there will be federal enforcement of standard pension rights and obligations. All these have an effect on how you and your customers, competitors, and suppliers do business and have significantly increased the cost of operations. Some Americans think that we alone face such controls, but studies of the situation in other countries show differences in degree, not kind. The concern for improving the quality of life is international.

Product-Related Actions

Regulations dealing with product safety abound. The cigarette industry must now include a message on packages and in advertising telling the public that its product is injurious to health and can result in death. It has been prohibited from advertising on television—an action that was considered impossible only 10 years ago. New laws are being introduced in Congress dealing with product obsolescence. Manufacturers will be required to state how long the product is expected to operate. There will be programs to bring about more standardization in warranties. At one time automobile dealers had the option of withholding information on the retail price of cars, which gave them the opportunity of implying that their price was a real bargain. Truth-in-advertising and truth-in-lending requirements are other examples of how the government is changing the old adage "Let the buyer beware" to "Let the seller beware."

Profits

Profits have come under greater government control and scrutiny. Even during the Nixon administration, businessmen were confronted, to their surprise, with price and wage controls. No longer were they free to pass on costs to the consumer without approval. Laws dealing with trusts, mergers, and place and form of product sale have become more and more stringent. Politicians are increasingly calling for companies to provide complete information on their profits. Such full-disclosure requirements will not only uncover which products are very profitable and which are only marginal; they will also force the conglomerate to reveal when it is funding its growth by milking one operation to nurture another. There is also pressure to prevent companies from moving out of a high-cost labor area into a cheaper region.

Exporting and importing is hedged around with a plethora of directives focused on encouraging the export of some products, keeping others at home, and protecting the domestic markets of still others. At times the government decides that it needs a more favorable balance of trade or payments, and so it sets incentives into motion. Some countries have extensive incentives for this purpose.

Taxation impinges on every aspect of a company's existence. All businessmen recognize the effect of sales and income taxes. Taxation is often multiple. Profits may be subject to federal, state, and local levies or to both domestic and foreign collections. Some countries impose a value-added tax. When the government wishes to spur the economy, it encourages business to spend by granting investment tax credits.

Regulatory Agencies

On the federal level businesses are kept under surveillance by the FTC, the FCC, the FPC, and the rest of the watchdogs in the alphabet soup. What was once a humorous set of metaphors has come to have a serious impact. At times some companies are regulated and inhibited from participating while others are left freer to compete. Then there is the problem of jurisdiction—which agency has authority over a given firm, operation, or product?

The list of regulatory bodies has grown enormously in recent decades. The increase in government involvement has forced companies to extend their staff functions to Washington, whether by opening offices there or by hiring consultant or information services, merely to track what is going on. More firms than ever before are feeling that they must lobby. You may think that these are luxuries you can't afford, things only the big guy can do. But staying abreast of matters vital to business survival is no luxury; it's a necessity.

You should also keep in mind that more than one government has a hand on your business. You can no longer track only what

is happening in Washington. You need some type of sensing operation to keep you informed as well of what is going on in the capitals
of states containing important markets of yours. This may mean
merely subscribing to a clipping service, or it may require contracting with an agency to represent you. Or you might encourage your
industry or trade association to establish or expand contacts with
state regulatory bodies.

Furthermore overlaps and conflicts are evolving among levels of
government, and these can affect your markets, customers, competitors, and resources. Note what has happened in the nuclear energy
arena. Here we find that state agencies have imposed regulations
above and beyond those brought to bear by the Atomic Energy
Commission. These regulations and restraints have resulted in a delay of nuclear plant startups. The impact on utilities and suppliers
of equipment has been heavy. The delay has also had an effect on
the cost of power, which ultimately must be passed on to the individual consumer and industrial user.

In addition there are conflicting roles and objectives among agencies on each government level that deal with the same area, such as
equal employment. This causes confusion and conflict and may
have a harmful effect on business profits.

Finally, you must stay alert to the difference between the law
and its enforcement to be fully aware of the opportunities and
threats entailed in government regulation. Business must focus on
the way the law is implemented as well as how it is written. A failure to recognize this distinction may lead to substantially increased
legal fees as well as fines and possibly imprisonment.

Government penetration into the business sector is still often
underestimated. As a result companies continually find themselves
exposed to new regulations and constraints—or missing opportunities.
Pressure and vested-interest groups are usually well organized and
persistent. Business waits too late and then reacts rather than anticipating change and moving to meet it.

THE INFLUENCE OF THE ECONOMY

Economic forecasting isn't new. Government agencies and economists have been making forecasts for decades. There have long been

projections of gross national product, inflation (the new buzz word is double-digit inflation), balance of payments, and so forth. Yet many businessmen don't make use of these indexes. They read them and then go on worrying about and reacting to short-term developments. They don't seem to try to relate the predictions to their operations. As a result economic trends can surprise them by overtaking their companies. Let's review some of the ways that changes in the economy affect the manufacture and sale of products and services, whether for profit or not.

The multifaceted impact of inflation is a subject on everyone's mind. It has increased the price you must pay for materials and labor. It means that your profits may be inflated and not real and that replacement costs may not be covered by your depreciation figures, especially if you have used the straight-line method. The problem is compounded if you have overestimated the true life of your plant or equipment. Your inventory may also be affected, as may your competitor's.

But inflation isn't the only economic fact of life you must track. Payments and trade balances may also have an impact on you. At home the U.S. government may change the export and import incentives or restrictions. Abroad the governments of countries where you have suppliers may curtail their firms' sales to you, and if these products or components are critical in your operations, this will at least drive up your costs.

We have all witnessed the effects of currency revaluations and devaluations. Suddenly overseas competitors are strengthened or weakened because the value of their currency in international markets has changed. Within a short period Japanese and German goods became more expensive in the United States, for example. This opened doors to domestic products they had been underpricing.

How the federal government especially handles its economic problems or opportunities is also becoming more important. There are a number of conventional monetary policies that affect the cost of borrowing and the amount of money available. In the early 1970s the Federal Reserve system tried to control inflation via the money availability route. Loan money got scarce and interest rates skyrocketed. At other times the government has resorted to such fiscal measures for stimulating the economy as increasing government spending and granting tax cuts or tax credits to consumers and industry. Different government policies have different effects, and you must anticipate their impact on your company.

Not all businesses are affected by an economic trend in the same way, of course. Thus I don't suggest that economic forecasts be taken at face value. But I do recommend that businessmen study these predictions and at least hypothesize what the impact of the forecast change might be on their market size, pricing, costs of labor and materials, and borrowing. If you feel that a shift is likely to have repercussions on your sales or operations, then it must be incorporated into your strategic thinking.

There are many services and publications that can be used for the purpose of tracking the economy. For example, the Wharton College of the University of Pennsylvania provides an economic forecasting service. Periodicals like *Business Week, Forbes, Fortune,* and the *Kiplinger Letter* as well as publications put out by the Departments of Commerce and Labor can be helpful. For those interested in more detailed approaches, there are subscription services using computerized economic models that answer what-if and what-then questions: If the GNP increases or decreases by a certain amount, what will happen then in your industry? These models handle many more dimensions simultaneously than the human mind can and thus enable you to see the impact of a possible change in broad perspective. Of course a model is only as good as the factual data and assumptions it has been built on. If you are going to apply one to your situation, you should make an effort to check its foundations.

THE IMPACT OF TECHNOLOGY

Forecasts of technology and its impact are another useful and sometimes vital part of strategic thinking. As is true of economic projections, these are iffy; the future is of course uncertain, and the methods for predicting technological change are not yet refined—they don't provide us with definite scientific weather vanes. But we can use them as thought and question stimulators.

Many professional forecasters have found that the Delphi Technique seems to work well for stimulation purposes. In simple terms this approach is built on the premise that experts in a certain field might be better prognosticators of future trends and events thinking as a group than as individuals.

The technique begins with a series of well-conceived questions presented in writing to the selected experts, perhaps in different locations and in different specialities within the field. Each recipient of the questionnaire is asked to complete and return it. After the answers are processed, the results are sent out with another copy of the questionnaire to the participants. This tells them how their thinking compares and who is promoting which theory or assumption. They are then asked to reconsider their opinions and answer and return the questionnaire again. The circuit is repeated several times more, with the respondents being encouraged each time to reevaluate their views in the light of others'. Thus the approach attempts to combine individual opinion and group consensus in order to come up with a more accurate perception of the future.* I personally don't believe that anyone has the power to predict the future very accurately, but I do believe it is smart to get others' opinions in making the forecasts on which you will build your strategy.

Be warned, however, that participants in an industry and current experts in a technological field are sometimes the last people to see changes coming that will affect accepted products. A new design or process disregarded by established companies can rapidly make a product obsolete or critically shorten its life cycle. Many examples illustrate this point: Leaders in the locomotive industry didn't anticipate or chose to ignore the potential of the diesel engine. The manufacturers of steam locomotives have all disappeared, and the industry is dominated by General Motors. In duplication processes a small unknown promoted the use of dry copying, and those in the field were left far behind, maybe never to catch up. Another dramatic illustration of a technological advance which has had significant impact is one I have used before in another connection: the case of the semiconductors.

*The Delphi Technique and other approaches are described well in James Bright, *Technological Forecasting for Industry and Government*, Englewood Cliffs, N.J., Prentice-Hall, Inc., 1968. I also recommend some of the materials issued by the Institute for the Future, in Menlo Park, California.

Most scientists and technical experts who are familiar with the development of semiconductors would probably agree that its impact could not have been predicted substantially in advance of its appearance on the market. But it is interesting how many people failed to recognize its potential even after it was introduced. Yet the semiconductor changed the sizes and life spans of existing devices and in addition created entirely new products and uses. It reduced the size of radios, television sets, and communications equipment, making it possible to develop portable models where none had existed before and to miniaturize established designs. Transistors require less power and have a longer life. Suddenly the number of units being marketed increased, and the number of applications for the new components expanded geometrically. Automation was enhanced as controls were made smaller and more compressed. Data processing equipment was redesigned to do things never envisioned with tube technology. There are those who say it was semiconductor developments that made it possible to explore space and put a man on the moon. And with all this, the exploitation of semiconductors seems to have only just begun. With new integrated circuits and other, more sophisticated components, such as microprocessors, it appears that we will be able to do even more in even less space.

As a strategist you must develop a system to keep you informed of technological advances not only in your own and related industries but indeed in unrelated fields. You must make someone responsible for tracking R&D beyond your perimeters. Then at the very least, you must ask yourself the what-if and what-then questions, "What if this breakthrough takes place? How could it change my customers, my market, or the way I currently do business?" Here are some instances:

- What if the source of most electricity changes? Are you prepared to use solar energy? Will this affect your markets or profits?
- What if improved communications devices come into use? Will they change the way orders are placed to or by you? Will they change your approach to marketing?

- What if automobiles are powered by electric rather than internal combustion motors? Will this have an effect on your products and services?

Many of us may skim over this type of question and say it will have no effect. But think for example about what the last possibility would do to existing businesses. It would hit the petroleum industry since gasoline stations would have to become recharging stations. It would affect producers of engine components and associated equipment. It might change the way electricity is produced and the cost of using it.

Overall, questions such as these may not shape your primary strategy, but they certainly will affect your contingency planning, especially if the risk of being unprepared is high and the results will therefore possibly be devastating.

THE INTERACTION PROCESS IN THE FOUR-DIMENSION OVERLAY

In discussing the four-dimension overlay on the business world, I have separated the sectors of influence and dealt with them one at a time. But in reality they interact with one another. Your strategic thinking must recognize this interdependence, and you must try to identify which event is the cause of a battery of developments in several areas. Then insofar as possible, you should act to influence the cause, not the effect.

A common causative sequence in recent years has begun with social forces. Pressure groups propel the government to enact legislation that affects a given technology, which in turn affects the economy. An example might be the use of catalytic converters on automobiles. We can argue that the real source of these components is the demands of environmentalist groups, who were concerned about the contribution of automobile exhausts to air pollution and who applied pressure to government for clean-air legislation. The new laws that resulted affected the automobile industry, which had to develop new technology aimed at emission control. Moreover the catalytic converter requires the use of non-lead gasoline, so that oil companies must provide this type of fuel. Consumers are forced to pay for both the converters on their cars and the more expensive gasoline. And all these extra costs are being sustained at a time that the nation is experiencing rapid inflation and continuing to suffer the consequences of petroleum shortages. Figure 7-1 illustrates this sequence of repercussions, which are of course far more extensive and complex than I have described.

The fact of these interactions is well known. The *origin* of a given sequence, however, can be hard to pin down. For purposes of illustration, I have just argued from a societal cause, environmentalists' demands for cleaner air, to several economic effects. Yet are the additional costs of purchasing, maintaining, and running a car attributable primarily to those demands? Or are they mainly the effect of an inefficient engine, which would mean that American technology is at fault? Is the higher price of gasoline the result of the oil companies' trying to make a killing? Or should we question a basic pattern in our culture and ask whether we as a people need so many cars or need to use them so much? This last assumption—admittedly a very problematic one to pursue—ties in with the possibility that consumers might be receptive to substitute services, a question explored briefly in Chapter 4.

Although the four-dimension overlay makes up only part of your strategy formation, identifying causes and effects permits you to anticipate opportunities and threats at remote distances. If a potential action to meet such a change is also suggested by other aspects of your analysis (for example your competitor assessment), it should be evaluated further.

PARTICIPANTS IN NONPROFIT SECTORS

In the past few decades, the public has developed intensely heightened levels of expectation about nonprofit organizations.

Colleges and universities have been called on to make numerous changes, some realistic and some impossible. Higher education has become the right of anyone, regardless of race, creed, sex, and even

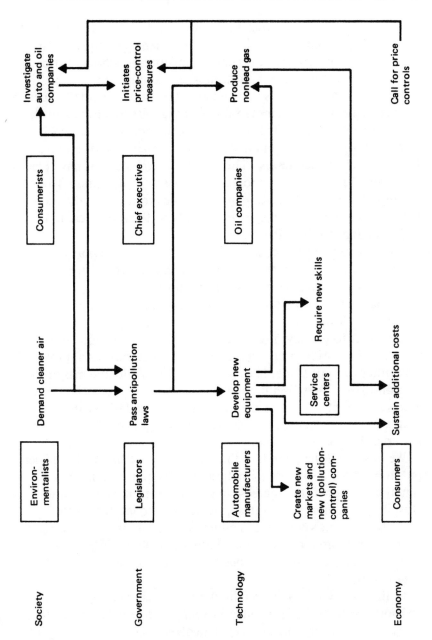

Figure 7-1   An interaction process among social, government, technological, and economic forces.

ability, rather than the privilege of the few. Public institutions have been required to provide open enrollment. All these changes have resulted in new pressures and opportunities, which in turn have caused further changes in strategies and missions.

Health services have also moved into the rights category. Special-interest groups have promoted the idea that all citizens are entitled to equal medical care. This has led to Medicare, a movement toward national health insurance, and new demands for the prevention and cure of sicknesses. The increased expectations have placed hospitals and the medical profession under new pressures. These trends offer new and exciting opportunities to those ready and willing to respond but frightening threats to those who cannot or will not adapt to the changed conditions.

As the levels of public expectations have risen, the political structure has reacted with corresponding legislative requirements. Some laws that have been passed in recent years challenge the right of colleges and universities to discriminate among candidates for enrollment through tests and admissions policies. Others, based on the right to privacy, prohibit an education institution from giving out information pertaining to a student without his approval. Still others permit students to have access to all documents in the files on them. These requirements have brought about changes in admission practices and in the use of recommendations and critical evaluations. In some states the professor's right to use specific text materials has been curtailed.

We have seen the quandary that medical practitioners have been put in by the massive rise in malpractice insurance premiums, a function in part of the increase in malpractice suits and awards. Hospital admission procedures have become so legalistic that at times the patient's suffering is inhumanely prolonged because permission for treatment isn't immediately available. Even religious institutions have increasingly been pressured to conform to legal regulations.

In the last two decades, public funding of education, medical, and social services has expanded in keeping with public expectations. The more the organizations involved rely on the use of government funds for their operations, the more subservient they become to the state. These groups must take a good look at their financial strategy and mission to determine whether this is the direction they wish to take.

Technological changes also need to be tracked by the nonprofit organization. With the advent of new communications techniques, for example, education may become more and more an in-the-home activity and less and less an on-campus program. Some institutions already broadcast courses on television that are professionally produced to optimize the use of the medium. This can result in a loss of matriculated students, and it obviously reduces the use of the school's physical facilities. The same mechanism has probably contributed to the falloff in religious attendance by enabling congregations to meet and worship in homes. Medical care may be improved by telecommunications, which may also enable less-trained paramedical personnel to substitute for the doctor or the clinic. The day may not be far off when tests can be performed in the home using audiovisual and data-transmitting devices to send the results to a computer for diagnosis. This could change the whole approach to medical care.

Thus in the nonprofit as in the business sector, every leader must think about the social, government, economic, and technological changes that are happening or impending and ask, "Do these events have a real or potential impact on my organization?"

APPLICATION TIME

Pause now and try to identify issues on the four dimensions that may affect your operations. Think through how they may change some of the characteristics that you have already defined relating to your customers, markets, competitors, products, warranties, distributors, suppliers, and internal resources. To determine whether these might create new opportunities and threats or affect those you have already identified, here are some questions that may prove helpful.

Regarding societal concerns: What groups, official or unofficial, are seeking changes that will intrude on your product, customer, or industry practices? Are there any controversies over your prod-

Summary of Macroenvironment

Societal Factors	Government Factors (national, state, local; domestic, foreign)	Economic Factors	Technological Factors
Values and priorities	Legislation	Inflation/deflation	Changes
Environment and ecology	Areas of current impact: composition of workforce, health and safety, product standards, advertising and promotion, etc.	Level	Type
Life style	Bills in preparation	Impact	Degree
Industry practices (social responsibility)	Ties to pressure groups	Revaluation/devaluation	New applications
Product standards and costs	Regulation	Country	Existing technology
Needs and expectations	Agencies with jurisdiction	Impact	New technology
Goods	Overlaps of jurisdiction	Fiscal policy	Lag of technology
Services	Conflicts of jurisdiction (intralevel and interlevel)	Increased spending	Technological obsolescence
Pressure groups	Interpretation and enforcement practices	Tax cuts	
Areas of concern	Taxation	Credits	
Spokesman status	Kinds and rates	Monetary policy	
Demographic changes	Collection and payment requirements	Balance of payments	
Population shifts	Special incentives	Controls	
Composition of workforce	Production supports	Price	
	Exports and imports	Wage	

uct, justified or not, that could become the banner of a pressure group? Are changing public needs, expectations, priorities, or values supportive of or antagonistic to your methods of doing business? Can or should these be countered?

Regarding government action: Are there current laws that can affect your business? Will their application be the result of enforcement or interpretation in each case? Consider all aspects of the regulatory power that government at all levels—federal, state, and local, foreign as well as domestic—has over your various functions. What about jurisdictional conflicts among agencies on one level or between authorities on different levels?

Regarding the influence of the economy: How does your industry growth compare with GNP growth? How would a major deflation or further inflation hit your industry, your markets, your competitors, and your own firm individually? Is your industry affected by changes in decretionary spending?

Regarding the impact of technology: What technological changes do you see on your horizon that are related to your product or your industry? What new patents or processes might give your competitors an irreversible market lead? Are there R&D programs outside your immediate bailiwick that might produce innovations you can adapt?

The checklist suggests the range of focuses that your exploration of the four-dimension overlay should encompass.

8

NOW LET'S STRATEGIZE: THE INVESTMENT DECISION

There are many managers and businessmen who think that data collection and analysis are synonymous with strategic thinking and planning. The result of this misconception is that they fail to develop meaningful and creative strategic alternatives because they stop the process too soon.

In order to get the proper perspective on the sweep of strategic thinking, let me review what we have done and describe the steps that remain. If you have conscientiously followed the process as described up to this point, you now have answered the following questions:

1. What has your business been, what is it now, and what would you like it to become? This is the first phase of your feasibility study—mission development—and your probing has enabled you to determine how extensive your planning process must be as well as what planning resources you require to obtain the information you need.

2. What will your environment permit you to become? This exploration of your setting has included in-depth analyses of your microenvironment—your customers, markets, and competitors—and your macroenvironment, the four interacting force fields described in the previous chapter that overlie your operations. From these findings you have drawn positive and negative implications, or prospective opportunities and threats.

3. What is the status of your competitors and their strategies, past, present, and future? This is the second phase of your feasibility study, and it has enabled you to uncover your current and potential rivals' key resources and skills.

4. What abilities and resources have been, are now, and will be available to you? This third phase of your feasibility study has allowed you to list your assets and liabilities.

The combination of these three major analyses enables you to proceed from determining feasibility to formulating viable strategic alternatives. You are now in a position to answer the following questions:

- What investment options do you have? How do you rank them?
- What are the options available to pursue the investment strategy you have chosen?
- What are the opportunities and threats which will enable you to pursue the management strategy you prefer?
- How will you use your strengths and correct or minimize your limitations effectively in pursuing your most important opportunities and threats? (Operating strategies and key programs are described in the next chapter.)
- What will be the results of the decisions you have made? Will these results conform with the overall objectives you would like to achieve? Do you need to change your strategies or your objectives?
- What potential events or trends can prevent your organization from achieving the objectives you have in mind?

The answers you record pertain to the selection of investment, management, and operating strategies for your company. Regarding the latter, you will recall that in Chapter 1 I stressed the need to recognize levels of strategy makers: the chief executives, the rest of the management team, and those who implement. One functioning without the other makes even the best-laid plans incomplete and possibly worthless. This chapter will deal with the development of investment strategies, and Chapter 9 will take up the management and operating levels.

The pages that follow will describe how to summarize the massive data you have collected in a way that highlights the key facts and assumptions that should mold your investment priorities. I will develop a decision matrix that will uncover the positive and negative aspects of your choices. The discussion will then outline how to specify the opportunities and threats that bear on your investment options and how to crystallize the "success factors." Using your evaluations of your competitors' and your own resources, you will move from the isolated overviews to comparative assessments, which will permit you to identify your real strengths and limitations. At this stage you will be able to construct all the viable options and their rewards and risks—in short to strategize.

THE INVESTMENT SUMMARY

"What I really need is a way to highlight the critical path and pull out what is relevant." This is the reaction of many businessmen once they have completed the three analytic phases. The reaction is understandable since, if the work has been disciplined and comprehensive, it has inundated them with facts, opinions, and assumptions. The approach I will outline helps you, your staff, and your subordinate managers to be selective and boil down the volumes of data into key displays.

The concept is very simple. You set down on one side of a page the environmental characteristics and assumptions about a total business or market segment and on the other your corresponding status and position. You treat the past and future as well as the present under both headings. Since this is a synthesis, the recorded information is the result of each data compiler's judgment of what is important to include. Some characteristics and assumptions may be omitted that have strategic significance. Do not be disturbed over this. A review procedure to be described in Chapter 11 will allow you to pick these up.

The investment summary covers (1) market factors, (2) competition factors, (3) financial and economic factors, (4) technological factors, and (5) sociopolitical factors.

Market Factors

Here is the information to record in your investment summary concerning your market and your customers.

YOUR ENVIRONMENT	YOUR STATUS/POSITION
Size (dollars, units, or both)	Share (in equivalent terms)
Size of key segments	Share of key segments
Growth rate per year:	Your annual growth rate:
Total	Total
Segments	Segments
Diversity of market	Your participation
Sensitivity to price, service features, and external factors	Your influence on the market
Cyclicality and reasons	Your sales lag or lead
Seasonality	
Captive customers	The extent to which your sales are captive

To illustrate this compilation, let's suppose we're a (fictitious) bicycle company surveying our market performance since five years ago and forecasting for the next half-decade. Here are our findings (figures are rounded and the environmental data are purely illustrative).

BICYCLE INDUSTRY ENVIRONMENT	OUR STATUS/POSITION
Past five years, average:	
$200,000,000; 3,000,000 units	$20,000,000; 350,000 units
$67 average price	$57 average price
10% growth rate	12.5 growth rate
Next five years, average:	
$350,000,000; 3,500,000 units	$40,000,000; 445,000 units
$100 average price	$90 average price
12% growth rate (in dollars)	15% growth rate (in dollars)
European and Japanese market larger but growing at a slower pace.	We don't participate overseas

Not price-sensitive; growth even with price increases

Our growth greater than average because of lower prices

No cyclicality observed in past 10 years, though market is seasonal

Our sales typical of industry's

No captive segments

Thus in a few lines we have outlined the market and its key features as well as our performance, summarizing the elements of customer and market analysis studied earlier. We could add other aspects of our resources, but it seems preferable to keep the example simple.

Competition

The next step is to summarize what is significant about the competitive situation.

YOUR ENVIRONMENT	YOUR STATUS/POSITION
Types of competitors	Where you fit, how you compare
Degrees of concentration	
Changes in type and mix	
Entries and exits	Segments you have entered or left
Position changes in share	Your relative share change
Functional substitution	Your vulnerability
Degrees and types of integration	Your own level of integration

Let's see now how our bicycle company looks in relation to its competitors.

BICYCLE INDUSTRY ENVIRONMENT	OUR STATUS/POSITION
Four major producers account for 70% of sales.	We are No. 4 in our market.
Five companies have entered through acquisition in the past five years. All are diversified, which has decreased	We are a single-industry company, and our future depends on this market.

the number of single-industry competitors to two.

Two other new entrants are anticipated in the next five years.

The top four producers' positions have remained relatively stable.

The top company has 25% of sales, a drop from 30% five years ago.	Our share has increased from 9% to 10%, and we expect it to increase to 12.5% in the next five years.
Bicycles compete against other sports and leisure-time activities. The biggest substitute has been the exercise bicycle, which is made by most competitors.	We don't make exercise bikes.
One company has integrated backward. This was Peerless Sporting, a retailer that purchased one of the manufacturers. Some of the large mass merchants may do the same.	We are not integrated.

We now have a snapshot of the competitive environment and our position in it. A little later we will make judgments about the attractiveness of this situation and our relative position in it.

Financial and Economic Factors

This synthesis highlights financial characteristics that influence the desire to invest further.

YOUR ENVIRONMENT	YOUR STATUS/POSITION

Profitability:
  Ratios
  Dollars
	Your profitability performance:
	  Ratios
	  Dollars

Contribution margins	Your contributed value
Leveraging factors, such as economies of scale	Any competitive advantage you possess
Barriers to entry or exit (both financial and nonfinancial)	Problems you would have in entering or exiting
Capacity utilization	Your utilization

With regard to ratios, it is important to select those that are relevant to the industry in question. Different industries measure themselves in different ways. The most commonly used ratios are return on investment (ROI), return on sales (ROS), and return on stockholders' equity (ROSE).

Here is the picture of our bicycle business, which, along with other industry participants, relies mainly on ROI and ROS calculations for purposes of comparison.

BICYCLE INDUSTRY ENVIRONMENT	OUR STATUS/POSITION
Past five years, average:	
ROI: 12%	ROI: 16%
ROS: 6%	ROS: 4%
Next five years, average:	
ROI: 10%	ROI: 12%
ROS: 5%	ROS: 6%
No significant economies of scale because of number of models; this will change.	We are strong in the private brand market, and this increases our models and inventory levels.
The industry requires cash for inventory.	We have a good cash position to finance dealer inventories.
Few barriers to entry	It would be difficult to exit (since this is our key business).
95% utilization	100% utilization

As you can see, we have combined various data from our analyses of the industry and our own company to find out where we stand in relation to others' financial performances.

Technological Factors

The following describes and anticipates the technological situation in the industry and deals with your status and position from that perspective.

YOUR ENVIRONMENT	YOUR STATUS/POSITION
Maturity and volatility	Ability to cope with change
Complexity	Depths of your skills
Differentiation	Types of your skills
Patents and copyrights	Your position
Processes or manufacturing technology required	Your resources

Let's illustrate how this might work in our bicycle business.

BICYCLE INDUSTRY ENVIRONMENT	OUR STATUS/POSITION
Bicycle technology is long established and relatively simple, and bicycles can be produced in a simple factory. Only speed-gear changes are somewhat complex.	We have good speed-gear-design capability.
Patents don't mean much because they are easy to bypass.	Our company is a follower, and we don't do much R&D.

Our own and our industry's technological setting is relatively stable and uncomplicated, but in some industries the technology summary might furnish the key to understanding what it really takes to be a winner.

Sociopolitical Factors

Here you draw information mainly from the analyses of the macroenvironment which pertains to the industry and markets you serve.

YOUR ENVIRONMENT	YOUR STATUS/POSITION
Social attitudes and trends	Your company's responsiveness and flexibility

Laws and government agency regulations	Your company's ability to cope
Influence with pressure groups and government representatives	Your company's aggressiveness
Human factors, such as unionization and community acceptance	Your company's relationships

Applying the sociopolitical outline, we can complete our data displays for our example company's investment summary.

BICYCLE INDUSTRY ENVIRONMENT	OUR STATUS/POSITION
Societal concern with pollution and physical fitness has helped expand the market.	Our sales have been helped.
Government has been supportive, allocating funds for bike paths in cities and suburbs.	We have no assets to deal with pressure groups or the govment.
Safety of bikes is becoming a public issues.	Our design people are abreast of the industry on this.
Unions are small and local.	We don't have a union.

Thus you can see that just a few pages suffice to condense a mass of environmental and resource information into a form that makes it easy to survey as a whole and use as a basis for decisions. The summary is an instrument that helps you determine whether the business is worth further investment and if so how much. The list can be expanded if you want to compare one segment of the market with another. For instance, returning to our bicycle example, our sales of $20 million would derive from an array of products across several segments. Included in our offerings might be tricycles for little children, two-wheelers for eight- to twelve-year-olds, larger recreation bikes for teenagers and adults, and racers for this last pair of groups. Since each segment has its own characteristics (if it didn't it wouldn't be a segment), we would find it useful to outline each with the five-part summary just described. Thus instead of one summary, we might have four. However, for purposes of making the overall investment decisions, the single summary is best because it is concise but not overly general.

THE DECISION MATRIX

Having completed the summary, your next step is to make some judgments about the attractiveness of the external environment and your position in it. Let's examine how to go about this in terms of our bicycle company.

The market for bikes has grown, on the average, twice as fast as the gross national product in the last five years, and it is expected to grow even faster in the next half-decade. It doesn't have any sensitivity to price, as well as not having large cyclical swings. This is a very healthy situation, especially when we look at the performance of our hypothetical company. The one notable negative aspect is that our average price is lower than the competition's. This is O.K. if this is what we want to do since we have the cost structure to sustain our price strategy. So we now can review the bidding, determine how we feel about the situation, and rank it *high, medium,* or *low* in terms of its attractiveness. We can then rank our position as *strong, medium,* or *weak.*

Reviewing the summary of the competition, again we determine the attractiveness of our environment and our standing. The competitive situation is in a state of flux, and it will remain unstable for some time. There is a high degree of concentration, which in itself isn't either good or bad; our own position in this regard isn't bad at all, since we are among the top four and gaining. A thing that may be a problem is the entry of the multi-industry companies, which have considerably more resources than the average among other participants. The exercise bike market is also a potential problem; it may inhibit the growth of sales of traditional models. But this product would be simple to make, so the threat isn't serious.

Let's assume we have completed the evaluation of each part of the summary and have made the judgments listed in Table 8-1. We rate each aspect of our industry for its attractiveness (high, medium, or low), and we rank each aspect of our performance or condition according to our relative position (strong, medium, or weak).

Table 8-1.

	Bicycle Industry Environment	Our Position
Market	High	Strong
Competition	Medium	Medium
Financial and economic factors	High	Medium
Technological factors	Medium	Medium
Sociopolitical factors	High	Strong
Overall	High	Medium

If you want to increase the sophistication of your assessments, you can use a weighted-score approach. This will require further judgments, since you will have to rank the relative importance of each element. Is competition a more important feature of comparison than market? Are the sociopolitical factors more important than the technological? If more important, how much more? Although the techniques for weighting scores are not hard to master, I'm not persuaded of the need or the value of doing so. I have found that weighting clouds the real issues and generates a reverence for numbers that may be unwarranted. In effect it tends to make a pseudoscience out of an art.

Equipped with your judgments, you can now use a simple graphic aid to help you make your investment decisions. The reason for this overview format is again that it allows you to review all major variables at one time. The basic decision matrix merely plots your judgments. It is shown in Figure 8-1.

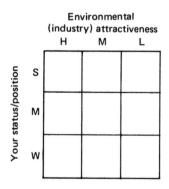

Figure 8-1 The basic decision matrix for investment strategy.

The horizontal axis will display your judgment of whether your industry overall has high, medium, or low attractiveness. The vertical axis will show how you rank your company's overall position—as strong, medium, or weak. This chart gives you guidance on what investment strategy is most appropriate for you according to how your standing combines with your industry's ranking. Let me describe how the decision matrix is used:

Step 1

Evaluate the investment summary for the past and current situation and decide whether your environmental situation is essentially high, medium, or low and whether your status/position is strong, medium, or weak. Plot your decision on the matrix. For example, if your environmental situation is medium and your own position is strong, you will plot them with a dot, as shown in Figure 8-2.

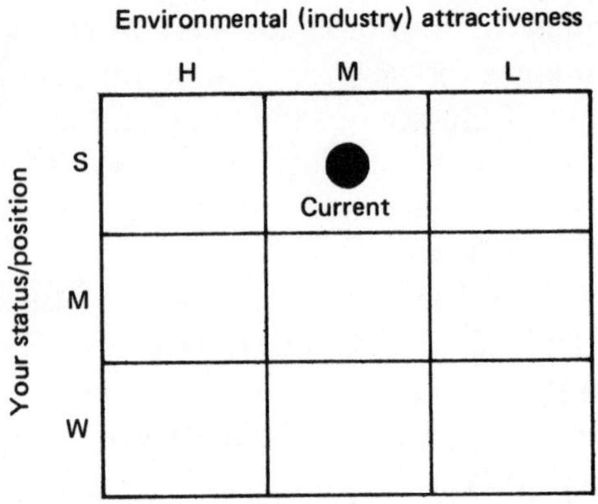

Figure 8-2 Past and current investment evaluation.

Step 2

Return to the investment summary and determine whether the environment and your position will change. Assume that you will continue to follow your current strategy and that your resources will be only as good as they have been. Figure 8-3 shows where you will be (the rectangle) if you started with Figure 8-2 and continue to follow your current investment strategy. It illustrates that the environment is not expected to change in attractiveness and

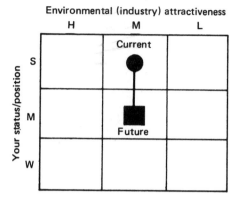

Figure 8-3 Where your current strategy would take you.

that position will be lost. In other words your company would arrive there by trading its future for present earnings.

Step 3

The next question to consider is future strategy. Where would you like to be in the next five years (or whatever time period is relevant)? There are several choices:

Invest to hold. The star in Figure 8–4 is used as the strategy indicator. It illustrates a desire to stop the position erosion represented by the rectangle and to maintain the current position. This "invest

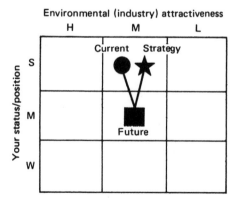

Figure 8-4 The "invest to hold" strategy.

to hold" strategy could also be illustrated by having the current, future, and strategy indicators all in the same position, "Invest to hold" calls for enough investment to keep up with the environmental forces, and may be expensive if the environment is changing rapidly. There are several other choices:

Invest to penetrate. This is an aggressive strategy, demanding investment and yielding probably little or no earning growth. It is illustrated by moving the star upward and/or to the left. When you intend to move in both directions, you are taking an expensive option with high risk.

Invest to rebuild. This situation is familiar to the manager who has taken over a business whose profits have been extraordinarily high because his predecessor was "milking" the business, or harvesting it prematurely. Investing to rebuild requires an understanding of where you were, are now, and will be if the strategy is continued. In Figure 8–5 the indicators show that the firm was strong, has lost position, and, if the same amount of resources are applied, will erode even further. At the same time the environment has remained, and will containue to remain, attractive. Management has several choices. It can continue the same strategy and use the erosion to generate cash, or, as Figure 8–5 demonstrates, it can reverse the trend to regain lost position.

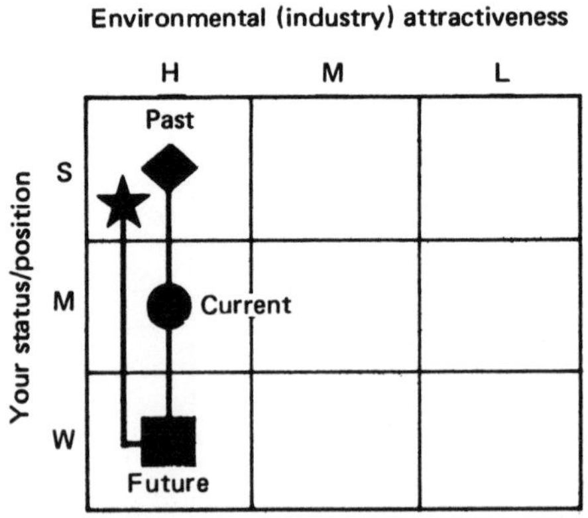

Figure 8–5 The "invest to rebuild" strategy.

Little or no investment. The fourth option can be classified as a "harvest or divest" strategy. This doesn't automatically mean no investment, since even if you intend to divest you may wish to invest to make the business more attractive to potential buyers. This is like painting the house before you sell it so that you get top dollar. Figure 8–6 depicts the exit situation.

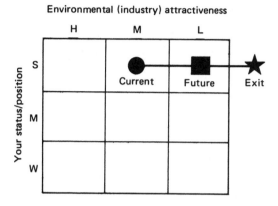

Figure 8–6 The "harvest or divest" strategy.

Advantages of this classification system. This system of classification provides insight into the extent of and reason for the investment. It also enables the strategist to understand the types of results that can be expected. For instance, investment for penetration yields market share or volume growth; investment to hold strives to increase earnings and hold share; investment to rebuild aims at regaining share or market position and may be an earnings drain in the short range. Investing very little or nothing at all should provide short-term earnings and excess cash. Looking at this from another perspective, you can see that these are all growth strategies, but some of them grow sales, others grow earnings, and still others grow cash for reinvestment in the growth of others or for paying off the debtors.

APPLYING THE MATRIX TO SEGMENTS OR PRODUCTS

The same options are applicable to market segments and product lines, and the decision matrix may be plotted for either of these. Figure 8–7 positions three major segments of a firm. The circles

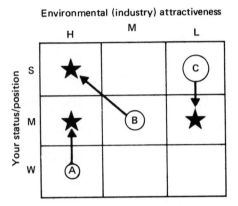

Figure 8–7 The decision matrix as applied to market segments.

show the relative sizes of the segments in terms of sales, and the arrows show the investment decisions. Segment C is being used to generate cash for the other two segments. Segment B must change its position while keeping up with an increasingly attractive environment.

You are now well equipped to compare your desires with the results of your feasibility analysis. If they agree, you know that you are on target and can move to developing management and your operating strategies. If they don't match, you have some pondering to do. If your decision matrix indicates that you should be investing more heavily but you are less ambitious, this shows that you are being conservative and missing opportunities, but it doesn't mean that you must change your desires. What you need to discover is how far your desires are out of tune with reality. The greater the gap, the more difficult it will be to do what you want. For example you may want to invest heavily but find that your position is poor and the industry a poor attraction. In this case you really have problems and must do some serious rethinking. Again, you need not automatically give up your ambitions, but you will need to look outside your current industry or conceive of how to change its attractiveness or your position in a dynamic way. Although both of these possibilities entail high-risk strategies, both have been carried off.

APPLICATION TIME

This is the appropriate point to test your understanding of, and the utility of, the investment summary and the decision matrix:

1. Summarize your business in terms of market, industry/competition, profitability, technology, and sociopolitical factors. Remember to describe the current situation and note changes anticipated for the future. It may be helpful to complete one summary for past/current and a second for the future.

2. For each element of the summary make a decision as to its attractiveness and your status. Be sure to note reasons for the decision you have made. Figure 8-8 illustrates what I mean. Note that Figure 8-8 is not a complete investment summary; it comprises only the factors which influenced your decision regarding attractiveness and position.

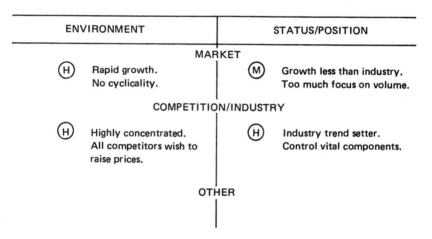

Figure 8-8 Your investment assumptions (current).

3. Plot the results of your decision on the investment decision matrix. Use a circle for current results, a rectangle or box for future results, and a star for your strategy.

4. Determine the type of investment strategy you have to or wish to follow: *invest to penetrate, invest to hold, invest to rebuild,* or *little/none (harvest or exit).*

5. Compare your investment strategy with the mission you developed earlier. That is, is your present strategy comparable? Does it fall short (is it less aggressive)? Does it come above (is it more aggressive)?

OTHER INVESTMENT DECISION APPROACHES

The matrix I have just described and applied represents a multidimensional approach to investment decision making. It takes into account five major aspects of a business and its total environment. Because the matrix is multidimensional, it is complex and requires a great deal of judgment, which puts the emphasis on qualitative thinking. Some prefer to use more quantitative approaches. Here are a few suggestions.

Share and Market-Growth Matrices

There are several organizations which emphasize the need to evaluate market growth rates and market share in making investment strategy decisions. A four- or eight-celled matrix is used to record market growth vertically and market share horizontally. Each segment of the business and the business in total are plotted, and the completed matrix can then be used as a springboard for projecting net income and cash flow. For instance, a combination of low share and slow market growth indicates that the segment or business will provide low net income and low or negative cash flow. On the other hand, low market growth and a high share, relative to competition, indicate that the unit will most likely be a financially sound winner and will contribute to the financing of other opportunities. In short, these matrices are built on the premise that share and growth are closely correlated to cash flow and that cash flow is the key financial indicator of any business.

I personally like to use these matrices in conjunction with the investment decision approach I have just described and to compare the results. If the results are identical, I recognize that I am weighing market share and growth very heavily in my decision criteria and possibly not properly recognizing the complexity of the environment and my position. Share/growth matrices are an aid, but they overemphasize these dimensions and make the decision making overly simplistic, because, as we all know, the world of business is more than a marketing and share game.

Financial Ratio Matrices

Another popular display utilizes a variety of financial ratios, including return on sales, return on stockholders' equity, return on net assets, and total return on investment. The ratio chosen should reflect the prime means by which management wishes to measure itself.

Figure 8-9 shows a matrix using ROS and ROI. Obviously those segments, products, or total businesses which provide high yields on both dimensions are to be considered the most desirable and deserving of reinvestment. But the figure also illustrates that some businesses may have high investment returns and low sales returns. A good example of this situation is aerospace and defense businesses which require small or no investment because the government owns the buildings, machinery, and land and the contractor operates them under contract. The low ROS of these businesses, on the other hand, is due to the combination of lowest bid awards and many hungry bidders. On the other side of the financial ratio coin are instances where the supplier must lease his equipment or provide liberal terms and conditions, all of which reduce the ROI but may allow a high ROS.

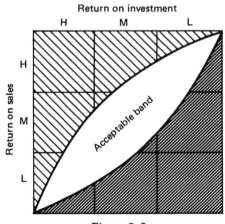

Figure 8-9

There are other matrices which plot the cash flow on one axis and net income on the other, thus providing additioı al insights for decision-making purposes.

SOME WORDS OF CAUTION

Before I close the discussion of investment decision aids, let me make a few observations about their uses and potential abuses. These matrices are merely guides for decision making and should not be applied mechanically. I have seen situations where the charted position and the actual performance of the business didn't match. This is fine, since a major purpose of such devices is to challenge your thinking. In one case the business occupied the lower right corner of the share/market matrix. It was only half the size of its nearest competitor, and its industry's growth rate was only 5 percent per year. Still, its earnings were high, and it generated a favorable positive cash flow. An observer might react, "It doesn't make sense." But it does when we probe deeper. In this instance the reason the results and the graph didn't conform is the unusual conditions of the company's market. The firm participated in an industry comprising only two manufacturers, and the leader held a price umbrella, making the company very profitable. This doesn't mean that the concern's position was solid; as the matrix showed, the company was vulnerable, and if the market slowed further or the leader decided to reduce or remove the price umbrella, the firm would be a loser.

Applying a few rules of thumb will help you use decision models to best effect. I would suggest that you use all three of the matrices described and not fixate on one, for they measure different aspects of a business. It is therefore worthwhile to work with them all and try to explain any deviations. In addition be careful to prick a representative time period. Since business results normally fluctuate, be sure you don't use a period that is the exception and not the rule. In some cases the last two or three years may be enough to give you a true picture of what has happened and what will happen. In other situations you may have to use 20 or even 50 years. Such a lengthy time run may make it impossible to predict the future, but the matrices will at least give you a rough estimate.

These techniques are merely aids to your examination and judgment. They are never to be used as substitutes for tough, comprehensive strategic thinking. Never let the matrix make decisions for you.

INVESTMENT DECISION MAKING IN
NONPROFIT ORGANIZATIONS

Leaders of nonprofit institutions might be willing to accept the strategic thinking process, with some modifications, covered in the previous chapters, but many would very likely reject the need for investment decision making. I assert that investment strategizing is equally relevant and useful to them. All organizations must make tradeoff decisions and set priorities, for all have limited resources. Let's take a few illustrations.

Colleges need to assess the attractiveness of each field in which they participate and their position in it. Is it really profitable to remain in the fine arts, pharmacy, or medical sciences? If it isn't profitable are there other benefits from maintaining a position in the specific discipline? Just as for a profit-making business, profit or loss isn't the only reason for a nonprofit enterprise to remain in or exit from a market segment or to continue or discontinue a product. The offering may add prestige or other support to the whole institution and may be justifiable on this ground alone.

Hospitals should determine the attractiveness of specific medical specialties. If one is too great a drain on the total resources of the organization, it may have to be dropped and others making a greater contribution may have to be added.

The major difference between a company's and a nonprofit organization's use of the decision matrices may be the criteria on which the decision is based. In some cases this is merely a matter of translation. "Market" may be replaced by "discipline" or "specialty" and "competition" by "alternative offerings," both positive and negative. The financial, technological, and sociopolitical factors appear to be relevant as they stand. Whether the process is structured or not, each leader needs to understand what sectors of his service have high, medium, and low priority. If faced with a need to limit resources, he should feed the most attractive and starve those with little future.

The checklist summarizes the process of defining investment decisions and related strategies.

INVESTMENT SUMMARY		
Your Environment		*Your assets and liabilities*

Market Factors

Size
Size of segments
Growth rate
Diversity
Sensitivity and features
Cyclicality
Captive customers

Competition Factors

Types
Concentration
Changes in types and mix
Entries and exits
Position changes in share
Functional substitution
Integration

Financial and Economic Factors

Profitability
Contribution margins
Leveraging factors
Barriers to entry or exit
Capacity utilization

Technological Factors

Maturity and volatility
Complexity
Differentiation
Patents and copyrights
Processes

Sociopolitical Factors

Social attitudes and trends
Laws and government
  regulation
Influence
Human factors

9

THE MOVE TO MANAGEMENT
AND OPERATING STRATEGY

"I'm glad the planning job is done and I can get back to running the business." This is a typical reaction of operating managers. It is understandable to want to get the strategic decisions behind and concentrate on operations. Most managers are uncomfortable with planning as such, and the fact that it is complex, time consuming, and highly conceptual doesn't make the task any more appealing. I am personally sympathetic, but I feel very strongly that it is necessary for strategists to spell out exactly *how* they will achieve the investment results they want. They must avoid the temptation of stopping too soon.

In this chapter I will point out that the answer to the question how? has two dimensions, one related to the management thrust and the other to the operating implications. I will explain techniques for converting the generalizations of the investment strategies to concrete alternatives. This will make use of the analyses and forecasts we have made in previous completed work.

KNOWING WHERE YOU WANT TO PUT
YOUR MONEY ISN'T ENOUGH

Before we examine each of the steps of operating strategy in more detail, I would like to demonstrate why they are important to perform by showing some of the ill effects of skipping them.

The global opportunity syndrome. I have observed that many businessmen have no trouble spotting an opportunity or threat but do have trouble describing it in specific enough terms to understand what resources are really required to meet it and how they stand in relation to these resources. For example several U.S. firms have recognized that there is a growing consumer market in Europe and have decided to enter it without detailing the timing, cyclicality of growth, locations, and extent of participation they desire. Lacking these specifications, you can't communicate what you mean to your company, and subordinate executives will each be free to interpret your intentions for themselves. The result will be mottos instead of plans.

Failure to understand the price of admission. Even if the specifications of the opportunity or threat under consideration are defined, it is unlikely that you will be able to carry out your plans unless you know the cost of the game. How many times have you read about companies that took the plunge into a new market segment or business arena only to find that it cost more than they had thought and that they could invest? There are many instances in the capital-intensive markets with long payout periods. In other cases management has suddenly discovered that the distribution network is different from their own. If these facts of life are recognized too late, many options will be nipped in the bud, and the probability will increase that the effort will fail.

Failure to take stock of the competitors. There are two ways this can happen, and again both affect results. On the one hand the rivals may be entirely different from those you have competed with previously. Perhaps they are unknown to you because they come from another industry or geographic region—or because you do, for they may not be the aggressors; it may be you who are entering their traditional turf. Whatever the case these companies may have strengths or limitations that you are not familiar or used to competing with. On the other hand you may know the other participants and have competed with them in the past, but now you must evaluate their abilities and yours in relation to the opportunity or threat you are examining. Again, without this comparison you may be unsuccessful.

Fixation on "the best strategy." A businessman may become convinced that he has *the* magic formula or that the only way for his company to operate is as it has in the past. Either type of fixation inhibits his creativity as it leads him to refuse to consider alternatives. This failure prevents the organization from adapting to the new situation, which in turns leads to inappropriate strategy and ultimately to failure. Many companies have tried to invade foreign markets practicing "the way we do things back home." During the 1960s a number of U.S. giants failed in Europe because they didn't develop suitable approaches. Other instances of fixation include companies that have continued to do it themselves, when joint venture or acquisition made more sense, and concerns that have continued to finance growth internally when it would have been better to increase debt.

THE MANAGEMENT STRATEGY COMES FIRST

The first step aimed at avoiding these pitfalls is to think through the options available which will enable you to execute the investment strategy you have selected. It's easy to conclude that you wish to grow sales, or net income, or even cash, but it becomes believable only when you determine whether growth will come from intensifying or modifying your marketing efforts, or from introducing new products or new applications of existing products or technologies, or from improving the manufacturing capability. In other words, the next step is to determine how you might pursue the investment thrust and then select those opportunities or threats which will yield the final results.

Management strategy is built on the premise that the decision maker will be selective; that is, he must decide on which part of the business will be the lead function. Unless there are unlimited resources, it is not possible to simultaneously innovate, improve marketing, acquire, joint-venture, increase manufacturing, and so on. Therefore some one of these thrusts must be prime and the others supportive. The relative importance of these thrusts will vary from one segment to another, and it is important to specify which is leading and which is following. When this decision is made, you can spell out all the other functional, or operating, strategies and describe how strengths will be used and limitations corrected.

Let's outline the management options available:

Marketing-led options can spearhead the investment strategy by concentrating on new geographical areas or a new type of distribution, or by emphasizing more price aggressiveness or additional advertising, and so on. The point is that marketing can be the lead and other areas of a company will support it.

Product innovation can come in many shapes or forms. It can be founded on new products—to fill out the line or to force the competition to follow. Or it can stress new applications, designs, models of existing products. Or it can be based on the development of a brand-new technology. All of these are viable options whether they are intended to increase sales, hold position, rebuild, or even harvest.

Capacity/manufacturing strategies can be employed to add capacity in advance of demand so that share can be increased when the market demand turns up. Or it may be a cost reduction thrust in order to increase earnings or to position the company for a more aggressive pricing policy.

Financially based strategies may be used to create a competitive advantage by leasing equipment at attractive rates to users, or by increasing the amount of inventory or receivables that is required to participate in an industry. Acquisition might also be classified as a financially based strategy.

Management directed strategies which can be employed include, for instance, takeover of or merger with another company or joint-venture agreements which permit growth.

At this stage of the process I recommend that you merely recognize that these options are available and then determine which makes the most sense for the business based on the evaluation of selected opportunities and threats.

The next step, then, is to select opportunities or threats which can contribute to the investment strategy you wish to pursue.

SELECTING OPPORTUNITIES AND THREATS TO SCRUTINIZE

Not all opportunities are worth analyzing. This is a truism, but it bears emphasizing, because the process I have been describing demands a great deal of time and manpower. Here are some guidelines for determining those worth the effort.

I divide opportunities into those pertaining to your entire industry and those favorable more specifically to you. Obviously those that arise from the fact that you are stronger than the competition should appear high on the list. The same classification can be made of threats. If a change will have a significantly higher impact on your current position than on your rivals, it can't be ignored and deserves intensive scrutiny.

An opportunity or threat suggested by one aspect of your environment or resources and repeated by others should also be carefully looked at. For instance suppose the customers you serve are very interested in safer bicycles for their children and that this is likewise a concern of the general public and its elected government representatives. This is an opportunity that shouldn't be neglected. The multiple sources of interest increase the probability that a safer bike will sell even at a premium price. If you don't offer one, the competition may beat you to the punch.

Another situation to look for is an occasion where you can take advantage of more than one opportunity or a combination of opportunities and threats with one strategic move. Again the bicycle business provides an illustration of what I mean. Suppose you see the chance to participate in a market in a country without indigenous manufacturers. This opportunity area is very close to the home market of a major foreign competitor, who you believe intends to strengthen his position in your major market. By moving into the third country, you will be positioning yourself to move into the competitor's home market as well as forcing him to spend some of his financial and human resources to defend himself, which may in turn weaken his ability to attack you. Thus in one strategic action, you are taking advantage of the third-country opportunity, preparing to move into competitive territory, and reducing a threat to your home base.

SPECIFICATIONS

Once you have ranked and matched your opportunities and threats, you can take up the following questions, which are expressed in terms of positive openings but pertain to dangers as well. The sample answers again relate to our bicycle company.

What is the opportunity?

To participate more heavily in the market for multiple-speed bikes, which is anticipated to grow from $250 million to $350 million by 5 years from now.

Where is the opportunity?

In the eastern United States, especially in the metropolitan areas of Philadelphia, New York, and Boston.

When do (or did) you expect the opportunity to materialize?

Since 1974 the market has been growing 14 percent a year, a rate it will maintain through 1976. Thereafter growth will decline to an 8 percent annual rate.

What share of this market do you wish to have?

A 15 percent share of the urban markets by 1978.

Why will (or did) the opportunity materialize?

The increasing desire for more exercise by urban dwellers along with the increasing number of bike paths and the cost of gasoline for automobiles.

Each of these questions has operating and resource implications that the management team must understand. Obviously the next to last question holds the challenge. If we had no share of our target market now, it would take a great effort to get to 15 percent, whereas since we have a 12 percent slice, it should be easier.

The timing of the opportunity will also determine what options are realistic. If it is imminent, then you may have no time to develop your own product line and sales force and may be forced to acquire, enter into a joint venture, or brand privately.

Another key question is why there is an opportunity or threat at all. This question also forces you to identify the causative assumptions that have led to the conclusions about timing, cyclicality of growth, locations, and extent of participation. Since successful plans aim at cause and not effect, the question is fundamental. The causative assumptions will help you identify the *success factors*.

CRITICAL SUCCESS FACTORS

This phase of strategic thinking requires that you ask, what does it take for *anyone* to succeed in the opportunity area or effectively reduce or eliminate the threat? What it takes may be physical, monetary, human, even attitudinal, or any combination of these. To develop a comprehensive list, it would be helpful to review the questions in the chapters on competitor and resource analysis. To relate these questions to your specific situation, review the investment summary you developed in Chapter 8 on the market involved.

Conceive/design success factors. Is any special research or engineering talent required to participate? Do you have to make technological breakthroughs or be able to license patents? If you were to decide to enter the dry-copy market, you would have to gain access to patents held by Xerox. If you were to want to produce a cola drink, you would need access to one of the cola manufacturers' formulas or else do extensive development on your own in order to offer a substitute.

Let's return to our bicycle example. The multiple-speed bike doesn't require any really complicated technology, though the design of the gear mechanism is critical. It must meet the expectations of the consumer and be relatively easy to repair. This technical know-how is equally appropriate for rural, urban, and foreign markets. The only factor that might introduce some differentiation is legal requirements for some specific safety devices. Such regulations may be local or state rather than federal. So one of the resources our company may need is a specialist to track legislation that can have an impact on the design of bicycles.

Production success factors. Do you need certain manufacturing or process abilities? Process sophistication is critical for success in the chemical industry. So is it in the production of drugs and some consumer materials and the refinement of precious minerals. Do you need large plants and equipment that demand heavy capital investment? Without high bays and cranes in the electrical apparatus industry, you can't make the sizes of generating equipment now being marketed. How about your materials or components? Are they simple or complex, easy or hard to procure? And so on down the list of resources listed in earlier chapters.

To apply this to our example company, the manufacture of bicycles in general and multiple-speed models in particular isn't a highly complex process. It consists primarily of bending and shaping metals into precise sizes and forms and of making the gear components. Often the factory merely packs the parts, relying on the dealer or retail buyer to assemble them. In the future substitute materials like fiberglass may be used in place of metals. If so, the manufacturing equipment and processes will need to be altered, and the production success factors will change. Moreover the types and mix of competitors may also differ.

Manufacturing scheduling is a key to success in obtaining a share of the northeastern market. Bicycle sales are very heavy in the late spring and fall, the spring in anticipation of summer and the fall in anticipation of Christmas. If our company doesn't have inventory in the stores at these times, we will miss sales.

Capacity is also worth analyzing. Since the market is seasonal and there are so many models and sizes of bikes, we must have the correct model mix in production in the plants.

Marketing success factors. By now you can see that identifying success factors requires thinking through the implications of your company's environment and internal condition in terms of resources of all sorts. The complexity of marketing is often underestimated by businessmen, especially those who are product- and technology-oriented. In many cases the right product hasn't made it because of the producer's lack of marketing expertise. Even more often the wrong product is introduced at the wrong time in the wrong place, this too being the result of marketing ineptitude.

Success factors in this function are tied closely to customer and industry characteristics, both past and future. Going back to the question of customer needs and expectations provides the interconnections.

In our bicycle case we would evaluate our prospective new dealers and retail purchasers. In regard to dealers, since the ultimate customer is a city dweller who in our experience doesn't have the tools or the patience to assemble and repair bikes, we should have distributors who are able and willing to provide these services. This may be the most important characteristic they possess, which may mean in turn that it isn't important to have mass-merchant distribution for this product segment.

Product knowledge may also be useful in this opportunity situation since the consumer may be interested in knowing how brands differ, especially if there is a price spread.

Another critical factor on the marketing side might be the ability to reach consumers through advertising. For example, if we are targeting the middle-class, moderate-income urbanite who needs the bike to exercise, then we must know which publications he reads and what aspects of the product will strike his fancy. The advertising must also tie in with the product features and the type and locations of dealers. It makes no sense to concentrate on quality and reliability if the dealers are oriented toward price, not performance or service. Thus the consistency of the success factors needs to be checked.

Consumer financing may also be a swing item. Most people want to be able to charge. Thus you should choose dealers who permit charging, whether to a personal account or through a credit card or bank-charge plan. This means your dealers must have credit ratings good enough to qualify for centralized charge services.

This last factor prompts me to point out that what may be crucial for one opportunity may be unimportant for another. Credit may not be vital for selling in rural or foreign markets. Service and assembly may have little bearing on sales to lower-income or young customers.

Financing success factors. Some opportunities require the ability to finance the customer's inventories; others require huge outlays of capital; still others require management flexibility to prevent losses due to inflation, revaluation, and taxes. We could say that some are cash-intensive, some capital-intensive, and some both. It is vital to take the financial situation of long-payout businesses into account in times of inflation, devaluations, and high interest rates. In recent years the ability to serve overseas markets has been based on obtaining funds overseas and not taking money out of the United States.

In the bicycle industry the most critical financial factor is the necessary financing of inventory and receivables, which results from making the product available for the summer and Christmas rush. This means that the company needs to buy its materials, produce its bicycles, and ship them to dealers at times when its revenues are low. It has to grant dealers payment terms that enable them to sell the goods before they pay for them. Thus this is a cash-intensive industry for certain periods of the year.

Management success factors. We are all familiar with the difficulty American managers have participating in foreign markets. Different culture patterns—and specifically the different ways business is conducted and legally regulated—cause the problem. This applies to the home scene too; I discussed earlier the implications of moving into an industry with a different value structure.

Until recent years bicycle markets were stable, and management style did not change. The entry of foreign producers and their agents has made some modifications, but mostly in the low-price segment. In the opportunity area we are now considering, there don't appear to be any major discontinuities from the past. The attribute managers need most is agreement with the quality and reliability standards held by the customer. This means we must be willing to stand behind our product and assure satisfaction in deed as well as word.

I have found it useful to subcategorize success factors as musts, high wants, and desirables. *Critical* success factors are musts. They should be carefully screened, for if you list too many, this will impair your creativity in generating options. Some consultants assert that there are very few of these critical factors, whatever your line of business or service, and that if you identify too many, you haven't done your homework. The definition of "critical" lies in whether or not a given factor is vital—whether you are doomed to failure if you don't have it.

WHO IS POSITIONED BEST?

Now that you have defined the specifications of major opportunities and threats and have determined their success factors, you are ready to examine your current capabilities and tangible assets and those of your most important competitors. This step also banks on the analyses you have made previously. The hooker is that an opening or danger may involve companies you have no previous experience with. An example is smaller banks moving into the lucrative automotive credit markets dominated by such concerns as big commercial banks, the General Motors Acceptance Corporation, and Ford Motor Credit Corporation. These companies too have expanded their scope and penetrated market segments previously reserved to other lending institutions.

Challenges like these abound today because of the ongoing trends toward merging and diversification. In these cases the task of ascertaining position is more complicated and requires you to obtain more information about each competitor. The type of data will depend on whether the company is single- or multi-industry and foreign or domestic. If it is regulated you must assess whether this is a help or a hindrance. An interesting story in the major business press explored the effect of regulation on AT&T's ability to compete against IBM in the communications arena. The article pointed out how AT&T was impeded by certain accounting procedures required by FCC and state agency regulations.* But the information you seek should relate to success factors, not just to the competitor's general condition.

Another point to keep in mind is that you should also evaluate potential competitors if the probability of entry is high. This is particularly true of a newly emerging and dynamic opportunity. By covering both potential and existing rivals, you will be in a better position to strategize to prevent entry.

Objectivity is a word that must always be kept in mind. It is very easy to see yourself as superior and underestimate the enemy. An outside point of view may be necessary. I have often enough observed a tendency as well to call a potential deficiency an asset. A good illustration of this is the financial evaluation made by many a manager in a subsidiary that his concern is stronger than its smaller competitors because it is part of a bigger, financially more flexible corporation. There is no disputing that the parent organization has larger financial assets, but there may be a big gap between this fact and the manager's ability to obtain the financial support he needs. If the corporation has other commitments or has no desire to underwrite the manager's plan to the degree he wants, then his capabilities are no greater than the smaller company's. He is like the millionaire who can't use his millions because they are all locked up in trust accounts. His strength is thus hypothetical, not real.

Let's return to our hypothetical bicycle company to see how this works. We know we have two major competitors in the Northeast urban market we are focusing on. One of them is part of a sporting goods chain, and the other is a large national mass merchant (like Sears or Montgomery Ward). Of course, companies of this type

*Business Week, July 27, 1974, pp. 42–45.

must be considered on the competitive list even if they aren't manufacturers.

In conception and design we are the only company of the three that produces its own gear mechanisms. The sporting goods competitor makes its own bikes but purchases its gears from another manufacturer. The mass merchant doesn't even make bikes but buys the completed product from overseas vendors and private-brands it. So we have strength in terms of availability and quality control. But whose gears perform the best? Suppose Consumers Union rated the three brands last year and ranked our gear design second to that of the sporting goods competitor. Thus we have a strength in two aspects of design but nonetheless come out second.

We know that all three of us need to keep abreast of legislative and regulatory actions that may impose new safety requirements. Since both of the other companies are much larger and both have Washington representatives, they are much better positioned to keep track of what is going on in this area. So we rank No. 3.

There are three production factors we feel are critical. One is the ability to use fiberglass or other substitutes in the manufacture of bikes some time in the future. Since our company is the only single-industry competitor in this opportunity area and the other two have other products that utilize synthetics, we are behind and should consider this a liability. We have been in the business for years and have been able to meet the seasonal swings. This is a standoff. Our capacity is already in full use, and we are straining to meet current demands. The sporting goods manufacturer has a new factory and is utilizing only 75 percent of its capacity, and the mass merchant has numerous sources around the world. We are again low man on the totem pole.

As regards dealers to reach the affluent, we have the lead since we sell through bike shops while the competitors have more generalized distribution. Of course their outlets are in their own stores, so they have more control. If they feel that service isn't sufficient, they can remedy this easily and quickly. Thus we have a current strength, but it could wash out. Both of the competitors have at least the required levels of product knowledge and advertising ability, and if they wish to improve on either count, they have the responsiveness to do so. The major disadvantage of the mass merchant is that it must spread its attention broadly and can't concentrate so much as we can. On the opposite side, however, it can use bikes as loss leaders to pull customers into the store and so gain share even without profit on the bikes.

Although we would appear to rank low in financing factors, things may not be so cut and dried. We think that the sporting goods chain has moved more rapidly than it had the funding to do, for its line of credit is lower than ours. The mass merchant may also be having liquidity problems and may be less capable of underwriting the inventory and receivable levels. So we are in the best position even though we are the smallest. Of course if we get too ambitious, we too may be unable to meet the challenge.

Considering management success factors earlier, we didn't see anything unusual in this category. But now as we compare ourselves with these two competitors, we have some different thoughts. Both management teams are more aggressive than ours, and both are able to use the bike business to increase total sales. Thus even in this high-quality area, they can apply strong pricing pressures, and they are able to give more liberal consumer terms and conditions. This may mean a new ball game for us, and the issue is whether our management can meet the characteristics of the environment.

The comparison with competitors enables you to make some judgments about the situation you face. In the last aspect of our example, it added some new perspectives to the requirements for success. As you rank yourself and your competitors, you can also indicate why you think the ranking is fair or not. The use of numerical rankings without these notations can be useful but next to impossible to explain or replicate in the future.

Is the Opportunity Feasible in Context?

In comparing your abilities with those of your competitors, you convert general assets and liabilities into specific terms. You couldn't do this earlier because a strength or limitation is relative to the particular opportunity or threat facing you, its key success factors, and the competition involved in it. What is a strength in one situation may be a limitation in another. History is full of examples of great armies being defeated by small, unorganized, poorly armed bands of rebels. For instance the British were defeated in the American colonies because they weren't accustomed to the terrain and the methods of fighting. The superiority of the U.S. air power in Vietnam wasn't really the critical element of the conflict. The Germans overran the French in good part because the invaders had a flexibility the defenders were unable to match.

A consumer product designed for the U.S. market, whether it is an automobile, a television set, or a mixer, may be inappropriate for markets in Europe. The leader in one country may be unsuccessful in another. A styling lead in Italy may not be transferable to the United States or vice versa. I have observed some highly automated businesses that were unable to make a go of it in segments or whole markets because these require low volumes and flexibility. Having financial strengths geared to capital-intensive businesses may be of limited value in those requiring large cash reserves.

If you have evaluated an opportunity and the competition and discovered that you are weak in the majority of critical success factors, you need to consider seriously whether the opportunity is viable for you. Starting from ground zero in most resource areas may be more that the organization can achieve, so that it may be the better part of valor to scratch the challenge off your list and look for others in which you are better positioned. This shouldn't be an automatic response, since even though the odds are low, the rewards may be so great that you should pursue the opening. Or you may have reserves of cash so large that the risk is worth it. Or you may have the creative power to come up a winner. Keep your thinking flexible.

In this connection, as you assess your position in relation to one opportunity (or threat), be on the alert for further openings that the evaluation brings to light. This may appear to contradict my advice to be selective in which opportunities and threats you analyze since the process takes time and manpower. Actually it doesn't because better options can appear than the one you are exploring. Or you may find that by preparing for one prospect, you can position yourself to take advantage of another at little or no cost.

Our bicycle story may be used to illustrate what I am saying. Suppose that as we are investigating the nationwide market for multiple-speed bikes, we find two opportunities in addition to the Northeast urban opening that have lower potential rewards but also fewer risks. Suppose also that we elect not to pursue the urban opportunity but rather to focus our attention on one of the alternatives, the expansion of the market in smaller midwestern communities. We now decide to joint-venture with a department store chain that also has outlets in large urban areas across the country. Therefore, though we are joining forces specifically for the midwestern market area, we are gaining a potential ally for the Northeast urban penetration at a later date.

As I commented regarding earlier phases of strategic thinking, you might consider using planning teams to review specific opportunities and threats. This approach enhances your ability to look broadly. Working independently, each team may come up with several possibilities, which later can be matched with the findings of the others. The multiple-team approach increases the number and variety of openings perceived and normally yields creative ideas for tackling them.

BUILD ON STRENGTHS AND CORRECT LIMITATIONS

Most successful strategies are those that maintain and build on existing strengths. The point is worth emphasizing that a strength is not a gift of God that can be counted on without some attention to keeping it healthy. This isn't always recognized. Any company can lose a strength over time because of complacency and neglect.

There are five major ways of correcting limitations. Not all of these are available or workable for every opportunity (or threat), and to be achievable, they must be converted into meaningful actions.

Self-development. The first and most obvious means of correcting a limitation is to strengthen your own resources. If you need specific types of people, you can hire them, transfer them in from elsewhere in the organization, or set up a training program for existing personnel. All these approaches enable you to build competence for the long term. But all take time and expenditure. Time can be critical. You can't always readily find the right people to hire, and special skills need time to develop and measure. Numerous companies have spent months or even years finding the right person only to discover later that he couldn't do the job. Training is very costly and also time consuming. Building complex skills requires properly selected trainees, sophisticated teachers, and possibly equipment. Learning is a slow process. In some situations this may be the only option that will bring you the strength you need, but it shouldn't be the only solution considered.

Acquisition. Acquiring another company or piece of a company is another possibility. This enables you to move quickly, and it will effectively correct a limitation if you are careful about the selection of the acquiree. Your list of success factors and your assessment of your abilities provide the criteria to be considered in determining what the incoming organization must possess. Rarely are your deficiencies and the available company's strengths a perfect match. The word "available" is worth underlining, since as in hiring you must often settle for what you can find, unless you are willing to pay a large sum for the takeover. For some companies acquisition choices are limited by government rules and policies against restraint of trade.

Another critical element is the decision on whether you need or wish to retain the acquired company's managers. If you want to retain them, you must think out why they will wish to stay. If they are incompatible with your company's way of doing business, values, or compensation policies, this should be noted and contingency plans drawn up for implementation if they leave. There are numerous examples of the company built on one man whose departure left it with minimal assets. Beware of the innovating entrepreneur who began his firm on his own and now wishes to sell it. He will be hard to keep, and if he stays he will be harder to control.

Unfortunately acquisitions are more unsuccessful than successful, and though the option is worth considering, it should be carefully evaluated.

Joint venture. This may be a combination of acquisition and self-development, and it has become a rather popular move in recent years. The European coalitions have actively sought ways of using competence economically and avoiding duplication of effort. This approach works best when the partners are compatible and both have a need they can't fill on their own. Suppose you evaluate your resources and find that you have a good product but poor marketing ability. You may find it worthwhile to join with a company that needs a product and has a good sales force. This makes a win/win combination. Like all the other ways of building on strengths and correcting limitations, it will take a great deal of searching and negotiating to develop a working joint venture. Again you must assess the compatibility of the partner firm's management, for you must determine whether both of you want to lead and neither to follow. If this is the case, the venture will fail because of internal tugs-of-war that make a disciplined attack on the problem impossible.

A favorite form of joint venturing used particularly in international markets is the consortium approach to major projects. For instance suppose a developing nation wishes to build an entire city from the ground up. It might be interested in having a single bid on the whole project. Of course no one company has the ability to do the entire job itself, so it may bid together with other companies, each representing a specific skill. This is the way many of the large aerospace contracts were handled, and the practice has moved into the commercial markets.

Subcontracting. The best solution in case you are faced with a short lead time may be to subcontract with a company that has a strength not otherwise available to you. This may take the form of buying a component or complete product to fill out your line and enable you to participate in the market quickly. For example suppose our bike company needed to offer a windshield on its motorized models in response to a sudden fad in the adult urban market. We could go to a company producing windshields for motor scooters and ask it to produce a design we specify. Many large merchants have come up with their own brand of consumer products by the subcontracting route. This practice is popular in the credit card business, where the card issuers provide all the central administration and indeed capital required to fund the accounts of companies honoring the cards.

The subcontracting option, like the others, also has limitations. It gives your supplier a chance to increase his experience in your field, and he may decide to become a competitor. If you depend on a single source, you not only sustain a potential future competitor but open yourself to the danger of losing your whole supply line if he turns rival.

I have found that subcontracting is primarily a short-term solution and should be supplemented with another move for the sake of longer-term security. For instance you might subcontract until your firm can develop its own product, take an equity share in this or another supplier's business, or even merge with a supplier. In short subcontracting is an excellent way to buy time for the present and position yourself for the future.

Licensing. In cases where you identify a technological limitation, licensing may be the answer. To be really useful a license must ordinarily include the know-how that goes with it. As with subcontracting I believe licensing is a short-term solution. You should recognize that licenses are of advantage to the licenser unless you bring some other strengths to bear that give you leverage not available to anyone else, including the licenser. An example might be superlative marketing abilities that will enable you to increase sales if you have access to certain products. This could be the case when the owner of a patent is much smaller or wants merely to obtain additional income, not to participate in the market to which the patent pertains. There are many cases of a company stumbling onto a new concept or product and having no interest in capitalizing on it. Several years ago General Electric established an organization to market patents, copyrights, and products to other companies purely to obtain income from items that otherwise would go unused.

Of course you may choose to combine some of these approaches or change from one to another in time. You might decide to buy some components from subcontractors and work on enhancing your existing resources in areas that represent the greatest potential market gains or cost savings; you might choose to acquire a small company to obtain its key people and dismantle the rest of it; or you might plan to hire and train people to get a foothold and later do some licensing or acquiring.

The more combinations you identify, the more options will be available for you to assess. In addition you will create alternatives that may be used later as contingency strategies. Table 9–1 shows some of the moves our bicycle company might make to tackle the opportunity in the Northeast market.

HOW WILL YOU EMPLOY WHAT RESOURCES?

Having analyzed your opportunities and threats and outlined the alternatives for building on strengths and correcting limitations, you should easily be able to define explicitly what resources you must employ and how in order to meet each specific opening and danger. This completes your development of your *operating strategy*. Your task now is to formulate detailed presentations that will communicate your prospective plans to your operating managers. Aware of what you need, what you can and will use, and what you will do to improve your position, you and your financial organization should be able to articulate the following:

- *The rewards*, that is, the sales you can expect in terms of both units and dollars. This provides you with the ability to determine market share and position.
- *The costs* of hiring, training, acquiring, licensing, manufacturing, distributing, motivating—everything that is directly or indirectly related to the sales volume you have projected.
- *The risks* involved. What is at stake? Who will be affected? How uncertain is the future? These can be expressed at least to the extent required for decision making. If you think you have found a riskless option, beware. Nothing comes free of risk, and you probably haven't evaluated the situation thoroughly enough.

If you have applied the entire thinking process you will have achieved the following:

- Determined your *investment strategy*.
- Decided the lead thrust, that is whether it is going to be based on marketing, innovation, cost takeout, acquisition, disposition, joint venture, and so on—this is the management strategy.
- Identified the opportunities you will pursue, the strengths you will build on, the limitations you will correct (as well

Table 9-1. Selecting alternatives for bicycle opportunities in the northeastern United States.

	Strengths		Correction of Limitations			
	Use Strength	Enhance Strength	Develop Self	Acquire	Joint-venture	Subcontract
Conceive/Design						
Gear availability (+)	Use as is					
Gear design (–)			Use own engineers	Buy Co. X design		
Gear safety legislation (–)					Jointly lobby with other suppliers	
Produce						
New material know-how (–)			Hire new material applications engineers		Develop with fiberglass company	
Capacity (–)			Add plant	Acquire Company Y		

	Strengths		Correction of Limitations			
	Use Strength	Enhance Strength	Develop Self	Acquire	Joint-venture	Subcontract
Dealers servicing affluent users (+)		Add franchised dealers				
Control of dealers (-)				Accept limitation–do nothing		
Advertising power (-)				Accept limitation–do nothing		
Pricing flexibility (-)			Emphasize cost takeout			
Financial						
Liquidity (+)	Use as is	Add more lines of credit				
Management						
Aggressiveness (-)			Hire new general manager			

as the means of correcting them), and the threats you will avoid. These elements will combine to describe the key programs which will be the heart of your operating strategy.

- Finally you will be in a position to estimate the rewards, costs, and risks associated with the decisions you have made.

In summary, you have now specified the three levels of strategy and their implications to the future of the business. The next step is to compare these with the objectives and goals of the key stakeholders involved in the business.

THINKING OPPORTUNITIES THROUGH
FOR NONPROFIT ORGANIZATIONS

A university or college may discover that a local company would like to use its facilities and faculty for management training and development during the summer months. The possibility appeals to the school since it will increase the utilization of its plant and provide supplementary income to its faculty, which may enable it to retain its top teachers. The arrangement is attractive to the company because it permits it to enhance the skills of its workforce without fixed costs. The opportunity for the school can be summarized thus:

What? To provide management seminars for a local company.
Where? In the school's surrounding community.
When? July and August.
What share? The company's 50 top and middle managers.
Why? The company's interest in improving the abilities of its employees and the unused capacity of the college and its faculty.

This opportunity seems straighforward, and the school administrators could assume that it doesn't require further study and planning. But I can assure you it does. In terms of conception and design, the institution must determine the managers' needs, which means assessing their current levels of know-how in relation to their company's expectations. Operating a seminar for an intensive period is very different from offering one-hour sessions for a semester. The seminars must be designed to evoke an optimum level of involvement, taking into account the executives' years of experience.

The faculty will need to understand how to teach adults, a different proposition from teaching undergraduates. This is a matter of marketing as well as of design. Instructors for these sessions can't use last year's course notes, rely on textbooks for homework, or lecture at the participants for hours on end. Participants expect to be challenged, see relevance, and determine how to put the material to work when they return to the job.

Production involves keying facilities and equipment to the seminars. In today's executive education programs, it is important to have rooms that enable participants to engage in face-to-face exchanges. Audiovisual equipment has become a must, and trained operators are required for sophisticated machinery. Coffee breaks and lunches must be prompt and short, which means that food-service areas must be close by seminar rooms and food preparation must be streamlined. As strange as it may seem, the accommodations may make the difference between a program's being highly lauded and considered mediocre.

So you can see that for a college to become a successful management training center requires an understanding of the success factors critical to that opportunity. After all the institution does not have a monopoly on the product or captive customers for it; there are many competitors. There are other colleges, perhaps some nearby. There are professional organizations like the American Management Associations and Advanced Management Research providing executive training programs. There are individual consultants and consulting firms. There are specialized conference facilities that can arrange to offer training as part of a conference "package."

Hospitals, social service groups, and religious communities are also faced with new opportunities and threats that must be scrutinized. If a religious organization decides to go into low-cost housing, it too, like a business, must determine the success factors involved and how well prepared it is. If a hospital decides to open a rehabilitation facility or nursing home, it too must assess its position. In short every nonprofit organization, whatever its field of endeavor, must spell out its investment decision in the alphabet of operating strategy in order to achieve its aim.

APPLICATION TIME

1. Identify the type of investment strategy you have chosen and record your reason for this choice.

2. State the management strategy option that can contribute to the investment results you desire. Remember that management options focus on either market, innovation, production, or the like.

3. Identify opportunities or threats which relate to the investment and management option you wish to pursue, or at least those which appear to be worth further analysis. These may be related to your strengths or result from environmental forces. Will your management option enable you to pursue several opportunities, now or in the future?

4. For each selected opportunity or threat, answer the questions What? When? Where? How much? Why?

5. Determine "success factors" based on future industry or market conditions.

6. Compare your resources/abilities with those of each major competitor, in the light of the success factors.

7. Identify your strengths and limitations and then develop alternatives which will use your strengths and deemphasize your limitations.

8. Evaluate costs, rewards, risks of each alternative.

9. Select your preferred alternative and then note the management and operating strategy implicit in your selection.

10
WHAT HAPPENED TO OBJECTIVES?

You will recall that in Chapter 2 I emphasized how this strategic approach differs from others, which formulate strategies from objectives and from existing strategies. The sequence I have been describing begins with a broad statement of your vision for the organization and follows with a systematic evaluation of the environment, competitors, and resources to determine whether your goals are feasible. In the last chapter you saw the method for identifying alternatives, making a selection, and then assessing its rewards, costs, and risks. These hypothetical results can be equated with the objectives and goals that you can realistically expect to achieve.

But that was merely the financial expression of the strategy, whereas the objectives of businesses and other institutions transcend the financial and are qualitative as well as quantitative. These organizations, as we know, are expected to serve more than their financial stakeholders.

This chapter will describe another, separate step of the thinking process, a step which will permit you to evaluate the alternatives in light of the stakeholders of the organization. The approach will build objectives based on the expectations and needs of the key stakeholders and then separate those which are absolutely critical from those which are merely desirable.

Before we begin, let's be sure that you understand what I mean by a *strategy,* an *objective,* and a *goal.* You have probably attended, at least once, a business or organizational meeting in which there was an argument as to whether a statement was an objective, goal, or strategy. I'd be very surprised if you haven't had this experience, since it has become almost a ritual in planning and thinking meetings. I have come to believe that this debate is the means used by many managers to sabotage the whole thinking process and to avoid having to plan at all. Of course, I may have become cynical or overly sensitive. In any event, to avoid this waste of time I suggest we define those three terms by means of these key questions:

- What do you want to achieve or avoid? *The answers to this question are your objectives.*
- How will you go about achieving your desired results? *The answer to this you can call strategy.*
- How will you know the results have been achieved on time and to the degree desired? *Answering this will provide you with measurable and understandable goals.*

GENERATING OBJECTIVES

One of the best ways I have found to generate a comprehensive list of objectives is to ask yourself what you would like to achieve for all your organization's stakeholders, and, if you have to make some tradeoff decisions, to ask yourself which stakeholders will receive the highest priority.

Who are the stakeholders? They are all those individuals or groups who have a stake in the business and its results, that is, those whose future is affected by the organization's performance. Specifically, they include:

Stockholders and other investors	Community
Management at all levels	Customers
Board of directors	Vendors and suppliers
Employees	Unions
Governments	Public

Each of these groups has unique expectations and needs related to the organization. The problem is that the wants of some of the groups are in conflict with those of others. If the company were to satisfy all of the needs and expectations of employees and their representative, the union, it would be forced to eliminate dividends, reduce profits, and possibly forgo the repayment of its debt. Thus, the employees would be satisfied but the stockholders and investors might become so unhappy they would withdraw their support, possibly causing the company to go bankrupt.

The key to stakeholder evaluation is to understand the impact that a specific alternative strategy may have on all groups of stakeholders and then to decide the priorities you wish to set for these groups. Of course, it is also important to determine whether any one set of stakeholders can *prevent* the effective implementation of a strategy. In short, you wish to optimize the positive effects of the strategy on the stakeholder groups while making sure that none can prevent its execution. Here's how to generate objectives with the stakeholders in mind:

1. *Inventory your current objectives.* Start by listing your current objectives and classifying them in terms of the stakeholder groups which benefit the most. If an objective aims at more than one stakeholder, put it under more than one category. This will enable you to visualize which of the stakeholders have been benefiting the most from your business and its current strategy.

It is quite normal to find that most objectives are aimed upward in the organization, toward either the board of directors, the top management, or major stockholders or investors. This is the way it is and probably the way it will always be. The main problem with this situation is that it may cause some stakeholders to become so upset that they will try to prevent the organization from achieving its objectives, and in so doing may even succeed in (usually inadvertently) destroying the organization itself. This is quite apparent in the labor-management scene. Some strikes have been so costly to the companies involved that they have been forced to close their doors permanently. In such cases the workers, instead of achieving their group objectives, have found themselves thrown out of work.

2. *Record what you think each stakeholder group wants now and will want in the future.* This second step involves determining what stakeholders really expect and how these expectations can impact on your business. Interestingly, most managers and businessmen fail to scrutinize the wishes, let alone the minimum needs,

of those whose contribution is vital to the success of the enterprise. Instead, they fall back on a series of cliches which often go unchallenged and may even be incorrect. We have all heard that stockholders only want high dividends and couldn't care less about the organization's contribution to society. Or that dividends don't really matter since the key to stockholder satisfaction is the price/earnings ratio, which is reflected in the price and value of the stock. This type of generalization clearly reflects a lack of analysis.

Determining the Stockholders' Expectations

One of the first probes you should make is to analyze who the owners of the company's stock actually are. Ownership is often divided. It may include large investors—such as banks, investment companies, and mutual funds—interested in only short-term results, and if the results don't happen then they will dump the stock and invest elsewhere. There may also be individuals who are investing for the long haul and interested in the dividend income for retirement. This type will be interested in visible and steady growth and may shy away from the high-risk glamour investments.

Owners may also be members of other groups and as such may have divided loyalties. For example, as investors, employees who own their employer's stocks want the company to make a dividend payout. However, as employees, they may also be demanding increased salaries and benefits, which, if granted, could reduce the size and frequency of the dividend.

And then there are the nonprofit institutions which, in recent years, have become stockholders in order to exert pressure for change. Churches, social awareness groups, and even pressure groups fall in this category. Though such investors may not have large blocks of stocks, they have the power to cause unrest and to organize others to influence decisions. Thus you can readily agree that "a stockholder" isn't "the stockholders"; investors vary and have different expectations.

Since stockholders are changing, it behooves the businessman to keep in touch with and to analyze what they are thinking and demanding. If he does this, then the objectives pertaining to this class of stakeholder will be realistic and he will be more effective in making the tough strategic decisions, which are based on those objectives.

Determining the Employees' Expectations

There are many books about the evaluation and motivation of employees, but they normally view employees as a valuable resource, not a decision-influencing stakeholder group. This is ironic in light of the fact that this group, above all other stakeholders, has the greatest effect on a company's ability to capitalize on opportunities and avoid threats.

As with stockholders, you can't make generalizations about workers. There are management employees who want to be treated as participants in the decision-making process, whose needs go beyond the financial remuneration they receive. There are professional employees who may be more loyal to their profession and specialty than to the company and may want to work only for an enterprise that is the leader in its field. They may rebel and refuse to implement a strategy that they consider makes the firm a follower. There are white collar workers, the backbone of the organization, who may be more interested in the preservation of their status than the salaries they obtain. Finally, there are hourly workers who seek pay increases along with job security.

To really understand this stakeholder group you must segment it not only by type of work but by demographic and personal characteristics, like geographic motility, years of service, age, sex, race, educational background, and marital status. With this scope of information, you will be able to see how the group is composed and what this may imply in terms of the members' desires and demands.

Finally, all other stakeholder classifications should be examined and assessments made of what those stakeholders need as a minimum. This includes both local and national unions, government at all levels, and so on. We could take each of these groups and pull it apart, but I think this is unnecessary, since I have made the point clear that sound strategic decisions depend on clear perception of what each group of stakeholders wants from your organization.

APPLICATION TIME

Let's pause here and take some time to record your current business objectives, classified by stakeholder groups. To reiterate, these include:

Stockholders and other investors	Communities in which you operate
Management (all levels)	Customers
Board of directors	Vendors and suppliers
Employees	Unions
Governments	Public

How have you been doing? Have some stakeholders been ignored? Have some received too much emphasis?

Consider now who your major stakeholders are and what their expectations have been and are now. Don't rush it! The time you take now and the depth of your thinking, especially about changes, may be vital to the salvation of your business.

CONVERTING STAKEHOLDER EXPECTATIONS INTO OBJECTIVES

In developing objectives based on the needs and wants of the stakeholders, three points must be borne in mind:

1. It is impossible to satisfy all stakeholders.

2. It isn't necessary to have an objective for each of the stakeholder groups; this would produce an unrealistic number of objectives.

3. To be useful for making decisions, objectives should be specific and classified into two categories: *critical* and *desirable*.

I will elaborate on each of these points in order to guide you in application:

Don't Try to Satisfy All Stakeholders

As I said before, you can't try to be all things to all people and remain in business. This becomes abundantly clear when we review the federal government's unsuccessful attempts to provide social programs for the poor and needy while it simultaneously strives to maintain a strong military posture throughout the world, to balance the budget, and to reduce taxes. Each of these objectives aims at a specific stakeholder audience, and each, in itself, is commendable. But taken together they are nonviable. Businessmen nod their heads when you use this illustration, and then they go about making essentially the same mistake as the government. For example, they may simultaneously try to satisfy:

Top management, by increasing profits.

The stockholders, by increasing dividends.

The suppliers, by increasing capital expenditures.

The union and employees, by increasing the number of jobs.

The investors, by reducing debt.

Each group will be happy with the objectives, but some are bound to be disappointed because it is unlikely that all those objectives can be achieved.

You Don't Need an Objective for Each Stakeholder

Don't feel compelled to state an objective for each group. I have witnessed this compulsion in action and it yields so many objectives that you practically need a computer to keep track of them, let alone use them to evaluate alternatives. I have observed situations where management has felt compelled to have numerous objectives and they became, in effect, more of a "wish list" than a means for making decisions.

If you do consider it necessary to have objectives pertaining to all or most of the stakeholder groups, then be sure that they are stated specifically and placed in some order of priority. Normally it is better to omit those objectives with a low priority or inconsequential impact on the results.

You Need Specific Objectives

Even when you have, as recommended, a limited number of objectives, you must make them specific. Since the purpose of objectives is to guide in the selection of the preferred alternative strategy, they should be clear, precise, and measurable. By "measurable," I mean that the decision maker should be able to know whether the objective is being met or missed. There are four questions to answer before you can rest assured that your objectives meet the criteria of clarity, precision, and measurability:

1. What will be achieved or accomplished?
2. To what extent will it be achieved?

3. When will it occur?
4. Where will it occur?

Some will argue that these questions are more pertinent to the establishment of goals than objectives. My retort is that it shouldn't make any difference whether these are called objectives or goals as long as they are specific and useful in making a decision. The degree of specificity of a given objective will depend on whether it is qualitative or quantitative in nature. Some of the key objectives are bound to be qualitative, and these will have to be delineated according to the feelings or judgment of management. But it is important that management communicate such definitions of objectives in advance to those responsible for making the decision and implementing the strategy. Objectives are really only as useful as they are helpful in selecting a course of action and, later, in measuring performance, and if an objective is not formulated until after the fact, it hasn't guided and in fact may become a negative motivator.

Some objectives are vital and must be met; I call these *critical objectives.* Others, which I call *desirable objectives,* are merely *beneficial* and have relative, not absolute, importance. A *critical* objective is indispensable to the survival of the enterprise. Financial solvency is an illustration of a critical objective for a private enterprise. The organization will not be able to continue if it isn't financially secure enough to pay its bills or to get credit to do the job. This doesn't mean that it can't have one or two loss years, and in fact it might be necessary to have a few loss years over the long term.

Desirable objectives pertain to the stakeholders' desires and expectations. The key question to ask is, What do I want the business to achieve for the stockholders? for the investors? for the employees? and so forth. You should test these objectives against your perceptions of the stakeholders' expectations and then determine whether what you wish to do is consistent with their expectations. If there is consistency, then you will have an objective supported by the stakeholder in question; if there isn't you may find a potential problem exists with the stakeholder group. Let's assume you want to increase net income over the next five years in order to make the company more attractive to sell. An objective like this is not consistent with the needs and expectations of employees and the union, who expect larger salaries and benefits during the same period and also seek long-term security. Coupled with your objective, those expectations have the potential to invoke conflict. Therefore, employee needs must be at least partially satisfied by the implementation plan. So the use of stakeholder expectations not only helps in developing objectives but also provides a checklist of specific, feasible courses of action which will convert the strategy into the operating plan and guidelines.

USING OBJECTIVES TO SELECT THE ALTERNATIVE

The objectives you set can be useful in choosing the preferred alternative. You have generated the alternatives by carefully analyzing the implications of your environment, competition, and resource position. Since this evaluation included the identification of the success factors and the relative position of all participants, it should have enabled you to produce viable options.

Now the question is, How do these options compare with the objectives and goals you have identified as being at least satisfactory to the stakeholders involved? In short, alternatives result from one set of evaluations, and objectives from another; they stem from separate and distinct thought processes. Now we will put them side by side and compare the desires with the possibilities. Since it is unlikely that they will match perfectly, it will be necessary to make a tradeoff; that is, you may have to set the objectives and goals lower on the scale or recognize that the alternative you choose may be very difficult to do but worth the price.

If you have developed the type of alternatives described in earlier chapters, they should be easily converted to financial costs, rewards, and risks. Thus you should already have a feeling for comparing the quantified results of each alternative and seeing how they stack up with the objectives you had in mind. If you intend to make your decision on the financial and other quantified results, such as market share, rates of growth, and the like, then you really don't need to go any further. But I will predict that if you do limit your assessment to these traditional criteria, you may miss some very vital aspects of the problem of surviving and doing business in the future.

Using Critical Objectives

The first step in this assessment process is to be sure that the alternative meets the bare essentials, the "musts." Critical objectives are very valuable since they quickly reduce the number of alternatives you have to consider and allow concentration on those which will optimize results. On the other hand they must be carefully selected or some very good alternatives, most likely the more creative ones, will be eliminated too early in the process and not given proper evaluation.

Alternatives unable to pass what I call the *critical screen* aren't really options at all and will be eliminated at that point. Consider these examples:

1. You have been told by your creditors that you will not be given any additional credit. This means that any strategy which requires additional external financing isn't viable.

2. In your evaluation of the government, you have determined that it will not permit you any further large acquisitions or mergers in the industry you now serve. As a result, strategies requiring this type of activity will be declared null and void.

3. In evaluating your wish to move to a lower-cost, nonunion region of the country or the world, you have decided that your employees and their union would vehemently oppose this and they have the economic, public, and government support to succeed in preventing the move. In that case, those options which call for such a move will be eliminated.

Just on the basis of those few examples it is apparent that the critical screen has the power of elimination, and if even the seemingly best options are wrong, they soon disappear. So the words of caution are these: have only a few and be sure they are truly critical. In the past, businessmen used to worry only about the quantifiable areas and were justified in doing so. Today they must be more aware of the power of stakeholders to prevent execution.

Using Desirable Objectives

Objectives which don't fall in the critical class automatically become desirable. These are not absolute, but relative, and so need to be placed in some order of priority. If you wish, you can rank them and place weights on their relative value. I normally put higher numbers on those considered more important and vice versa.

I could recommend such a weighted-score system for choosing the alternatives. However, although this works in theory, I have found it to be too complicated for practical use on the strategic level of planning and more appropriate for the tactical decisions which need to be made. There are benefits in systematically thinking about the relative fit of the alternatives and the objectives, but there is no need to quantify them and make the decision of "best fit" on a numerical scale. Further, I have observed that quite often the numbers are misused, that is, they—rather than the qualitative analyses and evaluation—come to dominate the decision making. Numbers lead the decision maker to believe that he is dealing with a science rather than an art and, therefore, that the future is certain and predictable, rather than built on uncertain assumptions. The fact that one alternative receives a higher score or is chosen by the computer doesn't mean that it is the best alternative. The choice of the strategy is and must be a personal process. The preferred alternative is most often the one that management feels most comfortable with and is based on the combination of intuition, judgment, and analysis. The process we have been discussing is an aid to all three of these human factors.

Let's illustrate how desirable objectives are used by supposing you are managing the bicycle company described earlier and have arrived at the following list of such objectives:

Increase our market share by 5 points worldwide.

Increase our profits to 8 percent return on sales after taxes.

Hold employment steady in the Cincinnati area (our main plant).

Help the U.S. balance of trade by a $150,000 contribution.

Maintain labor peace, keeping worker actions down to only minor walkouts.

Further assume that these are in order of priority and reflect the best of the list of all desirable objectives. The situation shown in Table 10–1 is fairly typical since neither set of alternatives is perfect. Neither approach achieves the desired share or income targets. If they were based on desirable objectives, both alternatives would be unacceptable, but the objectives are wants, and so each alternative is viable. Approach 1 trades income for share, employment stability,

Table 10-1. Alternate approaches for the bicycle company.

	Yields	
Objectives	Approach 1	Approach 2
Share	Increase by 2.5 points	Increase by 4.6 points
ROS	Increase to 6.5%	Increase to 4.5%
Employment	2% decline	No decline
Balance of trade	Contribute $250,000	Contribute $125,000
Labor peace	Three walkouts	One walkout

and labor peace. Approach 2 does the opposite, providing more share at the expense of income—though still less than the desired level of the objective—and meets the target of employment and labor stability better than Plan 1. So as manager, you must decide between two options, neither of which meets all your objectives. But this is a dilemma of all leaders, since it is generally impossible to do everything at once. The issue you must resolve is whether to choose between these two alternatives, reiterate the process and develop some new options, or readjust your expectations and settle for objectives which seem to be possible.

OBJECTIVES FOR THE NONPROFIT ORGANIZATION

Setting objectives for the nonprofit institution requires the same procedures as the foregoing, with two key differences. First, the list of stakeholders will be more extensive, and second, you should expect more qualitative than quantitative objectives. Here is a list of stakeholders for two typical nonprofit institutions:

HOSPITAL	UNIVERSITY
Trustees	Board of regents
Top management	Top management

Administration	Administration
Department heads	Department heads
Physicians	Faculty
Nurses	
Paraprofessionals	
Service employees	Service employees
Patients	Students
	Alumni
Benefactors	Benefactors
Medical Associations	Professional associations
	Professional institutions
Accrediting/certifying bodies	Accrediting bodies
Insurance companies	Companies who underwrite tuition
Blue Cross/Blue Shield	Lending institutions
Medicare/medicaid	
Government	Government
Community organizations	Community organizations
State (e.g., Maryland) cost control boards	
Cooperating institutions	Cooperating institutions
Special interest groups	Special interest groups

Unlike businessmen, the leaders of these nonprofit institutions are more dependent on their stakeholders for continuing support. Each of these stakeholder groups has the power to close the institution. At the same time, as with stakeholders in business organizations, not all can be satisfied to the same level. My own experience with nonprofit institutions suggests that they tend to want to meet everyone's demands, and this normally results in the institution's becoming overcommitted and, in some cases, in its shutting down entirely. Therefore, if you are in this field, when you develop your objectives, recognize the need to be selective. Though you can expect to have more qualitative objectives than a businessman, this does not relieve you from the responsibility of determining how you will measure them. This is particularly true of the must variety. Since a critical objective is a *go, no go* test, you need to be able to determine if the alternative meets the essential criteria.

The checklist sums up the selection process developed in this chapter.

Selecting Alternatives Based on Stakeholder-Oriented Objectives

First: Develop an inventory of your stakeholders.

Develop a survey of their expectations.

Convert their expectations into your objectives.

Second: Classify your objectives by whether they are critical or desirable.

Third: Evaluate your strategy alternatives in light of the critical and desirable objectives you have set.

Fourth: Eliminate any alternative that doesn't meet the "critical" objectives.

Fifth: Determine which alternative best fits the "desirable" objectives. If you must make a compromise, recognize that you are either modifying the alternatives or the objectives.

Sixth: Select your preferred alternative and note its rewards, costs, and risks.

11

KEEPING IN TOUCH WITH REALITY: STRATEGY REVIEW

"Unfortunately," as one executive remarked, "you can't tell for sure whether a strategy will really work until it is tested over time." This is true; you can't guarantee that a strategy will produce its promised results until it is implemented and the results are known. But this doesn't mean that you can't review the strategy and assure that it is viable. In this phase of our thinking, I will discuss some of the major reasons that strategies fail and suggest some ways of reviewing the strategy you have selected to determine its feasibility.

WHO SHOULD DO THE REVIEW?

At this point in your strategic thinking activity you have a clear, concise description of what you wish to do with your business and its potential results. This has been done by you, with the assistance of associates and staff. If you haven't asked for an outside opinion, it is now time to do so.

Strategy review requires a critical, unbiased look at what you say you will do and why. This objective critique must be done by someone who was not involved in the analysis and formulation process. It can't be done by someone who has his mind already made up or an ax to grind. I personally have found that someone outside your organization can be most helpful, since he can ask probing questions and will not be intimidated.

CAUSES OF INEFFECTIVE STRATEGIES

Before I recommend review approaches, it will probably be helpful to discuss why strategies may fail to be implemented effectively. In this way I think it will become apparent why more than one review may be needed, and also how you may select from among them.

PITFALL 1: MISMATCHING OR ERRONEOUS ASSUMPTIONS

As you now recognize, strategies are built on assumptions about the future behavior of customers, competitors, governments, and other external factors, as well as assumptions about internal resources and your ability to use them. These assumptions evoke your opinions about opportunities and threats, and, ultimately, your planned strategic response.

Assumptions are related to ineffective strategies in two ways: (1) The original assumptions are valid but the strategy somehow develops along different lines so that it is based on other, shakier assumptions. (2) The original assumptions are either faulty from the start or eventually become so because of changing conditions. To avoid failure in either case, you would have to reconstruct or replace the troublesome assumptions. Let's deal with these factors one at a time.

Valid Original Assumptions

Although all strategies are based on assumptions, a strategy as it finally evolves may no longer be consistent with the assumptions that initiated it. This can occur—during the interval of time between the recording of the assumptions and the finalizing of the strategy—in several ways:

1. New information may be acquired or new ideas may occur which serve to alter the strategy. New information, if reliable, will

probably help to improve a strategy, but new ideas can have either positive or negative effects.

2. Discussion or negotiation with or persuasion by others in the organization may also change the original strategy. The need for consensus often plays an important part in bringing about such changes. Modifying a strategy is not harmful per se, but it can be if the changes are based on faulty or misguided assumptions.

3. Both 1 and 2 may occur, either consecutively or simultaneously.

Faulty Assumptions

There's no point in discussing those assumptions that are O.K. at the outset but are proven wrong when a strategy fails due to unanticipated changes in external conditions. Avoiding these would require an infallible crystal ball. But it's far more common for a strategy to fail because it is based on assumptions that are shaky from the start *but are accepted without question.* Let's take an example. Suppose the recorded strategy calls for opening a new distribution network in the Far East. This element *implies* that there is a market for your product in that part of the world, that dealers can be convinced to carry and sell the product, that consumers will want to purchase it, that both dealers and consumers can finance their purchases, and that there will be service available for the pre- and postsale period. Some of these assumptions are based on research and fact, and others are based on feeling and intuition. Many of the key assumptions are never explicitly stated, and it is these tacit assumptions that are likely to cause the most trouble.

It is amazing how many decisions about moving into new markets have been based on untested or unrecognized assumptions. One major company moved aggressively into foreign markets assuming that its brand name was a worldwide emblem, only to discover that it wasn't known to the foreign consumer. This fundamental assumption was erroneous and was enough to cause defeat. There are numerous instances in which a company met with failure because it assumed that its current dealer and distribution network was appropriate for a new, but different product, or that electricity, oil, and other sources of energy would remain plentiful and relatively inexpensive.

There is no question that assumptions are the basis of strategy because nothing in the future is certain. But the point is that we make many tacit assumptions that have no solid basis in fact, and it is often these assumptions which spell the difference between success and failure. To avoid this pitfall, we must be careful to identify what has been thought through in depth and what may have been given short shrift.

PITFALL 2: FAILING TO ANTICIPATE A COMPETITOR'S RESPONSE

Strange as it seems, businessmen may fail to think about the competitor's response to their strategy. Some seem to think that the competition is within their control and will lie down and play dead. Even worse, some others think they have a monopoly on brains and ability and that the competitor isn't very smart. These attitudes can be fatal.

A useful review device is to lay your total strategy alongside the one you have determined to be your competitor's. For example:

YOUR OPERATING STRATEGY	OPERATING STRATEGY OF COMPETITOR X
Marketing	Marketing
Use direct sales	Use independent distributors
Focus on specialty shops	Focus on department stores

Next, it is important to evaluate which of these approaches will be more effective and why. Then determine how the competitor may react if you are successful at his expense. This last step will enable you to identify potential contingencies, which we will review in the next chapter.

RESPONSE OF COMPETITOR	CONTINGENCY OPTION
Switch to direct sales and move in our dealers. Reduce prices to regain share.	Hold line on price but increase incentives to our dealers to make our line more attractive.

This should be done for all your strategy elements and those of your major competitors, that is, those which are either a threat to your position or the targets of your aggression. This is tough work and requires objectivity. A few words of caution: If you find that all your strategy elements rate high and seem to be invincible, you may be either overestimating yourself or underestimating the enemy. Further, if you find that your strategy compares equally well with all competition, you have a strategy that will probably fail. Competitors differ and their strategies will vary in effectiveness. You must choose which competitors you wish to challenge and which you wish to neutralize. Your review should make sure that your strategy is aiming at the right competitor. Finally, don't become overly reactive and start to change the strategy at will; this is only one of the tests and must be put in its correct perspective.

PITFALL 3: FAILING TO FIND THE STAKEHOLDER WITH VETO POWER

In the previous chapter I recommended the use of stakeholder analysis as a means of developing, weighting, and using objectives to *select* the preferred option. But I have found that many executives consider this approach too complicated and impractical. Though I disagree, I would like to suggest how the concept can be used in a more simplified review technique. It is another way to test the practicality and viability of the strategy. The key to this approach is to recognize that your strategy can't satisfy everyone equally and to make sure that there isn't one stakeholder group or even individual that in effect has veto power and can prevent implementation. If you fail to recognize this, you may find that your strategy is like a presentation made by a junior executive which his associates think is great but isn't acceptable to the boss.

The question to ask is, "If I began to execute this action or strategic element, what would be the likely reaction of each of the major stakeholder groups, and could they prevent it from being carried out?" One of the stakeholders who would be positively affected might be helpful in the task of implementation. Could a potential enemy be changed into an ally? Or could an ally help to change the reaction of a potential enemy? Even when you are planning a plant relocation, you can reduce the impact on the community and the workforce by giving them advance notice, by working with other employers to place those who will be displaced, by assisting the government to attract other employers to the area, and so on. In any of these ways you can at least be seen as someone who, although he will be leaving, is concerned about the employees, community, local government, and even union, and is not just running away.

Strategy element: Exit Product X

STAKEHOLDERS	IMPACT
Employees	150 employees affected
Union	Fewer members
Community	Unemployment increased
Government	Unemployment increased
Suppliers	5 small suppliers
Other company components	Sold to same dealers as component Z

Reaction: Strong possibility of a strike by all plant employees. Government is strongly prolabor and needs to be handled with care. Develop new element of the strategy to handle this product exit.

One of my favorite illustrations involves management's continuing desire to increase productivity or decrease labor costs. During the 1950s and 1960s this was strategically addressed by moving to the lower-cost, nonunion South or to the offshore havens in the Far East. The reason for this strategy was relatively clear. The Northern cities were becoming more and more expensive, and the unions were difficult to deal with. Businessmen in those days were more able to do as they pleased. Who could stop them from closing plants and moving?

As the laws began to change and the unions became more effective, the freedom to move became more limited. Unions and sympathetic organizations appealed to government at all levels, they organized boycotts, they picketed other company locations, and they even went to court. Management was forced to recognize the rights and expectations of stakeholder groups which in the past had been given only a passing look. Even lower-level company managers reacted to the strategy of moving, many of them refusing to move and either obtaining other employment in the same area or going to the competitor. Thus, basic assumptions that the professional and lower management skills would be retained were proven incorrect.

The issue this raises is that management and the chief strategist must learn to assess in advance the impact on the stakeholders and not be caught unprepared by their reaction. I am not suggesting that elements be discarded because they make people unhappy or create conflict, but there is a need to identify those stakeholders with the most to lose who will fight and may prevent execution. What is required is to ask whether there is something which can be added to the strategy which will help reduce the impact on those stakeholders, who can be negativists, or to accept their anticipated reaction and be prepared to respond before they prevent execution.

This illustrates the benefit of this type of analysis since it results in the addition of an element or program or contingency plan aiming specifically at problem prevention or at least impact reduction.

PITFALL 4: UNDERESTIMATING THE DEVIATION FROM THE PAST

The big, bright, beautiful tomorrow, as reflected in the financial forecast of the strategy, may be only a figment of our imagination and have no basis in reality. For many years, college professors and Wall Street analysts have noted a common phenomenon that they call the hockey stick effect. This normally emerges when a business has been in trouble and has just appointed a new management team. The new managers realize that they have a few years to prove their ability and that they will be forgiven if they show losses or poor results during the first year or two. Thus they will take the opportunity to write off everything they can, which sends the slope of the earning curve down. This, the new team reports, is necessary to get future results and rejuvenate the business. However, they stress that the downturn is only temporary and that in a few years sales will move upward and take off like a rocket. If you were to plot this pattern, it would look just like a hockey stick—hence the name.

Theoretically, there is nothing wrong with this argument. Normally a business must be cured if it is sick, and this causes less profit. However, the optimistic outcome predicted by the hockey stick effect does not necessarily apply to all businesses. And even when such performance is projected from a strategy, there needs to be an assessment of how it is to be obtained and whether it looks probable as well as possible.

Gap Analysis

There is a simple but effective way to depict the type of performance necessary to achieve the promised results. This device is called a gap analysis. You make this analysis by viewing the future in the light of the past and determining trends that will enable you to reach your objective. The charts in Figure 11-1, which show the sales and net income results of a hypothetical company, can help to demonstrate the technique more clearly.

Step 1. Look at the past four years of sales and net income performance. In the period 1972 to 1976 sales grew from $3.25 million to more than $11 million while net income increased from $95,000 to $400,000. Also note that the sales moved consistently upward through the whole period while net income was erratic and in fact declined in 1975.

The point to keep in mind is that you want to understand the past so that you can estimate how the future performance may look. This is not to say that the future will be a carbon copy of the past or that it can be predicted by extrapolation from the past. But you do wish to determine how much future change is necessary and whether it is possible.

Step 2. Having reviewed the past, you will now determine the size and shape of the promised results. The forecast shown in Figure 11-1 is that sales will increase from $11 million to the $24 million level in the next three years. This growth is faster than that achieved in the past four years, and the 1972 to 1976 sales are projected to increase by 50 percent in one year alone. On the net income side of the ledger, the growth projected is even steeper and the same year also shows a 50 percent gain. Both these curves are much steeper and reach higher levels than in the past. Does this mean that they are wrong or impossible? Not necessarily. Before

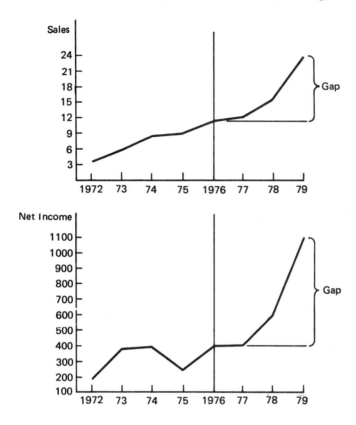

Figure 11-1 Sales and net income results for a hypothetical company.

you make your judgment, you must understand how you intend to achieve these objectives. This is the next step in gap analysis.

Step 3. Figure 11-2 shows the way the gap would be filled. On the sales side, Product X is expected to grow from $10 million to $16 million, a 60 percent increase. This isn't impossible given the growth projected in the number of consumers and the total sales in the market. Product A is expected to provide $2 million, which isn't unreal if the company can obtain a source of the product and if the popularity of the product among consumers continues as expected. The last $6.4 million will be obtained from the entry into a new product segment.

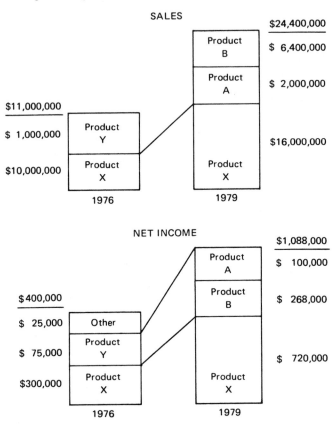

SALES

		$24,400,000
	Product B	$ 6,400,000
	Product A	$ 2,000,000
$11,000,000		
$ 1,000,000	Product Y	$16,000,000
$10,000,000	Product X	Product X
	1976	1979

NET INCOME

		$1,088,000
	Product A	$ 100,000
$400,000	Product B	$ 268,000
$ 25,000	Other	
$ 75,000	Product Y	$ 720,000
$300,000	Product X	Product X
	1976	1979

Figure 11-2 How management expects to fill the gap.

On the net income side, Product X will contribute $720,000, an increase from the current level of $300,000. Product B will provide $268,000 and Product A $100,000.

Thus you now know how the management plans to reach the target numbers and is in a position to evaluate the assumptions it has made which will provide the results.

Step 4. The process thus far has shown the projected results. The next logical question is, Why will the sales and income levels be achieved?

It is assumed that some of the rise in sales will result from market growth, share gain, and price increases, and some from new products, new market segments, or a change in strategic decision.

This ties in with the management strategies that were selected. It is helpful to group these reasons on a single-page display form, such as shown in Table 11–1.

Table 11–1. Sales gap analysis, Product X.

Product/Segment	Factor	Millions of Dollars	Assumptions
Product X	Market growth	4.0	Market will grow to $33 million; we will hold 50% of the sales. Average price will hold, even in face of substitute product and new competition.
	Market share growth	2.0	Can gain share from lesser competitor because of stronger dealer network and higher quality. Substitute material will not hurt current product sales.

Comments: You can see that this analysis helps to clarify how much of the Product X sales will result from the market and the share of the company. Thus two-thirds of it will be the result of market growth with current share and the other third from gaining share. If we test these assumptions from the past, we might question the validity of gaining share when they already have over 50 percent. Based on other experience, I might have a serious reservation about the price holding for a product which is declining as percentage of the total and also coming under increasing pressure from the substitute product.

Comments: Product B (see Table 11–2) means a brand new ball game for the company, and so the past doesn't provide much guidance. The company has made several fundamental assumptions

Table 11-2. Sales gap analysis, Product B.

Product/Segment	Factor	Millions of Dollars	Assumptions
Product B	Share in new segment	6.4	Can obtain source of private brand products from quality supplier. Can use existing sales force. Own brand name will pull through new product.

which, if wrong, will be costly. There are considerable differences between selling Product A and Product X, and these differences must be recognized. Can the salesmen increase the Product X volume, while at the same time selling the new product and the one substituting for Product X?

The analysis of net income growth follows the same pattern. The difference lies in those factors which can contribute to this growth. Normally income is affected by:

Cost reduction
Productivity increases
Pricing increases
Volume
Materials and purchasing savings
New markets and segments
Substitution of materials, processes
Tax changes
Unusual sales of property, assets extraordinary
Extraordinary Income (like licensing)

Now that we have completed the gap analysis of the hypothetical company, we ask how we feel about the probability of its achieving the promised results. If we were considering a loan to this company on the basis of what its management has told us and the evaluation we have done, we would have to conclude that it is highly doubtful that it will be able to perform as its management would like. Thus, this company might not be a good investment. Even if the sales and net income targets are met, the returns on sales and investment are only in the medium range, and if you believe that these two are optimistic forecasts, our decision would probably have to be no. The explanations of how the sales and net income gaps will be filled should be done separately.

You can also record the major programs which will contribute to understanding the key actions to produce sales or net income. Programs are equivalent to the key operating strategies, and the last column surfaces the assumptions underlying the required resources and your ability to obtain and use them.

The value of this approach goes beyond its usefulness in assessing the odds of reaching the financial objectives. It is also a means for management to tie financial results, plans, and assumptions together. The critical assumptions on which the business is built are identified. These are the ones that need to be monitored and that may require contingency plans.

PITFALL 5: PLANNING FOR TOO MUCH TOO SOON

Attempting to make too many changes too quickly is a deadly pitfall. We see this danger threatening our fictitious company in the preceding section. The marketing organization will be asked to increase the number of dealers, continue to sell its existing product at the same price levels, enlarge the product offerings to include a substitute product, and move into a line that is completely outside its experience. If we were to examine the changes required of the rest of the company's functional area, we would see heavy demands being placed on them too. The manufacturing group must increase automation, expand machining equipment and skills, and learn new materials processing. The changes aren't reserved to these functional areas; the entire management level team will also be in a state of flux. New positions must be added, new organization elements established, and new people from outside the industry and company recruited.

In a situation like this, it is very likely that the strategy will never be implemented as planned unless the complexity and degree of the changes are fully understood and taken into account in the execution of the strategy. For instance suppose management could determine the optimum sequence of events and make provisions to have the most important tasks done first and the less important ones delayed. This indicates that timing must be considered and modifications based on criticality. Thus the fact that the company is biting off a big mouthful doesn't mean that the strategy must be changed, but it does suggest strongly that timing and execution may be the key to success.

PITFALL 6: MISMATCHING HUMAN FACTORS AND STRATEGY

Although the thinking process you've followed in formulating your strategy has required that you carefully scrutinize the critical skills needed to meet opportunities and threats, your human resources should also be reviewed. If the original evaluation was a conscientious job, the task won't be that difficult and will consist more of a check than of a detailed recapitulation.

You begin this review by asking yourself, "What kinds of people will I require to implement this element of strategy, and are they currently available?" The same question pertains to the system of organization and the systems of measuring and rewarding employees' performances. Is there a match between the strategy and the systems, and if not, which should change?

Numerous books describe the results of a mismatch between people and strategy and between strategy and organization methods. These issues pertain to all functions in an enterprise and all personnel levels from the top down. A strong, aggressive entrepreneur will have great difficulty executing a plan that requires him to focus on administration and cost reduction; he will have even greater difficulty discontinuing operations. I once observed a young manager move a business that he should have been harvesting into the invest/ penetrate category because he was not willing to pursue the goal his company had set. On the other side of the coin, an administratively oriented leader has considerable trouble expanding a business in an environment requiring entrepreneurial risk taking.

But the need for matching human resources isn't restricted to just the management function; properly selected and motivated people are necessary for the engineering, manufacturing, marketing, and financial aspects of a strategy. Will the designers be forced to perform as followers when they have been innovators and leaders? Will the manufacturing professionals be asked to automate and turn to volume output at the expense of the handcrafting and quality of the past? Will the finance people be required to focus on financial analysis and forecasting rather than the accounting and bookkeeping tasks they are accustomed to?

Theorists argue that free-form organization is to be preferred to the more traditional, tightly controlled structures of the past. But it is impossible, I assert, to know what type of organization is best if you don't understand the strategy selected. This means that organization must be adapted to meet the dynamics of the movements toward objectives and not determined in isolation. For example suppose that a company wants to enter a new market that is currently occupied by large, financially stronger participants. This may mean that the management team will have to be quick and flexible in its actions. In this case decentralization and a loose form of organization will obviously be best. In other situations the game will require a tight control over expenses and cash flow, in which case the preferable type of organization will be closer to a hierarchical, centralized form. The point is that you need to know where you are going and how you will get there before you decide how to organize.

Performance evaluation and reward systems should also be tailored to fit the strategy. If you have decided to follow a high-quality/low-volume thrust, your salesmen and managers must be rewarded in such a way as to make this happen. There are cases where the strategy called for a restricted share but the measurement system rewarded those who obtained large volume and high share, regardless of the profitability of the others. Concentrating on short-term results demands performance standards that are different from those aimed at the long haul. An invest-to-penetrate business should be emphasizing market share and position. This will only happen if salaries and other incentives propel managers toward these objectives. If there are too many performance criteria and their relative importance isn't made clear, management will either become paranoid or merely average the total. Again the question that needs to be is whether the current rewards will produce the results promised by the strategy.

There are other pitfalls besides the six we have just examined— a miscalculation of customer needs, inattention to macroenviron- mental trends, a failure to spot a critical resource deficiency, and so on. Strategy reviews can be conducted in these areas as well. Each review looks at your objectives from a different standpoint, and just as when you take a picture from different angles, each will yield a perspective not visible from any other sight line. For this reason, when I do strategy reviews, I try to use as many of the proc- esses as possible. This doesn't mean that each will be pursued to the same depth, but all will be performed to some degree. I recom- mend this practice. Further, let me again counsel the use of an out- side consultant to add objectivity and completeness to your reas- sessments.

NONPROFIT STRATEGY REVIEW

Strategy review is equally useful to nonprofit institutions. Let's see how our six pitfalls endanger them.

There are many cases where an organization's planners have made assumptions about the environment and their resources that have proved incorrect or inconsistent with their strategy. Until recently school boards counted on a continuing increase in students. They also assumed that their communities and the taxpayers would sup- port education first, spending whatever the school administrators thought it took to provide quality education, and they equated ed- ucation with bigger facilities, more equipment, more teachers, and so on. Suddenly, they awoke to two changes. First, the number of students was declining. Second, education budgets were being seriously questioned. The assumptions underlying the objectives of expansion had not been challenged, so that numerous school boards found themselves caught with strategies that were no longer workable.

Competitor response review may not be relevant to all types of nonprofit endeavors, but many do need to evaluate competitive reactions. What happens when private institutions move into the public turf? The field of education provides a well-known answer. When private and parochial schools sought part of the tax dollar, which was to come out of the public schools' allocations, several emotionally charged issues emerged and competition was fierce. The reverse can also be seen—situations in which nonprofit and public-supported institutions move into those areas which were the sole concern of private, non-tax-supported organizations. The key point in either case is that nothing is static and competition must be anticipated by all institutions.

Stakeholders' expectations are also important to the nonprofit corporation. In fact, they may be even more critical, since the nonprofit institution depends heavily on goodwill. The reactions and expectations of stakeholders may prevent execution of a strategy and even threaten the survival of the organization.

Suppose a national organization decides to become more selective in the groups it serves or begins to concentrate on a specific geographic region to the exclusion of others. In a sense this is what many Catholic religious orders did when they recognized that they couldn't staff all of their schools. Thus, they chose to close some schools and to concentrate their declining resources on the others.

Regardless of the orders' reasons and whether their decisions were correct, many stakeholders became upset and reacted negatively. Certainly parents with children in the affected schools became unhappy. This is always the case with a retrenchment strategy. But other stakeholders—investors of two types—were also disturbed. The first group included those who contributed to the schools and the Church, some of whom stopped giving. The second group consisted of the banks and lending institutions involved, which were concerned because empty buildings meant further financial drains on already declining assets. The members of the religious orders also were affected and responded in various ways, some leaving the order and some leaving teaching entirely. And not only did the orders lose those members but, because of the adverse publicity, also found it difficult to attract new members.

The lesson to be learned is that understanding stakeholders and assessing their potential impact is very important, regardless of whether your objectives are related to profit or nonprofit activities.

Projecting past trends into the future is another procedure that is beneficial to profit and nonprofit organizations alike. Nonprofit organizations which depend on annual fund-raising drives, for example, can use assumptions about past contributions to help determine the probability of meeting goals. Let's look at the gap analysis for this purpose in Figure 11–3.

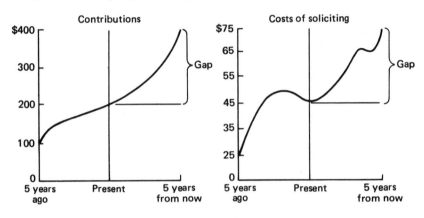

Figure 11-3 Gap analysis for fund raising.

The projections call for a doubling of contributions in five years and a 66 percent increase in soliciting costs. Let's examine how the additional revenue will be provided:

Corporate giving	$100,000
Major gifts	25,000
Individual donations	75,000
	$200,000

The increase since five years ago breaks down this way:

Corporate giving	$ 60,000
Major gifts	10,000
Individual donations	30,000
	$100,000

The rate of growth of total contributions is the same in both periods, but major gifts and individual donations are expected to increase faster than corporate gifts, though these will continue to make up the largest source. The figures prompt the question of why and force key assumptions to surface. Most likely these relate to rising incomes and the donors' continuing recognition of the organization's worth. Like the businessman, the nonprofit leader should explore the income gap and prepare contingency plans if any assumptions seem shaky.

Nonprofit organizations too can try to change too rapidly in too many ways. I recall the case of a university that opened two new colleges, one of which was highly experimental, at the same time that it was building a new campus many miles from the main campus and in a state where it had not previously operated. It was also attempting simultaneously to upgrade its faculty and change its institutional image. Within less than 10 years, both new schools were closed, the new campus was insolvent, the new and old faculty both were dissatisfied, and the university's image had deteriorated. Undertaking this magnitude of change brought the institution close to disaster.

Moving into a new social service, a new medical specialty, or a new type of educational endeavor without the right mix of people and strategy can be equally disastrous. New areas and ventures are exciting but normally require talents not presently in the organization. Because someone is an experienced specialist in one field, this doesn't qualify him for another. An excellent golfer isn't necessarily a competent tennis player.

APPLICATION TIME

Now that I have outlined the type of reviews I have used to evaluate the consistency, viability, and feasibility of strategies, it would be helpful for you to think about your own situation and apply the reviews. I have emphasized that each review looks at the strategy from a different perspective, and therefore the reviews as a group should provide a variety of insights.

Begin by reconstructing assumptions based on the implications of the strategy formulated. Ask about each element of the operating strategy, such as the conception and design of the products/services you plan to offer, and think through the implicit and explicit assumptions which relate to the environment, competition, and resources. Do the same thing for the marketing, financial, production, and management elements and then evaluate the assumptions in the plan in terms of your analysis. Do they make sense? Have you changed the assumption base without realizing it? Do you wish to revise the strategy or accept the new assumptions that you have made? The key is to be consistent and recognize the real assumptions underlying the strategy you have chosen to follow. Remember that there isn't a right or wrong assumption—there are only inconsistent assumptions.

The second review compares your strategy with the one you believe your key competitor will follow. This will force you to look objectively at both and determine whether your strategy will do what you expect of it. Again, this doesn't mean that you should change your mind. The review will merely point out where you are vulnerable and whether your competitor will react in a way that can hurt your chances of success. Remember this: The fact that you and the competitor decide on different strategies doesn't necessarily mean that you are smart and he is dumb. The differences may be a result of different resources, objectives, or desired results. Nor should you be disturbed that he has chosen another way. In fact it should be more disturbing to find that a key competitor intends to follow the same course of action or to move simultaneously toward the same target. The key questions are these:

- Which competitor are you aiming at?
- What is this competitor's strategy?
- How does your strategy compare, that is, where are there similarities and differences?
- Do you wish to change any of your key operating strategies?

Stakeholder review assures that you haven't overlooked a group that has the power to prevent successful implementation of your plan. If you used this approach to develop your objectives and assist in the final selection of the strategy, it may be redundant to do a stakeholder review. If you didn't think about stakeholders, then this review should be high on your list. Some key questions to ask include:

- Which stakeholder groups have the most influence on successful implementation?
- Which of these high-impact stakeholder groups will be adversely affected by the plan as a whole or by any specific elements?
- Is the impact so threatening that the group will take action that can inhibit execution or prevent the desired results?
- What can you do to counteract or minimize these stakeholders' impact?

Gap analysis evaluates the anticipated effect of the strategy on the financial performance of the business. It enables you to consider how specific strategic elements and programs will contribute to sales, income, and even cash flow. Start by plotting your sales and net income for the past five to ten years. Be sure that you go back far enough to assure that you illustrate normal growth. Next, plot what you expect to achieve in the next five- or ten-year period. The period you choose for the future should relate to the industry. Next, identify the gap between where you are now and where you think you will be. By the way, it will be helpful if you plot all of the figures in *constant dollars,* which are not affected by inflation. If instead you use *current dollars,* then it is important to estimate the impact of inflation, deflation, or even devaluation of the dollar.

Once you have estimated the difference between where you are now and where you expect to be, you should explain how the gap will be filled. How much of the change will be a result of merely keeping up with the industry and how much will come from share? What will be contributed by offering new products, moving into new market segments, and so on?

Next to each element contributing to the change, you should list the key assumptions you have made. For each assumption, note whether or not it is based on past events. If the assumption is based on your premise that future events will differ noticeably from past ones, explain why you think so. For instance, if you are assuming the market will grow faster than in the past, why do you think so?

This list of assumptions will help you very much to monitor your performance and to provide for contingencies.

Finally, perform the same task for the programs which will contribute the most to your financial results. This programs list will illustrate where your greatest challenges lie.

The "extent of change" review looks at the degree and type of change. It asks what changes are required of you, your key managers, and the workforce. Are you expecting a change of emphasis or a completely different type of behavior? Are you forcing the organization to undo the past and adopt new habits or perceptions? Is this change restricted to one part of the organization, or does it permeate the entire organization? Remember a simultaneous change in all levels of strategy will require a great deal of time and your personal attention.

Human factors follows the last analysis and probes the type of people, the organization, and measurement systems. Do you have the required number and quality of personnel? Is the current organizational structure appropriate to the new strategy? What about your compensation, incentives, and reward systems?

Remember that each of these reviews will require time, objectivity, and a different type of thinking. Don't be too ambitious. Select the reviews you think will pay the best results. I think it is better to use one or two of these completely than to be superficial in applying them all.

12
THE CASE FOR
CONTINGENCY ALERT SYSTEMS

Over and over again I have stressed that strategy is aimed at the future and built on assumptions. Assumptions are the platform or foundation of strategy. As with a house, if the foundation blocks come loose or slip, the structure will ultimately fall to the ground. Everyone knows this, but most of us tend to ignore it and begin to equate assumptions with facts. We therefore give little thought to contingency plans—what we should do in case of a damaging variance from our suppositions.

The reasons for this are easy to understand. We make our assumptions early in the strategic thinking process (as in any planning approach) and then subject them to review, argument, and modification. Because of all this and an unconscious concern that if we are wrong all our planning may be in vain, our minds put the uncertainty aside and raise the likelihood that the assumptions will occur to a high level. Thus it is important to take one more look at the assumptions and force ourselves to ask, "What if reality turns out different?" This is your starting point for building a contingency alert system.

To do an efficient job of thinking through plans for handling variances from assumptions, I would recommend the following steps:

1. Select your assumptions discriminately. Concentrate on those that have the most leverage.
2. Formulate other probable "what ifs."

223

3. Develop your tracking plans for keeping tabs on variances from your key assumptions.
4. Carefully define the triggers, and assign responsibility for monitoring them.
5. Outline the options; don't formulate them in detail.

SELECT YOUR ASSUMPTIONS DISCRIMINATELY

You can't monitor all assumptions. No one has enough time or resources to do this. Further, it isn't really worth the effort since some assumptions are not that important and others can be dealt with readily on the spot if and when they are proved wrong. So as with your strategic options, you should be selective in your contingency survey.

There are three criteria that you can apply to help uncover the assumptions you should lay contingency plans for. These criteria are the impact on your results if an assumption is wrong, the degree of confidence you have in the suppositions, and the degree of influence you have to make them come true.

Impact
If you used some of the review techniques described in the previous chapter, you have already determined which of the assumptions has the greatest importance for your objectives. Gap analysis points out the key factors that affect whether net income and sales forecasts will be met. If a market doesn't grow so fast as you anticipate or you do not obtain the share you expect, your sales and income will fall below your targets. Further, there are specific assumptions you have made about the users, competitors, dealers, and so forth on which you based your quantification of results. Each of the techniques of strategy review highlights a different aspect of the assumption platform and helps you identify the riskiest elements.

Your impact evaluation should reflect on positive as well as negative contingencies. For instance a variance in events may result in a bigger opportunity than anticipated. The market may grow faster than expected, giving you larger potential sales. This possibility deserves attention since a failure to prepare for it may make you miss sales or give a prepared competitor a leg up at your expense. Positive impact anticipation can yield dividends as well as negative.

Confidence

When I raise the criterion of confidence with businessmen, they normally equate this attribute with probability. They are partially correct. It is important to ask how probable it is that the assumption will turn out to be reality. Obviously the greater the probability is, the less likely it is that you will need to change your strategy. But there is more to confidence than probability. You should also ask, "Why do I think so?" Every assumption is based on either data from the past or analysis of the present, your intuition of how events will move, or your judgment of yourself or others. I have found it useful to record the source of each assumption, since the source may have a great bearing on how valid and reliable the prediction is.

This line of investigation starts with the question: "Where did the information come from?" Then ask yourself, "Why did I draw this conclusion? Was the information in conflict with input from other sources, and why did I accept these findings rather than others? What has the source's track record been? Is the assumption close to or far from my past experience?" When you have answered these questions, you specify the degree of confidence you have in the assumption. This can be recorded simply as high, medium, or low or expressed quantitatively as a percentage.

Many managers estimated some years ago that the economy would continue to grow at the rate of 5 percent per year and that inflation would be held within the 4 to 6 percent range. These assumptions were based on the past and were confirmed by many forecasts distributed by professional economists and the federal government. Had you questioned any businessmen who held these views, they would have retorted that they were perfectly logical since they represented overall trends for many years, though there have been cyclical swings. I am not suggesting that we argue about the validity of particular assumptions but merely pointing out that they should be recognized for what they are, uncertain predictions, and that it is important to understand why they have been made at all.

Influence

People and organizations outside your own enterprise are difficult if not impossible to influence and are ordinarily never within your control. For example many strategies call for some type of lobbying at either the state or the federal level of government. These efforts often fail to produce the desired results, and yet they are sometimes assumed to be automatically effective. This is not to say that lobbying should not be tried, but it does require careful planning and usually the cooperation of many other interested organizations. To take another example, even the degree of control managers have today over their own workforce is less than that exercised by businessmen two or three decades ago. Employees are less likely to follow an order to the letter, and more and more often they seek an explanation of it before they will act.

The point is that assumptions should be scrutinized to determine how much power you have to influence events in their favor. Those you have little control over may be worth including on your contingency list.

When you have applied the three criteria to your assumptions, you can decide how much each forecast needs a contingency plan, as Table 12-1 illustrates.

Table 12-1. Rating your assumptions.

Assumptions	Impact Rating	Confidence Rating	Influence Rating	Need for Contingency Plan
Dealers will carry our new line.	High	Medium (Source: sales force inquiry of dealers)	High	Low
Competitor X will exit from the medium-price market segment.	High	Low (Source: market manager's judgment)	Low	High

As you can see in this illustration, one assumption is rated high for impact, medium for confidence, and high for influence, while the other evokes low confidence and is less within control. It is thus not critical to outline a contingency plan for the first, but the second requires one. The next task is to determine how accurate the components of the critical assumptions are.

FORMULATE OTHER PROBABLE "WHAT IFS"

After the critical assumptions have been identified and ranked, the "what if" questions should be raised. There are some who argue that the most optimistic and pessimistic assumptions should be probed, stressing the need to prepare for the extreme possibilities as well as the most likely. This is an interesting exercise, but is otherwise a waste of time. I prefer that we think only about the *probable* possibilities.

Let's go back to Table 12-1 and the dealers' receptivity to your new line. Assume further that the sales force inquiry has turned up a 95 percent acceptance ranging from enthusiastic to lukewarm. This is the basis for the medium rating on confidence. Now, it might be useful to think about the effect of only a 75 percent acceptance. Many dealers carry multiple lines of merchandise, and if they aren't convinced that your new line is up to their standards, they can easily change their emphasis to competitors' products. In the long run this may mean that your position with them will decline, and it may even result in the loss of some of your top dealers. Thus you think through the consequences of the modified assumption so that you can decide whether you should be prepared to change your plan or construct an alternative approach if the level of optimism is inaccurate.

DEVELOP YOUR TRACKING PLANS

Deciding the *how* of your tracking procedures during the implementation phase of the strategy is the focus of your tracking plan, also called the monitoring plan. This step requires that you first specify the type of information that will enable you to know whether you are on target or not. In the case of the dealers in Table 12–1, this may mean surveys of end users that probe the reasons they are purchasing the product and further questioning of dealers to find out why they are enthusiastic or lukewarm. It may also require the services of outside agencies to collect data about the dealers' sales approaches and brand preferences. The second method involves the question of the reliability of the source of as well as the information itself. Will the source seek information directly or merely draw inferences from less specific mediums such as the newspapers? If we don't assess the source correctly, we may obtain misleading or inapplicable information.

You must next decide how much you want to spend on your tracking system. There is a whole area of decision theory dedicated to the question of the value of information. How much is it worth to you in dollars, time, and manpower to keep abreast of your environment or the condition of your resources? Information may be so difficult to obtain or so unreliable that it doesn't justify the effort required to collect it.

Finally, who is to be responsible for the monitoring? What will the person or group do to communicate the state of affairs? This assignment is critical to successful response, and it ties in with the next step in contingency planning, defining the trigger that signals when the variance from an assumption has reached the action point. There have been many cases where information was tracked well but communicated so ineffectively that the organization was still caught unprepared.

DEFINE THE TRIGGERS

Having thought out the system for monitoring assumptions, your next step is to identify the triggers that will activate the contingency plans. The need for these is obvious, but their definition is not. A trigger may be not one event or condition but rather a series.

A question in point: When should the president of the United States change his main strategy for dealing with inflation and use an entirely new game plan? Richard Nixon was elected president after campaigning as an economic conservative. He had repeatedly stated that government controls were ineffective and that the free enterprise system should be given a chance to operate without government interference. Yet he did a complete flip and resorted to controls. What were the events that led him to change his mind— or to put it in our terms, what were the triggers?

In his case there were several conditions that arose simultaneously. First, there was the extraordinary rise in the rate of inflation, which moved out of the normal bounds of 3 to 4 percent up to 8 and 9 percent. Then there was unexpected government deficit spending. In addition the public was becoming increasingly unhappy with the loss of purchasing power and choosing Democrats in a growing number of elections for executive and legislative posts on all levels of government. So Nixon resorted to changing his strategy and ordered the imposition of wage and price controls. The results of his about-face are now history—a continuing rise in the rate of inflation, distress in the business sector, job layoffs, public exasperation.

I'm not trying to develop a case for or against Nixon's actions, but they do serve to illustrate how complex triggers can be and how extreme the response they may provoke. Nixon's reaction was to abort his prime economic strategy. Not all contingency plans entail such radical change, of course; nor are triggers necessarily multiple or complicated. For example the fact that your competitors do not follow your new pricing policies may mean simply that you revert to a level halfway to the old levels, changing only this element of your original strategy.

Another aspect of trigger identification is the designation of the person or people who will be responsible for initiating the change. In the case of national economic policy, Nixon reserved this task to himself, even at the expense of having his chief economic counselor resign and losing support from his major conservative backers. In the marketing function of a business, the responsibility for price changes may be given to the marketing manager or one of his subordinates. The point is that someone must be made accountable in advance so that the contingency plan can be implemented.

The Pearl Harbor fiasco illustrates what can happen when triggers are either not set or ignored. There is considerable evidence that the possibility of a Japanese attack was recognized and that contingency plans had been developed. One of the problems was that no one was really sure who was responsible for the execution of these countermeasures. In fact, there are reports that indicate that the written plans were locked in a safe and the authorized officers were not available when the Japanese activated the trigger by launching their attack.

Of course, Pearl Harbor may also demonstrate that triggers can't be set which are so close to the event or condition that there isn't a chance to do anything to minimize the impact except perhaps to run. The point to keep in mind is this: To be useful, triggers, like any other early warning system, must provide sufficient lead time.

With your triggers identified and monitoring responsibility assigned, your contingency alert system is fully operative. It will enable your organization to change direction if and when this becomes necessary. By providing thought-out responses to variances from key assumptions, the system gives you the lead time and the means to minimize the impact on promised results.

PROVIDE OPTIONS NOT PLANS

I have mentioned the need to have a plan of response which will be executed at the optimum time. Actually, this may be somewhat misleading. What I mean is not that you should prepare a detailed plan but that you should give some thought to the options that are available. It is important to remember that any plan should be aimed at the cause of the problem and not at the symptoms. Suppose that you have a complete, well-developed plan to handle a contingency and that the plan is based on one set of assumptions about the causes of such a problem. If your assumptions are wrong, any response you would make to resolve such a problem might do more harm than no response at all. Having a varied set of options available, however, would give you more flexibility and allow you to quickly choose the response that seemed most appropriate to the actual problem.

CONTINGENCY PLANNING
FOR NONPROFIT INSTITUTIONS

Contingency options are equally important for the nonprofit organization. A hospital director may build his strategy on the assumption that Blue Cross or Blue Shield will obtain permission from the state commission to raise its rates. But suppose the commission grants only 50 percent of the requested amount or delays the approval for six to nine months. This may allow the "Blues" to reimburse the hospital only partially, which in turn may significantly reduce the hospital's cash flow. What are the options that the hospital could adopt if the assumption of total reimbursement was incorrect? How could the hospital trigger a change in its strategy before it was too late and it ran out of cash?

Universities, too, make assumptions which may prove incorrect—assumptions about the size of the student body, the professionalism of the faculty, and the continuing financial support of foundations, alumni, and government. What if the number of students dramatically increased in some disciplines and dropped off in others? This would mean the wrong mix of faculty and facilities. On the other hand, what if the government wanted to provide more funds for special research? Or a large company moved into the area and needed university training for their engineering or professional staff? The point I am making is that contingencies can be positive as well as negative and the lack of preparedness can mean a missed opportunity.

The 1975 fiscal crisis of New York City is an excellent example of the need for contingency options and for recognizing the complexity of making decisions. The "what if" question that should have been anticipated was the inability to continue obtaining financing. It was painfully apparent that options were not thought through. The crisis was compounded by the fact that the mayor's authority to change strategy was limited by the city council and even the New York state legislature. In institutions where authority or ability to act is restricted by law or the constitution, triggers should be set far enough in advance to provide the lead time to get the approvals necessary to avert a catastrophy.

APPLICATION TIME

Throughout this book I have stressed your need to think alternatives through and then select the one you.prefer. If you have been following this advice, you will have developed alternate investment, management, and operating strategies. Since you have already dedicated time and effort to this development of alternatives, you may find it beneficial to review them to determine whether any could be used as contingency options. The reward of having alternatives is that you may have already completed your contingency option list.

If, on the other hand, you need more help in developing those options, take a close look at the following example of an education equipment manufacturer. As you read through the example, apply the procedure to your own needs.

This manufacturer has developed a marketing strategy based on the assumption that its state government will continue to provide aid to local schools to purchase remedial language installations. The state has allocated more than $3 million a year to this effort in the past five years, and the company anticipates that the allocation will continue at this level for the next three years. As a result it plans to add new plant capacity in the state capital area to produce the language equipment. It has had 50 percent of that market segment, and this accounts for 30 percent of its total sales and 25 percent of its net income.

Using this and other information, the company constructs a contingency alert system as follows.

Assumption. The state government will provide $3 million per year for the next three years for remedial language equipment.

Impact: If the assumption is incorrect, this will seriously hurt the company's sales and net income. Conclusion: high impact.

Confidence: This assumption is based on past experience. There are conflicting reports on the total education aid budget, especially with the change of administration in the state. The allocation could be half of the original. Conclusion: low to medium confidence.

Influence: This is a small business and has no lobbying effort. Other companies in the education business are much larger, and they will be interested in preserving their segment size. Conclusion: low influence potential.

Need for contingency plan: This is a must for contingency planning.

What if? The state may cut the program budget in half and spend the balance on teachers rather than equipment.

Impact: Sales down by 25 percent and net income much smaller than projected.

Confidence: This is a more pessimistic possibility of what the state government might do. It is based on scattered but mounting opposition to the program in the legislature.

Tracking. Full monitoring is needed because of the high impact of both assumptions.

Information:
Government expenditures for education.
Budget proposals submitted by state officials.
Pressure groups that can influence the expenditure.
Local school remedial language programs.

Sources:
Budget documents.
National Education Association publications.
Speeches by educators, especially the head of the state Department of Education.
Speeches by state officials, especially the governor and his major opponents.
Reports on education to the legislature.
Documents of special interest groups.

Budget: $4,000 for the purchase of publications and visits to the state capital.

Responsibility: One marketing employee assigned full time.

Communications: Marketing manager will submit a monthly report.

Triggers. Three major warning signs exist:
1. The preliminary budget calls for less than $3 million in remedial language aid.

2. There is public indication that top state officials are changing their commitment to this activity.
3. Reports by top educators charge that remedial language labs are not meeting learning objectives.

If any of these trends develops into an active threat, one of the following options may be executed:

1. Tie in with other manufacturers to lobby for education funds.
2. Promote the value of remedial language labs among local school authorities across the state to stimulate them to apply pressure in the state capital.
3. Promote the use of general language equipment for advancement of skills and possibly for foreign language learning.
4. Do a feasibility study of strategies for entering other geographic markets or possibly the college market.

Strategic implications. Continue to base the strategy on the assumption of $3 million in funding but be prepared for change. The responsibility for change lies with the marketing and manufacturing managers subject to final approval by the president.

13

THE STRATEGY SUMMARY: A MEANS OF MANAGING BY STRATEGY

We have come to the end of a long and difficult journey, requiring large amounts of time and concentrated thinking. You have contemplated your mission, completed your analyses, carefully scrutinized your opportunities and threats, defined your potential objectives, and finally made your decisions. All these phases have involved your top managers and staff executives, and through discussion, reflection, and even compromise, you now have an overall business strategy.

This strategy provides you and your organization with a blueprint of the direction you want to take as well as the means to your goal. The blueprint shows you where you are and will enable you to determine as time passes how far you have veered off course—*if* the strategy is understood by those responsible for its implementation and those who must continue to allocate the resources necessary for success. The problem is how to communicate the strategy to these decision makers and insure that they understand it. I have known many businessmen to underestimate this task and even think it is an unnecessary luxury. This is a serious mistake. It may mean that all the work already completed will go unattended. There are two questions to think about: Why should investors put their money or managers their efforts into your business if they don't understand what you are doing and what they will get out of it? And how can managers below you implement something they don't understand?

In this chapter I will provide an illustration of a strategic summary. This summary may be used to communicate to your investors, whether they are higher-level management in a diversified company or bankers or backers outside the company. In addition, it will be useful as a means of familiarizing your subordinates with the strategy so that they can implement it effectively. Finally, since it will highlight the key elements of the strategy, including assumptions, programs, and contingencies, it should be extremely valuable for monitoring and tracking performance. In short, this concise document provides the means to *manage by strategy,* not merely *by objectives.*

The illustration portrays only one way to summarize. The way you select should fit your business situation and the message you wish to convey. As in a book, the style should fit the subject.

WHAT TO INCLUDE

A strategic summary should include the answers to the following questions:

- What type of business have you chosen to be and how does this compare with what you have been in the past (*your vision/ mission*)?
- What are the key assumptions you have made about your environment and your major competitors (*environmental assumptions*)?
- What are your investment priorities (*investment strategy*)?
- What is the lead thrust for each of your segments (*management strategy/segments*)?
- What are the major programs that will enable your strategies to work (*operating strategies*)?
- What are the results, costs, risks, and other key objectives and goals that will be achieved (*objectives/goals*)?
- *What if* the trends and events that actually occur are different from the assumptions you have made (*contingencies*)?

To clarify how each of these questions is presented, I will illustrate the key sections as they might appear for a hypothetical consumer products company. The numbers and comments do not pertain to any one business situation but are typical of the type of information that may be relevant to a company selling consumer products.

Mission Statement

Here is the mission statement of this company, which resulted from applying the entire process:

To continue as the quality leader in the U.S. market and build on our strong reputation for quality products and excellent service.

The management has decided to remain a product manufacturer in domestic U.S. markets, even though there may have been many other alternatives from which to select.

Environmental Summary

Figure 13-1 shows how you can condense the environmental assumptions made about the total industry, the consumer users, the market volume and selling prices, retail structure, and technology. These are not all the assumptions but those which the business managers have identified that will support the strategic decisions and have the greatest impact on the results, costs, and risks. Let's examine what the summary tells us about the business in the past and, as anticipated, in the future.

Total industry is expected to grow by $800 million or by 80 percent in the next five years. Note that all amounts given in Figure 13-1 are in constant, not current, dollars. The sector served by the company is expected to grow more rapidly and to represent 12, rather than 10, percent of the total. Since management isn't planning to move into the other sectors, it hasn't provided all of the data.

The consumer users section indicates that the total number of consumers will increase approximately 29 percent. However, the number of men will decline from 3.15 million to 2.9 million while the number of women will increase from 1.35 million to 2.9 million. This may be strategically important since the styling, type of retailers, form of advertising appeals, and so on, may vary depending on whether the user is a male or female. In addition, the portion of families in the total will also increase. This will also

TOTAL INDUSTRY SIZE

Total industry will grow from $1 billion to $1.8 billion in next five years.

The sector of the industry we serve will grow from $100 million (10% of the total) to $201 million (12% of the total) over the same period.

CONSUMER USERS

1975	1980
4.5 million	5.8 million

Demographics

1975		1980
70%	Males	50%
30%	Females	50%
85%	Singles; Young marrieds	75%
15%	Families	25%

OUR SERVED SEGMENTS

	1970	1975	1980
Average selling price per unit (1970 $)	$45	$55	$75
Units (000)	900	1200	1500
Totals (millions)	40.5	66	112.5

Comment: Our served segments will decline to 52% of the total market dollars, down from 66%. Styling and feature improvements will contribute to an increase in selling prices.

RETAIL STRUCTURE

☐ Department Discounters
▨ Sporting Goods
▤ Local Specialty
■ National Specialty

1970 — 25, 25, 50
1975 — 25, 25, 40, 10
1980 — 25, 25, 20, 30

Comment: The total number of retailers will decline, thus increasing concentration. Individual specialty shops will decline in importance, and their share of the total will be taken over by the national chains. The other types of retailers will hold.

TECHNOLOGICAL FACTORS

☐ Wood
▨ Metal
■ Synthetics

1970 — 15, 55, 30
1975 — 30, 50, 20
1980 — 5, 45, 50

Comment: Synthetics will continue to gain at the expense of both wood and metal. Metal will remain a key material in the product.

Figure 13-1 Environmental summary

have an impact and may determine the number of higher-price versus lower-price units. The first two items relate to the total industry and the overall sector which pertains to the business; the next three items focus on the specific segments in which the company participates. First, a historical and future comparison is made of the selling prices, units, and total segment sales. Following each exhibit there is a conclusion about the data presented. This is important since the data might lead to several perspectives, and it is useful to avoid any misunderstandings of what the management thinks is the proper interpretation of the information.

Management expects the selling price to reach an average of $75, which represents a 36 percent increase. The increase for the past five years was 22 percent. This projection is based on the assumption that there will be more feature and styling emphasis than price competition. The predicted change in user demographics also depends on this assumption, because women are expected to be more interested in the styling and features than are men. Since more families will be involved, there may be a willingness to acquire a product which is safe to use and will last longer. Also note that the selling prices have been indexed so that they aren't merely a result of inflation. Since inflation, a major problem in the past few years, is expected to continue, management should not deceive itself that it is in a rapidly increasing market whose only growth is a result of inflation.

Retail structure is vital to this business and therefore has been included. The illustration points out that national specialty chains will penetrate at the expense of the local shop. Since these chains tend to offer the same or an equivalent quality of goods, as well as before and after service, they will force the local merchant to compete on price. This will affect the margins and the volume of orders. It may also impact the type of service the company must provide, as well as guarantees and terms and conditions of payment. The historical data indicate that though department stores and discounters have been growing in the past, their growth is expected to be stabilized over the next five-year period.

Technology is a factor which can change the cost of maintaining or improving the position of the company in the segments it serves.

In Figure 13-1 the company management has illustrated that synthetic materials will increase and the two natural materials will decline. Metal however will not decline as much as wood. This raises some serious threats to those not able or not willing to provide the synthetic product.

Thus, in one or two pages management has summarized those assumptions that led to its decision and that deserve to be monitored. Other types of information—such as the customers' financial condition, service requirements, suppliers' and governmental regulations, and so on—weren't included in the illustration because though important, they weren't considered critical.

Competitive Situation

Competition and key competitors are the subjects of Figure 13-2. Here the management has noted that there will be fewer but tougher competitors. The foreign and multi-industry companies are expected to gain ground at the expense of their domestic, single-industry counterparts. Though this will result in more concentration, the short range will be more aggressive and require financial strengths.

The summary also describes the investment, management, and operating strategies of the company's three major competitors. Since share is a measure of position, the management has provided its estimate of market share changes over the five-year period. Two of the three competitors appear to be aiming at improving their share, while the current market leader is in a hold position. Since the leader is merely trying to sustain his position against two aggressors, you may question how long he will be number one. It is also worth nothing that two of the three intend to emphasize marketing, while Company Y is in an innovation mode. Overall, the combination of the changing environment and competitive scene means that it will require extensive investment and capable management to merely survive.

Strategic Decisions

The obvious question to put to the management of the XYZ Consumer Products Company now is, So what will you do? This brings us to a review of the strategic decisions that have been made. Figure 13-3 contains a concise outline of the investment strategy

	Percent of Market		
	1970	1975	1980
Single Industry			
Domestic	65	50	30
Foreign	5	10	15
Multinational	5	5	5
Multi-industry			
Domestic	15	20	25
Foreign	5	10	10
Multinational	5	5	15

Conclusion

The number of competitors will continue to be reduced. The number of single-industry competitors will decline the most and be replaced via acquisition and mergers by stronger, more aggressive multi-industry companies. This will increase the need to provide customer financing.

Major Competitors	Type	Investment	Management	Operating	Share (anticipated) 1975	1980
X	Domestic single industry	Invest to hold	Marketing thrust	New distribution Strong advertising Product quality	20%	20%
Y	Domestic multi-industry	Invest to penetrate	Acquisition; Product in-innovation	New materials application New capacity Aggressive pricing	15%	20%
AB	Multi-national, multi-industry	Invest to penetrate	Marketing and distribution	Distribution expansion Own sales force Aggressive pricing	10%	15%

Figure 13-2 Competitive situation.

for the total company and the key segments. The nine-block has been used to communicate the decisions that have been made. In this case there is only an indicator of the current situation with an arrow to point the direction in which the investment will lead you.

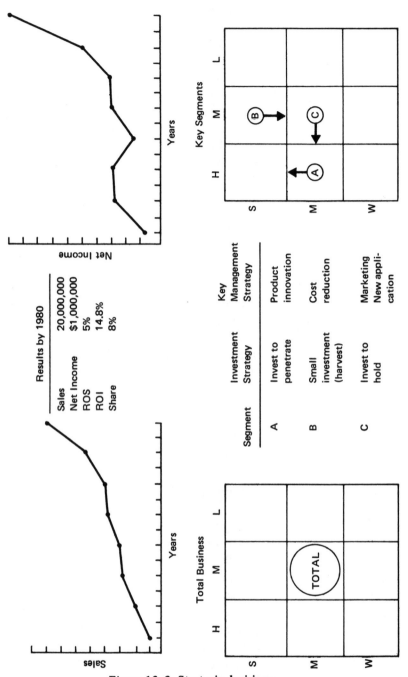

Net Income

Years

Results by 1980

Sales	20,000,000
Net Income	$1,000,000
ROS	5%
ROI	14.8%
Share	8%

Key Segments

	H	M	L
S		(B) →	
M	← (A)	(C)	
W		↓	

Segment	Investment Strategy	Key Management Strategy
A	Invest to penetrate	Product innovation
B	Small investment (harvest)	Cost reduction
C	Invest to hold	Marketing New application

Sales

Years

Total Business

	H	M	L
S			
M		TOTAL	
W			

Figure 13-3 Strategic decisions.

Of course, you could use the three or four indicators described earlier, when the purpose of the matrix was to make an investment decision. Though the nine-block is an oversimplification and has its limitations, it does provide a means for management at all levels to know what the decision is and the challenge it portends. Figure 13-3 also contains graphs of the sales and net income forecasts.

Finally, the investment and key management strategies have been outlined for each segment. For segment A, emphasis is on product innovation to increase share and stimulate volume growth. Segment B strategy is aimed at increasing earnings via cost reduction, and Segment C at combining marketing and new product applications for holding purposes. This exhibit ties in with the gap analysis reviews described in Chapter 11.

Operating Strategies

But the question of what management will do has only been partially answered. The next section of the summary fills in the operating programs as they pertain to the success factors. Table 13-1 represents the operating strategies for a specific segment of the business. In practice, there will of course be additional documentation for the other segments. Each of the functional resource areas is included, along with the programs, scheduling, and contingencies.

Since this segment focuses on product innovation, the other functions are programmed to support the engineering or conceive and design lead. Management has concluded that it has a strength in its design capability but intends to supplement it with a joint-venture partner. The timing of the production and marketing programs is built around this engineering design activity. This would be different if the marketing thrust were considered to be the lead and the design were to be adapted to meet sales requirements; so it should be apparent why it is important to specify both the investment and management thrust. Operating strategies must complement the higher-level decisions and not be permitted to merely satisfy the whims of the functional management. In the last columns I have noted some key contingencies or, if you wish, potential problems. This is the index to the contingency plans and isn't intended to describe the entire contingency alert system.

Table 13-1. Operating strategies, segment A.

Functional	Key Programs	Timing	Contingencies
Conceive/design Develop own capabilities in design and supplement with joint venture.	Design program, initiate. Select joint-venture partner. Initiate J.V. project. Complete prototype. Complete project/ deliver for production.	Jan. 1976 July 1976 Aug. 1976 Jan. 1977 Aug. 1977	Inability to find a compatible partner. Project delay for six months.
Produce Add new line in existing plant.	Order equipment. Receive delivery of equipment and install. Test equipment and train new workers. Initiate operation.	May 1976 Nov. 1976 Jan. 1977 Aug. 1977	 New equipment delayed by six months. EEO problems with new worker selection.
Market Add new distribution for the new line.	Identify new distributors. Initiate new franchise agreements. Train new sales force. Display new line. Initiate national sales campaign. Offer new line.	Apr. 1976 July 1976 Nov. 1976 Jan. 1977 May 1977 Aug. 1977	 Court decision prohibiting franchise agreements.
Finance Use financing from new stock offering.	Initiate new stock offering.	Feb. 1976	Inability to get 20 times earnings.
Manage Use existing management.	Transfer key managers with technical background.	Immediately	

The Payoff: Strategic Results

Since all strategy is aimed at achieving specific results, it is important to highlight results in our summary. In Figure 13–4 there are charts of sales, net income, market share, cash flow, and two return ratios (return on investment and return on sales).

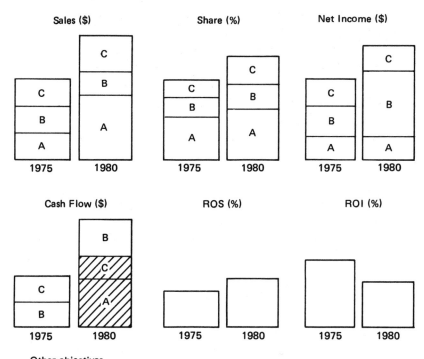

Other objectives

Dealers—Maintain "quality price premium" reputation.
Top Management—Position company for further expansion.
Employees—Retain and develop competent management and other professionals.

Figure 13–4 The payoff by segments.

This sales chart elaborates the one found in Figure 13–3. Each segment is plotted. The sales from segment A are expected to grow and represent a bigger slice of the total. Though segment C will hold, its sales will increase. On the income side, the situation is expected to be almost the reverse, with the percentage of net income coming from segment C declining while that of segment B is increasing.

From a cash flow perspective, management can determine whether the segment will be a cash user or contributor. Segments in a harvest mode will be cash contributors, and this is what the cash flow diagram shows about segment B. Segment C is illustrative of the holding strategy. It is expected to continue to provide its share of sales and a slight increase in net income. Since new applications need to be developed, segment C will require more cash than it contributes (shaded area). The point to be stressed is that the results should correlate with the strategies, and if they don't, information should be provided to explain why.

You will recall that an "invest to penetrate" strategy aims at sales and will result in poor income and a heavy cash drain. Invest to hold is most likely a sales standoff and a contributor to earnings. Invest to rebuild should improve sales and decrease short-term earnings. Depending on the rebuilding required, the cash needs could be as extensive as or even more extensive than those of the growth thrusts. Harvesting strategies are cash contributors and short-term earnings generators. But these rules can't be precise and the volume of sales, earnings, and cash will depend on the management strategy, the environment, and the current resources. Some companies *have* been able to increase earnings simultaneously with sales, but this is the exception rather than the rule. You should analyze any such deviations from the norm in order to understand how they happened.

At the lower section of Figure 13–4, management has listed objectives and classified them as to the stakeholder it is trying to satisfy. The first one pertains to the desired image, the second to an attempt to remain flexible, and the third to the management and professional staff. To be consistent, the operating strategy should have programs which are aimed at making these objectives a reality.

Discarded Opportunities

The strategic summary concisely articulates the mission, key assumptions, each level of strategy, the results and objectives, as well as the major contingencies. This is all that is really needed, but you may wish to add one more step which will wrap up the entire thinking process. This optional section diagrams the major opportunities you evaluated but elected to postpone or not to pursue.

The listing of opportunities serves two purposes: First, it may be monitored and implemented at a later date, and second, it may provide a list of contingency alternatives which can be executed if required to minimize profit or cash drain. Figure 13–5 illustrates this type of list. It utilizes a modified nine-block which plots the assessed attractiveness and ability to pursue the opportunity. Since opportunities can pertain either to your existing markets, unrelated markets, or related markets, they are classified in this manner. Remember the more we move away from our own markets, the more difficult and risky the opportunity may be.

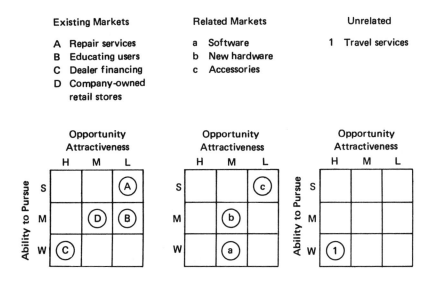

Future Potential

Monitor the dealer financing and com pany-owned retail outlets for possible entry at a later date when the economic conditions are more supportive.

Figure 13-5 Discarded opportunities.

THE STRATEGIC SUMMARY FOR THE NONPROFITS

The summary for the nonprofit institution should contain all the same ingredients I have just described, but the emphasis, specific categories, and type of presentation should differ. Let's briefly examine similarities and differences:

Mission. All institutions will have a mission statement. In many nonprofit institutions, this mission will be controversial. Dimension of changes in scope, size, variety, location should be highlighted.

Environmental assumptions. In this section management may wish to chart the level of student body, number and type of patients in the hospital, mix of parishioners in the church. These might include assumptions about sources of revenues, such as the percentage coming from donations, charges to users (students, patients), and grants from industry, foundations, and government; assumptions about the use of funds, depicting the amount for salaries, capital expenses, energy costs; assumptions about the type of services that have been provided and will be provided. Capacity and supplier assumptions may also be useful to include.

Competition. Though nonprofit leaders seem to resist the concept that there is competition, I believe it is important to surface and document the nature and type of the competition. This may be visualized in terms of the ownership of the competition, such as whether the hospitals or colleges are private, public, or quasi-public. It is also worthwhile noting the investment and management thrust of the key competitors. The capacity addition plans of these competitors may help anticipate the shortage or surplus of capacity. Is everyone taking advantage of the same consumer fad, such as their desire to become lawyers or engineers or medical paraprofessionals? Are all the hospitals in the area trying to become specialized leaders and is no one building community ambulatory facilities?

Investment strategies. This is similar in nature to the business portfolio approach and should be done on a segment or area of specialization basis. How much growth is anticipated? Is the investment aimed at the holding of capability? How much investment is for rebuilding? Is anything being harvested, pruned, or exited, or is all the action aimed at adding on and not taking anything out?

Management strategies. Is the area of specialization going to grow, hold, or rebuild because of an innovation in the specialty or in the method of disseminating the knowledge or skill? Or is it primarily a capacity-led thrust; in other words, will the hospital have more beds or the college more classrooms? Is the investment built on marketing and promoting? Do you anticipate the need to acquire, joint-venture, or buy know-how? Operating strategies describe your key programs, which build the understanding of what will be done in the conception and design, marketing, production, or financing of the product or service you provide. In other words, this section highlights your strengths and limitations.

Results, objectives, goals. Most likely this section will be more qualitative, but, as I emphasized before, this doesn't mean you must be generalized. Is the university going to turn out more specialists or generalists? Is the hospital going to decrease the cost of patient care, while maintaining quality service? Do you anticipate increasing revenue sources?

Contingencies. This section will include triggers. Options will pertain to the key assumptions and will help to assure that the results will be met as closely as possible, or to indicate whether the objectives need to be changed.

APPLICATION TIME

Take some time to write out your strategic summary, and don't underestimate its importance to the thinking process and its value to you. The key to documentation is to be concise. Don't worry about the format in the first pass. If you have trouble being concise and determining the most critical factors, you may not have a complete grasp of the business or institution you lead. There isn't any question that things are complex, but avoid the excuse that "my business is too difficult to summarize." Stick to the job and keep asking what is important and why. In a sense this is the final exam, and if you fail, it may mean that you need to repeat the thinking process in whole or part.

Though the form of the summary is secondary to the substance, it isn't insignificant. This summary must communicate effectively. If your investors don't understand what you are going to do, why you intend to do it, and what its results will be, then they may withdraw all or some of their support. Communicating downward is equally important, and again if the presentation confuses the implementers, they will implement poorly and have a negative impact on results. This document can be a powerful guide, but if it is too long, too complex, or confusing it will have only a limited value.

The message, then, is to complete the process and document your findings and strategies.

EPILOGUE:
CONCEPTS TO RECALL

As this book comes to an end, I thought it would be useful to summarize key ideas that have been covered. This will enable you to determine where and how you wish to promote the strategic thinking process in your organization.

Vital to all institutions. Strategic thinking is necessary to all institutions. Profit objectives are convenient measures, but whether or not profit is the goal, our changing world is increasing the need for the leader of any organization to think about its external environment and internal condition and isolate opportunities and threats that can affect its future significantly.

Assumptions are the foundation. Even though Chapters 11 and 12 spent considerable time on this notion and emphasized the need to identify the major assumptions and outline contingency plans, it is such a critical aspect of the art-*cum*-science of strategic thinking that it warrants reiteration early in this list. I have found that businessmen fail to recall that the future is uncertain and their views of it likewise. Thus assumptions must be recorded and then systematically monitored.

Three levels of strategy. Strategy is often erroneously considered to be solely the preserve of top management. This idea fails to recognize that there are three levels of strategy. Investment strategy focuses on the general investment decisions and the allocations of overall resources, which are limited and therefore must be selectively used. Management strategy is the concern of the top operating managers and clearly describes the main thrust of activity to be used in executing the investment decisions. Operating strategy answers the question of what will be expected of each major function of a business. It specifies how engineering, manufacturing, finance, marketing, and other operations will each do its share. A strategy is incomplete unless it covers all phases of a plan in terms of these two levels and their varying needs for specificity.

Healthy businesses, not sick businesses. The art of preventive medicine is just becoming understood, and so is the art of preventive strategic thinking. Some feel that you need to worry about the future only if there is a problem today. As a result they mistakenly believe that all the thinking about the competition, customers, resources, and what-if questions is pertinent merely to unhealthy situations. This thinking is just as fuzzy as believing that you don't go to the doctor or dentist until you are sick. If you wait too late to start the strategic thinking process, you may be putting yourself in the position of a person who has undiagnosed high blood pressure and waits for a heart attack to tell him his condition.

Knowing where you've been and where you are now. A good navigator starts his plotting by knowing exactly where he is at the present time. The same should be true for the navigator of an organization. Many managers have considerable uncertainty about the past of their enterprise, and even those who have experienced it together may not agree about what it has achieved and why there have been gaps between the desired objectives and the actual results. In the process we have been examining, the analysis of the past and present appears in many places. It begins in the mission development phase and continues in the steps of evaluating the organization's environment and internal resources. Finally, the exercise of strategy review is intended to help you select your future direction in relation to your previous and current history.

Customers are the heart of the market. Statistics about the market and its key segments are as useless for the businessman as test results are for a doctor without a clear understanding of the patient. There are many ways to classify markets and segments, but the most useful way to is start with a qualitative assessment of customers, both intermediaries and end users. In aggregate, customer data yield market data, not the reverse.

Knowing the rules. Someone who doesn't play cards could get the impression that all card games are the same. After all, they all use a deck of cards, and most require a number of players. But here their similarity ends. Poker is different from bridge, and both are quite different from rummy. Each has its own rules, and the stakes vary from game to game. Further, in the main, each attracts a different type of player, and each demands a different willingness to accept risk. The same is true of industries. All they have in common is that they require capital and participants. The rules of the games vary, the stakes vary, and so do the types of players and the types of acceptable behavior. It is critical for anyone who is contemplating entering a new market or participating in one undergoing drastic change to examine what it takes to win and how much it is possible to get out of the particular game.

Competitors—not just the obvious ones. Several chapters have dealt with competition and competitors. Remember that your products compete for the customer's dollar against not only other brands but other products and services as well. Further, never say "never" about the possibility of having to compete against companies from other industries and countries. Surprise can be deadly when it comes to the entry of new and strong rivals. Have you ever considered that you could be competing against the Soviet Union and not merely a company of that nation? Many have recognized that their Japanese competitors were not the companies but the Japanese government and its financial partner, the Bank of Japan.

Remember the four-dimension overlay. The microenvironment is where the action is for most companies. But this is increasingly being changed from the outside by societal, government, economic, and technological forces. Follow the national media with an eye and an ear for the implications of events in the macroenvironment for the industry and markets you serve. Try to resist the tendency to say, "That's interesting, but it's no concern of mine." Further, remember that government comes in different shapes and forms, not only the federal variety.

Know yourself. It is often said that each person sees his or her abilities differently from the way others see them. We may think of ourselves as the star first baseman; others may see us as quite inept in fielding. The same is true of any organization. It may have a distorted view of its capabilities and equate past success with a guarantee of repeating it in the future. Objectivity about current abilities and projected skills is vital to success. It often requires the help of an outside judge.

Success factors. Since it is impossible to evaluate all resources and learn all there is to know about a market or industry, selectivity is a must. At the minimum it is necessary to record and evaluate those factors *without which* failure will be inevitable. These are called success factors. All opportunities or threats, whether new or old, should be evaluated from this point of view.

Objectives—results, not merely guides. Objectives are the output of strategic thinking, and the planner must determine how they fit the expectations and needs of his organization's stakeholders. This phase of the thinking process should be done after strategic alternatives have been developed and are ready for a closer evaluation. This sequence should enable you to do a better job of identifying alternatives that are close to reality and have a greater chance of being achieved. It reverses the traditional management-by-objectives approach, which starts with objectives and then seeks ways of meeting them. My belief is that when objectives are set too early in the examination process, it force-fits the alternatives to the objectives and results in the selection of the "impossible dream," which most often turns into a nightmare.

Alternatives, not just one approach. The main reason that strategies haven't been wholly useful to management in the past is that they have locked in too early on the one "best way" and have not required planners to come up with several viable alternates. A manager should always be willing to ask if the business should be phased out or sold off. In addition he should be encouraging those under him to challenge the substrategies that affect their function or operation. Is it still useful to rely on the franchised dealers you have, or should you move gradually toward mass merchants? Is an innovative thrust always the best way to keep your share, or is it better to become a quick follower? These are some of the questions that should be probed at the operating strategy level. The point to remember is that all levels of strategy need periodic review to determine whether they still make sense. This means that alternates need to be evolved and assessed.

Does it really make sense? Chapter 11 provided some review techniques designed to assure that the objectives finally selected are realistic. There are checks aimed at increasing the internal consistency of the strategy on both levels and its conformity with the final objectives. If you are going to grow, it makes sense that the resources thrust and operating plans should enhance growth. Be warned though that the objectives of increasing cash, income, and share are rarely achievable simultaneously. I also suggested that you determine how competitors as well as major stakeholders might react to a major program. In addition, if too many changes are required in too short a time, this might spell failure. Finally, do you have the right type and mix of people, and do they have the correct motivations and interests?

Be prepared! This is the Boy Scout motto and should be adopted by every businessman today. The key to success is often the ability to respond quickly and decisively when adversity strikes. This is the purpose of an effective contingency alert system.

The next step. The best strategy in the world may be close to worthless if it isn't implemented adroitly. This seems so obvious; yet in case after case, leaders in all walks of life who do have carefully prepared strategies fail to make them operational. As a closing, I would like to specify some important aspects of the move toward implementing plans that will increase the probability of successful execution.

1. *Proper organization.* Look at the type of organization you have now and determine whether it fits the strategy you have adopted. An inappropriate organization structure is likely to cause failure.
2. *Measurement.* Do the current measurement systems encourage personnel to execute the strategy, or will they actually work against implementation?
3. *Rewards.* How do the rewards received for performance relate to the strategy? As is true of organizaton form and the measurement system, they can either support or distract.
4. *Understanding.* Do the key operating managers and professionals understand what has changed and why? Do they agree with the change, or will they only give it lip service? Do they know what is expected of them to make it work?

5. *Current plans and procedures.* If there are existing plans and procedures, these should be reviewed to determine their compatibility with your strategy.

These are a few of the key implementation reviews and actions that will pay dividends. Good luck in putting it all together!

INDEX

AMACOM Executive Books-Paperbacks

John D. Arnold	The Art of Decision Making: 7 Steps to Achieving More Effective Results	$6.95
Eugene L. Benge	Elements of Modern Management	$5.95
Alec Benn	The 27 Most Common Mistakes in Advertising	$5.95
Dudley Bennett	TA and the Manager	$6.95
Warren Bennis	The Unconscious Conspiracy	$5.95
Don Berliner	Want a Job? Get Some Experience...	$5.95
Borst & Montana	Managing Nonprofit Organizations	$6.95
J. Douglas Brown	The Human Nature of Organizations	$5.95
Ronald D. Brown	From Selling to Managing	$5.95
Richard E. Byrd	A Guide to Personal Risk Taking	$5.95
Logan Cheek	Zero-Base Budgeting Comes of Age	$6.95
William A. Cohen	The Executive's Guide to Finding a Superior Job	$5.95
Richard R. Conarroe	Bravely, Bravely in Business	$4.95
Ken Cooper	Bodybusiness	$5.95
James J. Cribbin	Effective Managerial Leadership	$6.95
John D. Drake	Interviewing for Managers	$5.95
Richard J. Dunsing	You and I Have Simply Got to Stop Meeting This Way	$5.95
Sidney Edlund	There Is a Better Way to Sell	$5.95
Elam & Paley	Marketing for the Nonmarketing Executive	$5.95
Norman L. Enger	Management Standards for Developing Information Systems	$6.95
Figueroa & Winkler	A Business Information Guidebook	$9.95
Saul W. Gellerman	Motivation and Productivity	$6.95
Roger A. Golde	Muddling Through	$5.95
Bernard Haldane	Career Satisfaction and Success	$5.95
Lois B. Hart	Moving Up! Women and Leadership	$6.95
Hart & Schleicher	A Conference and Workshop Planner's Manual	$15.95
Michael Hayes	Pay Yourself First: The High Beta/No-Load Way to Stock Market Profits	$6.95
Maurice R. Hecht	What Happens in Management	$7.95
Charles L. Hughes	Goal Setting	$5.95
John W. Humble	How to Manage By Objectives	$5.95
Jones & Trentin	Budgeting (rev. ed.)	$12.95
Donald P. Kenney	Minicomputers	$7.95
Ray A. Killian	Managing Human Resources	$6.95
William H. Krause	How to Hire and Motivate Manufacturers' Representatives	$6.95